An EPISTLE from the New Testament APOSTLES

The letters of Peter, Paul, John, James, and Jude, arranged by themes, with readings from the Greek and the Joseph Smith Translation

Arranged by John W. Welch

Bookcraft
Salt Lake City, Utah

Library of Congress Catalog Card Number: 98-74768

ISBN 1-57008-623-0

First Printing, 1999

Printed in the United States of America

For Alan and Karen

Contents

Preface

Dear reader,

This book takes twenty-one of the most important letters ever written in the history of the world and arranges them, as if they were a single letter. This thematic approach produces one consolidated epistle from the New Testament apostles. My desire is to give people a new way to understand the words of Peter, Paul, John, James, and Jude, to bring their messages more to life. These letters have many important things to say to the world, even two thousand years after they were first written.

As you open this book and turn its pages, I hope you will imagine for a moment how you might feel if you were to go to your mailbox only to find there a long letter addressed personally to you from the First Presidency and the Quorum of the Twelve Apostles as those church leaders were constituted shortly after the resurrection of Christ. How would you react to receiving such a letter? How curious and eager would you be as your fingers carefully opened the envelope?

What would you expect to learn from the testimonies of deeply committed people who had personally known or seen the Savior? What topics would they address? How would they present the gospel of eternal salvation? What moral instruction and spiritual guidance would they offer? Even if its lines were illegible or obscure in a few tattered spots, who would not count such a letter as one of the most precious treasures ever received?

This book sets out to give you just such a text: a letter from the earliest disciples of Jesus Christ. The New Testament contains two letters bearing the name of Peter, three of John, one of James, one of Jude, and fourteen that can be attributed to Paul. Most people rarely read them all, and even those who manage to get through them all often find it difficult to keep straight everything they say. This book takes each part of those twenty-one letters and sorts them by themes into a single composite letter. Hopefully, this organization will sharpen your understanding and reception of the messages of these significant New Testament epistles.

A Thematic Approach

In the process of studying these letters in this way, I have learned many things about the subjects taught by these early Christian leaders. I have found that a thematic approach to this letter collection offers many advantages.

Above all, this approach offers a synoptic overview of this collection as a whole. Seeing the big picture allows you as a reader to wrap your arms around the complete scope of these letters, grasping their meaning more comprehensively.

By seeing the big picture, readers can discover the profound consistency of doctrine presented in these New Testament epistles. The points made from one letter to the next reinforce each other and become mutually supportive. The consistency of advice given by Peter and Paul, of warnings given by Paul and Jude, and of exhortations by James and John show that these leaders were united in their faith and unified in their essential doctrine, grounded in the one eternal gospel of Jesus Christ.

Seeing the overall thematic structure of these letters discloses and clarifies the particular meaning of each individual section. Just as the individual pieces in a jigsaw puzzle take on purpose and clarity when they are put into place, each block of text in these New Testament letters speaks more distinctly when it is relocated thematically in the divine plan and order.

This approach also saves time. Instead of needing to flip back and forth between pages to compare the main cross-references from one letter to another, you will find the key passages on each main theme clustered together. This allows you to go directly to the subjects that are most interesting to you. You can locate those sections either by scanning through the outline at the beginning of this book or by consulting the indices at the end.

Finally, this method of studying the New Testament letters encourages you to read the words of the actual letters. While good commentaries and study aids are, of course, very helpful, ultimately the expert on John is John, and the expert on James is James. The best way to understand Peter is to read Peter. The best way to understand Paul is to read Paul. These men wrote articulately and precisely. The meaning of their words is not always transparent, but the best way to penetrate their intended messages is to read and ponder, reread and reponder, their own words. Reading their words, the primary and most direct source for the teachings of the early apostles, is the best way to access the words of divine inspiration and testimony that they so urgently desired to communicate.

By approaching these letters as if they were a single letter, we shift our attention, of course, away from the usual focus on the historical context and the individual authorship of each of these letters. Paul wrote one letter to the Ephesians, and another to the Galatians, and the writing style of James differs from that of Peter or John. Readers who wish to remain mindful of historical factors may still do so on a section by section basis. The original location of each section is noted in the margin at the beginning of each paragraph in this book, so that one can keep track of where every piece has come from. But our main purpose here is aimed more at understanding these letters as a whole.

Hopefully this book will allow you to hear the writers of the New Testament letters speaking in concert. Their parts work together in a manner no less amazing than any of God's other multifaceted creations. In forming one faith, one gospel, one Lord, one church, and one people with one heart, his spokesmen have offered us, in reality, not twenty-one letters, but one letter. By putting its pieces together, this book may bring the words of the New Testament epistles into brighter focus for you.

Formal Overview

Letter writing in the ancient world was a stylized art. Thousands of letters from antiquity have been discovered, and many of them bear common characteristics. Their general outline is also present in the New Testament epistles. That overall pattern has been used as the first key in organizing this book.

Ancient letters typically began with introductions, greetings, salutations, and well-wishes. Accordingly, the letters of the New Testament begin with personal greetings, often followed by expressions of thanksgiving, prayers, or congratulations. In contrast to most ancient letters, however, the New Testament epistles begin with greetings that are unusually personal, religious, and creative.

Friendship was extremely important in the world of the New Testament, and the language and courtesies of friendship shaped the composition of Greco-Roman letters. Ancient letters frequently expressed familiarity, loyalty, pain at separation, and the longing to see one another. Accordingly, many of the New Testament letters mention individuals by name and share personal experiences and biographical information. Paul refers to his own personal conversion and calling and speaks of his travels and concern for his friends. Several autobiographical statements bear testimony, disclose personal desires, reply to accusations, share sufferings on behalf of friends, and communicate sacred experiences.

Extending the circle of friendship beyond that of the writer and the recipient, the epistles of the New Testament speak of many other brothers and sisters within the Christian community. Paul, especially, was concerned with mentoring his fellow Christian servants.

Many ancient letters were philosophical in nature, offering discourses on theoretical topics as well as guidance for practical living. Similarly, the letters of the New Testament give precious doctrinal instruction and practical moral counsel for righteous living as a Christian.

The completeness and depth of these doctrinal teachings is striking. These letters speak powerfully of God the Father, magnificently of the Lord Jesus Christ, and emphatically about the need for the Atonement, which is made efficacious in the lives of Christians by faith and obedience to the laws and ordinances of the gospel. They articulate numerous gospel principles. They explain the salvation of the world historically, making sense of God's covenant with Israel in light of the mission of Christ. They also have much to say doctrinally about the apostasy, the Second Coming of the Savior, the resurrection, and the triumphal glory that awaits the righteous.

Turning to more practical instructions, the epistles also give important information about the organization of the early Christian Church, the ministry of the apostles, and instructions to Church leaders. Advice and encouragement to all Church members offers every reader wise and inspired counsel concerning prayer and worship, the sacrament, the use of wealth, abstaining from forbidden food, morality, family relationships, and other instructions which deal with the religious life and observances of the Christian congregation as a whole.

Not ignoring the individual, and the individual Christian's spiritual life and destiny, the New Testament letters also give extensive guidance on Christian virtues and living, as well as the cultivation of righteous relationships one with another. Love and unity within the Church are emphatically advocated, and strong counsel is given to avoid the wisdom of the world but rather to seek spiritual knowledge and spiritual gifts. In this way, though the struggle to overcome sin may be long and difficult, we are assured that through repentance and following the example of Jesus Christ it will surely be successful.

Most ancient letters concluded by bidding farewell and asking the addressee to extend greetings to others. Accordingly, the New Testament letters typically conclude with greetings, good wishes, final expressions of concern, exhortations, prayers, and blessings.

Doctrinal Overview

A glance at this book's table of contents should make all Latter-day Saint readers feel quite at home. The basic teachings of the plan of salvation permeate the New Testament epistles. These doctrines revealed by our modern-day prophets provide the second key to seeing the main themes of these letters.

Latter-day Saints believe in the restoration of the same organization and teachings that existed in the primitive church. The doctrines, practices, policies, and exhortations found in these New Testament letters read, in many respects, like an LDS handbook of instructions. The broad outline of their important doctrines—dealing with the Godhead, the atonement of Jesus Christ, faith and works, covenants, the great apostasy, apostles, bishops, elders, deacons, healing the sick, administering the sacrament, seeking spiritual gifts, sexual purity, the family, overcoming the world, and many other similar subjects—is particularly meaningful and relevant to Latter-day Saints. Even where time has changed the world in which we live (notably on women wearing veils and keeping a low profile in public, the economy depending on slaves, and worrying about eating meat that had been offered to idols), the underlying principles of modesty, respect, order, and purity remain in full force and effect.

Significantly, the Articles of Faith of The Church of Jesus Christ of Latter-day Saints, which encapsulate the fundamental beliefs of the gospel as restored in modern times, show special affinity toward the writings of the early Christian apostles. For example, the first Article of Faith speaks of God the Eternal Father, his son Jesus Christ, and the Holy Ghost. Paul similarly concludes his second letter to the Corinthians by invoking the blessing of "the Lord Jesus Christ, and the love of God, and the Communion of the Holy Ghost" (2 Corinthians 13:14).

The fourth Article of Faith outlines the first principles of the gospel as faith in the Lord Jesus Christ, repentance, baptism, and the gift of the Holy Ghost. Likewise, the letter to the Hebrews lists the "first principles" as the following: "repentance from dead works, and of faith toward God, of the doctrine of baptisms, and laying on of hands" (Hebrews 5:12; 6:1–2).

As in the fifth Article of Faith, Paul admonishes his young priesthood companion Timothy to remember the power that was given to him by "prophecy, with the laying on of the hands" by those in authority (1 Timothy 4:14).

The list of priesthood offices mentioned in the sixth Article of Faith is quoted verbatim from Ephesians 4:11, and four of the six gifts enumerated in the seventh Article of Faith are listed in 1 Corinthians 12:8–10.

Little wonder that the thirteenth Article of Faith concludes by mentioning by name "the admonition of Paul," which is found in

1 Corinthians 13:7, and speaks of "anything virtuous, lovely, or of good report or praiseworthy," directly recounting Philippians 4:8.

Articles of Faith	References in the New Testament Letters
1	2 Corinthians 13:14
2	Galatians 6:7; 1 Corinthians 15:21
3	Colossians 1:20; Hebrews 5:9
4	Hebrews 6:1–2
5	1 Timothy 4:14
6	Ephesians 4:11
7	1 Corinthians 12:8–12
8	2 Timothy 3:16; 2 Corinthians 13:1
9	1 Corinthians 2:10–11
10	Hebrews 12:22; 1 Thessalonians 2:19; 3:13
11	Romans 2:14–16
12	Romans 13:1–7
13	1 Corinthians 13:7; Philippians 4:8

Most of the teachings in the Articles of Faith can be found in the letters of the New Testament.[1] Many other similarities between the life and teachings of Joseph Smith and the acts and writings of the early apostles extend far beyond mere verbal echoes.[2] Indeed, one may see these apostles and prophets as virtual co-authors of the Articles of Faith with their common source in the Lord Jesus Christ.

Moreover, Latter-day Saints readily resonate to many LDS teachings that are found in the Bible only in the New Testament epistles. Thus, Peter alone writes about Christ's preaching to the spirits of those who had died. Paul makes the only biblical references to baptism for the dead and the three degrees of eternal glory. Herein also we learn such exclusive things as the qualifications of bishops, the distinction between the Melchizedek and Levitical priesthoods, prophecies about the last days, and

[1] John W. Welch, "Co-Authors of the Articles of Faith," *Instructor* 104 (1969): 422–36.

[2] Richard L. Anderson, "Parallel Prophets: Paul and Joseph Smith," *Ensign* (April 1985): 12–17.

declarations of the divine nature open to all human beings. Latter-day Saints take particular interest in these individual passages, as well as their composite configuration.

Presentation of the Text

The text used in this presentation begins with the King James Version of the Bible published by The Church of Jesus Christ of Latter-day Saints in 1979. For a number of reasons, I prefer the King James Version, even with its shortcomings. It is the version of the Bible that most Latter-day Saints hope to understand. By spending time with its vocabulary and syntax, readers will find it easier to understand than people often expect.

The base text of each New Testament letter has then been divided into sections, one main subject per section. Some are short and others are long. Each one is intended to represent something of a paragraph, although the use of paragraphs was unknown in the world when these letters were originally written. Each section is unified by a dominant theme or purpose. In dividing up these texts, I have also examined and benefitted from the divisions used by the editors of the United Bible Societies Greek New Testament and by the publishers of several modern translations of the Bible.

At the beginning of each section, a subheading has been added. These subheadings are suggestions to guide the reader by answering such questions as, "What is this section all about?" or "What is the main theme or point of this passage?" These subheadings should speed your reading and pinpoint your attention.

Using each subheading as a line in a topical outline, I then took all of the sections with common themes and clustered them into groups, and arranged the clusters into an overall organizational plan. I am grateful to Marny Parkin and Claire Foley for their work in carrying out the word processing to place all of these sections in their appropriate positions.

Regarding punctuation and editorial symbols, I have retained the King James punctuation for the most part, including the use of parentheses ( ), as those marks were used in the 1979 LDS edition of the Bible. When I needed to insert editorial comments, mostly to compensate for taking lines out of their original context, I included those comments in square brackets [ ].

Quote marks have been added to show which words have been drawn by our New Testament writers from earlier books of the Old Testament, which they knew from their Hebrew or Septuagint Greek scrolls. Scripture references for these quotations are given in square brackets [ ].

In addition, where the Joseph Smith Translation of the Bible modifies the text of the King James Version, I have included those changes in braces { }. Typically, these words are shown as alternatives to the immediately preceding word or words found in the King James Version. Words deleted from the King James Version by the Joseph Smith Translation are printed in this book in gray rather than black type with a strike-out line running through them. By ignoring all information in braces, the King James reading usually remains; and by skipping the crossouts, the JST reading emerges. I am grateful to Claire Foley for her careful work inserting these emendations by Joseph Smith. Our sources for the Joseph Smith Translation include its published versions supplemented by notes taken by Scott Faulring in connection with the JST Library Research Project. Our use of those notes is gratefully acknowledged.

Furthermore, where the King James Version offers one translation of a Greek word but other translations or meanings are possible, alternative translations are placed within forward slashes / /. The words found between these slashes suggest possible alternative translations for the immediately preceding word. In order to avoid cluttering this text unduly, only a relatively few of these alternative translations have been offered. Many more could have been provided. I have given those that are commonly found in marginal notes to the King James Version, and I have added others in order to clarify the literal sense of words or phrases or to draw attention to other potential nuances found in the Greek.

Finally, not all of the ancient manuscripts of the New Testament epistles are identical. Minor variations from one early manuscript to another can be found in the textual apparatus accompanying all standard Greek editions of the New Testament. Unless a person reads Greek, however, these textual variants remain completely inaccessible. This is not a major concern, because most of these variants involve differences in spelling, word order, or grammar that make little difference in meaning. On some occasions, however, it is interesting to look behind the English translation to see these variants. Such alternative readings are given between back slashes \ \. Words found in the back slashes are found in some, but not all, of the earliest manuscripts. I have not distinguished, however, between strong and weak manuscript readings. I am grateful to Daniel McKinley for his assistance in examining each of these variants.

A Letter to Read

I hope you will enjoy reading the epistles of the New Testament apostles arranged and presented in this fashion. I believe that, taken all together, they make a powerful and consistent statement. Even if you have read these letters before, I trust that you will understand each of their parts better by seeing how each fits into an overall structure and gospel framework.

In these words of the New Testament, I find the love of God, the gospel of Jesus Christ, the spirit of truth, the promise of eternal life, the plan of salvation, the essence of Christian virtues, inspiration for Christian disciples, the wisdom of the ages, the spirit of prophecy, and the testimonies of true and honest men. I hope you will too.

Symbols

( ) text inside parentheses is found inside parentheses in the King James Version (KJV)

[ ] information inside brackets gives editorial transition or cross-references for this edition

[ ] a scripture reference inside brackets following words in quotation marks identifies the Old Testament source of those words that were quoted by the original letter writer

LXX these Roman numerals indicate that the New Testament writer followed the Greek Septuagint version of the Old Testament, which differed from the Hebrew on which the KJV was based

{ } words found inside braces are added by the Joseph Smith Translation (JST)

~~text~~ crossouts in gray type are words deleted by the JST

~~text~~ { } words inside braces that follow crossouts indicate their JST replacements

{[1a]} raised numerals and letters in braces precede words to show the order [1a], [1b], [1c] that they had in a verse in the KJV but which was rearranged into another order {[1b]}, {[1a]}, {[1c]} in the JST; the words in this book are always presented in the JST order

[1a] raised numerals and letters without braces indicate that the order of these elements is the same in both the KJV and JST

/ / a word or phrase inside forward slashes offers an acceptable alternative translation for a Greek word where the Greek word itself is not in doubt but its meaning may vary in English translation

/ , / similarly, a string of words inside forward slashes offers a series of acceptable alternative translations for a Greek word

\ , \ two expressions separated by commas and inside backslashes give alternate readings that appear in various ancient Greek manuscripts (from the second century onward)

\ \ words or phrases inside back slashes are in some of the ancient Greek manuscripts but not in all

1

Introductions

Greetings

[1a]Paul, {[1e]}an apostle, {[1b]}a servant {[1g]}of God, {[1d]}called Rom.
{[1c]}of Jesus Christ {and} [1f]separated /set apart/ ~~un~~to {preach} 1:1–7
the gospel; [2](Which he had promised ~~afore~~ {before} by his
prophets in the holy scriptures,) [3]Concerning his Son Jesus
Christ our Lord, which was made ~~of~~ the seed of David according to the flesh; [4a]And declared /appointed, decreed, set forth/
~~to be~~ the Son of God with power, {[4c]by} the spirit ~~of holiness,~~
{[4b]}according to {the truth,} [4d]~~by~~ {through} the resurrection
from the dead \of Jesus Christ our Lord\: [5a]By whom we have
received grace and apostleship, ~~for~~ {through} obedience ~~to the~~
{and} faith {[5c]}~~for~~ {on} his name, {to preach the gospel}
[5b]among all nations: [6]Among whom ~~are~~ ye also {are} ~~the~~ called
of Jesus Christ: [7]{Wherefore, I write} To all ~~that be~~ {who are}
in Rome, beloved of God, called ~~to be~~ saints: Grace to you and
peace from God our Father, and the Lord Jesus Christ.

[1a]Paul, {[1c]}an apostle {[1b]}called ~~to be~~ [1d]of Jesus Christ 1 Cor.
through the will of God, and Sosthenes our brother, [2]Unto the 1:1–3
church of God which is at Corinth, to them that are sanctified
in Christ Jesus, called to be saints, with all that in every place
call upon the name of Jesus Christ our Lord, both theirs and
ours: [3]Grace be unto you, and peace, from God our Father,
and from the Lord Jesus Christ.

[1]Paul, an apostle of Jesus Christ by the will of God, and Tim- 2 Cor.
othy our brother, unto the church of God which is at Corinth, 1:1–2
with all the saints which are in all Achaia: [2]Grace ~~be~~ to you and
peace from God our Father, and ~~from~~ the Lord Jesus Christ.

Gal. [1]Paul, an apostle, (not of men, neither by man, but by
1:1–5 Jesus Christ, and God the Father, who raised him from the
dead;) [2]And all the brethren which are with me, unto the
churches of Galatia: [3]Grace ~~be~~ to you and peace from God the
Father, and ~~from~~ our Lord Jesus Christ, [4]Who gave himself for
our sins, that he might deliver us from this present evil world,
according to the will of God and our Father: [5]To whom be glory
for ever and ever. Amen.

Eph. [1]Paul, an apostle of Jesus Christ by the will of God, to the
1:1–2 saints which are at Ephesus, and to the faithful in Christ Jesus:
[2]Grace ~~be~~ to you, and peace, from God our Father, and ~~from~~
the Lord Jesus Christ.

Philip. [1]Paul and Timotheus, the servants of Jesus Christ, to all
1:1–2 the saints in Christ Jesus which are at Philippi, with the bishops
and deacons: [2]Grace ~~be~~ unto you, and peace, from God our
Father, and ~~from~~ the Lord Jesus Christ.

Col. [1]Paul, an apostle of Jesus Christ by the will of God, and
1:1–2 Timotheus our brother, [2]To the saints and faithful brethren in
Christ which are at Colosse: Grace be unto you, and peace,
from God our Father \and the Lord Jesus Christ\.

1 Thes. [1]Paul, and Silvanus, and Timotheus, {servants of God the
1:1 Father and the Lord Jesus Christ,} unto the church of the
Thessalonians ~~which is in God the Father and in the Lord Jesus
Christ~~: Grace ~~be~~ unto you, and peace, from \God our\ Father
and the Lord \Jesus Christ\.

2 Thes. [1a]Paul, and Silvanus, and Timotheus, {the servants [1c]}~~in~~
1:1–2 {of} God the Father and ~~the~~ {our} Lord Jesus Christ [1b]unto the
church of the Thessalonians: [2]Grace unto you, and peace, from
God our Father and the Lord Jesus Christ.

1 Tim. [1a]Paul, an apostle of Jesus Christ by the commandment of
1:1–2 God {[1c]}and {the} Lord Jesus Christ, {[1b]}our Saviour, [1d]~~which is~~

{and} our hope; [2]Unto Timothy, my own /lawful, true/ son in /a
true son according to/ the faith: Grace, mercy, ~~and~~ peace, from
God our Father and Jesus Christ our Lord.

[1]Paul, an apostle of Jesus Christ by the will of God, accord- 2 Tim.
ing to the promise of life which is in Christ Jesus, [2]To Timothy, 1:1–2
my dearly beloved son: Grace, mercy, and peace, from God the
Father and Christ Jesus our Lord.

[1]Paul, a servant of God, and an apostle of Jesus Christ, Titus
according to the faith of God's elect, and the acknowledging of 1:1–4
the truth which is after godliness; [2]In hope of eternal life, which
God, that cannot lie, promised before the world began; [3]But
hath in due times manifested his word through preaching,
which is committed unto me according to the commandment of
God our Saviour; [4]To Titus, mine own son after /a true son
according to/ the common faith: Grace, mercy, and peace, from
God the Father and the Lord Jesus Christ our Saviour.

[1]Paul, a prisoner of Jesus Christ, and Timothy our Philem.
brother, unto Philemon our dearly beloved, and fellowlabourer, 1:1–3
[2]And to ~~our~~ beloved Apphia, and Archippus our fellowsoldier,
and to the church in thy house: [3]Grace to you, and peace, from
God our Father and the Lord Jesus Christ.

[1]James, a servant of God and of the Lord Jesus Christ, to James
the twelve tribes which are scattered abroad, greeting. 1:1

[1]Peter, an apostle of Jesus Christ, to the strangers scattered 1 Pet.
throughout Pontus, Galatia, Cappadocia, Asia, and Bithynia, 1:1–2
[2]Elect according to the foreknowledge of God the Father,
through sanctification of the Spirit, unto obedience and sprinkling of the blood of Jesus Christ: Grace unto you, and peace,
be multiplied.

[1]Simon Peter, a servant and an apostle of Jesus Christ, to 2 Pet.
them that have obtained like /equally/ precious faith with us 1:1–2

through the righteousness of God and our Saviour Jesus Christ: [2]Grace and peace be multiplied unto you through the knowledge of God /of our God and Savior/, and of Jesus our Lord.

1 Jn. 2:12–14 [12]I write unto you, little children, because your sins are forgiven you for /because of, through/ his name's sake. [13]I write unto you, fathers, because ye have known him ~~that is~~ from the beginning. I write unto you, young men, because ye have overcome the wicked one. I write unto you, little children, because ye have known the Father. [14]I have written unto you, fathers, because ye have known him ~~that is~~ from the beginning. I have written unto you, young men, because ye are strong, and the word of God abideth in you, and ye have overcome the wicked one.

2 Jn. 1:1–3 [1]The elder unto the elect lady and her children, whom I love in the truth; and not I only, but also all they that have known the truth; [2]For the truth's sake, which dwelleth in us, and shall be with us for ever. [3]Grace be with you, mercy, and peace, from God the Father, and from the Lord Jesus Christ, the Son of the Father, in truth and love.

3 Jn. 1:1–4 [1]The elder unto the wellbeloved Gaius, whom I love in the truth. [2]Beloved, I wish above all things that thou mayest prosper and be in health, even as thy soul prospereth. [3]For I rejoiced greatly, when the brethren came and testified of the truth that is in thee, even as thou walkest in the truth. [4]I have no greater joy than to hear that my children walk in truth.

Jude 1:1–2 [1]Jude, the servant of {God, called of} Jesus Christ, and brother of James, to them ~~that~~ {who} are \beloved, sanctified\ {of} God the Father, and preserved in Jesus Christ: [2]Mercy unto you, and peace, and love, be multiplied.

Thanksgiving and Prayer

Prayer and desire to visit Rome

Rom. 1:8–15 [8]First, I thank my God through Jesus Christ ~~for~~ {that} you all {are steadfast, and} ~~that~~ your faith is spoken of /proclaimed/

throughout the whole world. 9aFor God is my witness, whom I
serve {9c}that without ceasing I make mention of you always in
my prayers, {9bthat you may be kept ~~with~~ {through} ~~my~~ {the}
spirit in the gospel of his Son. 10Making request {of you to
remember me in your prayers, I now write unto you, that you
will ask him in faith, that} if by any means ~~now~~ at length I
~~might~~ {may serve you with my labours, and may} have a pros-
perous journey by the will of God to come unto you. 11aFor I
long to see you, that I may impart unto you some spiritual gift,
{11cthat it} ~~ye~~ may be established {in you} 11bto the end; 12~~That
is,~~ that I may be comforted together with you by the mutual
faith both of you and me. 13Now I would not have you ignorant,
brethren, that oftentimes I purposed to come unto you, (but
was ~~let~~ {hindered} /restrained, prevented/ hitherto,) that I
might have some fruit /result, gain/ among you also, even as
among other Gentiles. 14I am debtor both to the Greeks, and to
the Barbarians; both to the wise, and to the unwise. 15~~So~~ {And},
as much as in me is, I am ready to preach the gospel to you that
are at Rome also.

Thankfulness for their testimony of Jesus

4I thank my God always on your behalf, for the grace of 1 Cor.
God which is given you ~~by~~ {of} Jesus Christ; 5That in every 1:4–9
thing ye are enriched ~~by~~ {of} him, in all utterance, and ~~in~~ all
knowledge; 6Even as the testimony of Christ was confirmed
/established, strengthened/ in you: 7So that ye come behind
/come short, miss, need/ in no gift; waiting for the coming /rev-
elation/ of our Lord Jesus Christ: 8Who shall also confirm
/secure, establish, strengthen/ you unto the end, ~~that ye may be~~
blameless in the day of our Lord Jesus Christ. 9God is faithful,
by whom ye were called unto the fellowship of his Son Jesus
Christ our Lord.

Thankfulness for their righteousness and prayer that it may continue

3I thank my God upon every remembrance of you, Philip.
4Always in every prayer of mine for {the steadfastness of} you 1:3–11

all making request with joy, 5For your fellowship in the gospel
from the first day until now; 6Being confident of this very thing,
that he which hath begun a good work in you will perform
/complete, accomplish/ it until the day of Jesus Christ: 7Even as
it is meet /just, right/ for me to think this of you all, because I
have you in my heart; inasmuch as both in my bonds, and in the
defence and confirmation /establishment, strengthening/ of the
gospel, ye all are partakers of my grace. 8For God is my record
/witness/, how greatly I long after you all in the bowels /affec-
tions, compassions/ of Jesus Christ. 9And this I pray, that your
love may abound yet more and more in knowledge and ~~in~~ all
judgment; 10That ye may approve /prove, put to the test/ things
that are excellent; that ye may be sincere /pure, spotless/ and
without offence till the day of Christ; 11Being filled with the
fruits of righteousness, which are by Jesus Christ, unto the
glory and praise of God.

Thankfulness for their faith and prayer for their good works

Col. 1:3–14

3We give thanks to God and the Father of our Lord Jesus
Christ, praying always for you, 4Since we heard of your faith in
Christ Jesus, and of ~~the~~ {your} love which ye have to all the
saints, 5For the hope which is laid up for you in heaven,
whereof ye heard before in the word of the truth of the gospel;
6Which is come unto you, as ~~it is~~ in all {generations of} the
world; and bringeth forth fruit, as it doth also in you, since the
day ye heard of it, and knew the grace of God in truth: 7As ye
also learned of Epaphras our dear fellowservant, who is for
you a faithful minister of Christ; 8Who also declared unto us
your love in the Spirit. 9For this cause we also, since the day we
heard ~~of it~~, do not cease to pray for you, and to desire that ye
might be filled with the knowledge of his will in all wisdom and
spiritual understanding; 10That ye might walk worthy of the
Lord unto all pleasing, being fruitful in every good work, and
increasing in the knowledge of God; 11Strengthened with all
might, according to his glorious power, unto all patience and
longsuffering with joyfulness; 12Giving thanks unto the Father,
which hath made /enabled, qualified/ us \you\ meet to be par-

takers /in the portion, share/ of the inheritance of the saints in light: [13]Who hath delivered us from the power of darkness, and hath translated us into the kingdom of his dear Son: [14]In whom we have redemption through his blood, ~~even~~ the forgiveness of sins.

Congratulations for their faithful example

[2a]We give thanks {[2c]}always, {[2f]}making mention of you 1 Thes.
{[2e]}all {[2g]}in our prayers {[2b]}to God [2d]for you; [3]Remembering 1:2–10
without ceasing your work of faith, and labour of love, and
patience of hope in our Lord Jesus Christ, in the sight of God
and our Father; [4]Knowing, brethren beloved /beloved of God,
your election/, your election of God. [5]For our gospel came not
unto you in word only, but also in power, and in the Holy
Ghost, and in much assurance; as ye know what manner of men
we were among you for your sake. [6]And ye became followers
/imitators/ of us, and of the Lord, having received the word in
much affliction, with joy of the Holy Ghost: [7]So that ye were
ensamples to all that believe in Macedonia and Achaia. [8]For
from you sounded out the word of the Lord not only in Macedonia and Achaia, but also in every place your faith to{ward}
God~~-ward~~ is spread abroad; so that we need not to speak any
thing. [9]For they themselves shew of us what manner of entering
in we had unto you, and how ye turned to God from idols to
serve the living and true God; [10]And to wait for his Son from
heaven, whom he raised from the dead, ~~even~~ Jesus, which
delivered us from the wrath to come.

Prayer for reunion

[3]I thank God, whom I serve from ~~my~~ forefathers with 2 Tim.
pure conscience, that without ceasing I have remembrance of 1:3–5
thee [Timothy] in my prayers night and day; [4]Greatly desiring
to see thee, being mindful of thy tears, that I may be filled with
joy; [5]When I call to remembrance the unfeigned faith that is in
thee, which dwelt first in thy grandmother Lois, and thy
mother Eunice; and I am persuaded that in thee also.

Thanksgiving and prayer

Philem. [4]I thank my God, making mention of thee always in my
1:4–7 prayers, [5]Hearing of thy love and faith, which thou hast toward
the Lord Jesus, and toward all saints; [6]That the communication
/participation, fellowship/ of thy faith may become effectual
/active/ by the acknowledging of every good thing which is in
you in Christ Jesus. [7]For we have great joy and consolation in
thy love, because the bowels /affections, compassion/ of the
saints are refreshed by thee, brother.

May all converted Saints rejoice

James [9]Let the brother of low degree /humble/ rejoice in that he
1:9–11 is exalted /given a high position/: [10]But the rich, in that he is
made low: because as the flower of the grass he shall pass away.
[11]For the sun is no sooner risen with a burning heat, but it withereth the grass, and the flower thereof falleth, and the grace of
the fashion of it /beauty of its appearance, face/ perisheth [is
lost]: so also shall the rich man fade away in his ways.

2

Biographical and Personal Statements

Paul's Conversion and Calling As an Apostle

Paul is forgiven

[12]And I thank Christ Jesus our Lord, who hath enabled 1 Tim.
me, for that he counted me faithful, putting me into the min- 1:12–17
istry; [13]Who was before a blasphemer, and a persecutor, and
injurious /violent, insolent/: but I obtained mercy, because I did
it ignorantly in unbelief [Acts 9:1–9]. [14]And the grace of our
Lord was exceeding abundant with faith and love which is in
Christ Jesus. [15]This is a \faithful, human or wide-spread\ saying,
and worthy of all acceptation, that Christ Jesus came into the
world to save sinners; of whom I am chief. [16]Howbeit for this
cause I obtained mercy, that in me first Jesus Christ might shew
forth all longsuffering, for a pattern to them which should
hereafter believe on him to life everlasting. [17]Now unto the
King eternal, immortal, invisible /unseen/, the only wise God,
~~be~~ honour and glory for ever and ever. Amen.

God calls and trains Paul to be an apostle

[11]But I certify /declare to, make known to/ you, brethren, Gal.
that the gospel which was preached of me is not after man. [12]For 1:11–24
I neither received it of man /from a man/, neither was I taught
~~it~~, but by the revelation /through a revelation/ of Jesus Christ.
[13]For ye have heard of my conversation /conduct/ in time past in
the Jews' religion, how that beyond measure I persecuted the
church of God, and wasted it /was ravaging, destroying/: [14]And
profited /was advancing/ in the Jews' religion above many my
equals /men of my age/ in mine own nation, being more exceedingly zealous of the traditions of my fathers. [15]But when it

pleased God, who separated /set apart, appointed/ me from my
mother's womb, and called me by his grace, [16]To reveal his Son
in me, that I might preach him among the heathen /nations,
Gentiles/; immediately I conferred /consulted/ not with flesh
and blood: [17]Neither went I up to Jerusalem to them which
were apostles before me; but I went into Arabia, and returned
again unto Damascus. [18]Then after three years I went up to
Jerusalem to see Peter, and abode with him fifteen days. [19]But
other of the apostles saw I none, save James the Lord's brother.
[20]Now the things which I write unto you, behold, before God, I
lie not. [21]Afterwards I came into the regions of Syria and Cili-
cia; [22]And was unknown by face unto the churches of Judaea
which were in Christ: [23]But they had heard only, That he which
persecuted us in times past now preacheth the faith which once
he destroyed. [24]And they glorified God ~~in~~ {on account of} me.

1 Cor. 15:9–11 [9]For I am the least of the apostles, that am not meet /ade-
quate, able, sufficient, competent/ to be called an apostle,
because I persecuted the church of God. [10]But by the grace of
God I am what I am: and his grace which was bestowed upon
me was not in vain; ~~but~~ {for} I laboured more abundantly
than they all: yet not I, but the grace of God which was with
me. [11]Therefore whether ~~it were~~ I or they, so we preach, and
so ye believed.

Apostles accept Paul at Jerusalem

Gal. 2:1–10 [1]Then fourteen years after I went up again to Jerusalem
with Barnabas, and took Titus with me also [Acts 15:2]. [2]And I
went up by revelation, and communicated /reported/ unto
them that gospel which I preach among the Gentiles, but pri-
vately to them which were of reputation, lest by any means I
should run, or had run, in vain. [3]But neither Titus, who was
with me, being a Greek, was compelled to be circumcised: [4a]~~And
that because of~~ {Notwithstanding, there were some [4c]}brought
in {by [4b]}false brethren unawares, [4d]who came in privily to spy
out our liberty which we have in Christ Jesus, that they might
bring us into bondage: [5]To whom we gave place by subjection
/yielding to them/, no, not for an hour; that the truth of the
gospel might continue with you. [6]But of these who seemed to be

somewhat, (whatsoever they were, it maketh no matter to me: God accepteth /shows favoritism to/ no man's person:) for they who seemed to be somewhat in conference /high reputation/ added nothing to me: [7]But contrariwise, when they saw that the gospel of the uncircumcision [to the Gentiles] was committed unto me, as the gospel of the circumcision [to the Jews] was unto Peter; [8](For he that wrought effectually in Peter to the apostleship of the circumcision, the same was mighty in me toward the Gentiles:) [9]And when James, Cephas, and John, who seemed to be pillars /as pillars supporting the church/, perceived the grace that was given unto me, they gave to me and Barnabas the right hands of fellowship /partnership/; that we should go unto the heathen /nations, Gentiles/, and they unto the circumcision. [10]Only they would that we should remember the poor; the same which I also was forward /zealous, earnest/ to do.

Paul rebukes Peter at Antioch

Gal. 2:11–14

[11]But when Peter was come to Antioch, I withstood him to the face, because he was to be blamed. [12]For before that certain [men] came from James, he [Peter] did eat with the Gentiles: but when they were come, he withdrew and separated himself, fearing them which were of the circumcision. [13]And the other Jews dissembled likewise with him; insomuch that Barnabas also was carried away with their dissimulation /hypocrisy/. [14]But when I saw that they walked not uprightly according to the truth of the gospel, I said unto Peter before them all, If thou, being a Jew, livest after the manner of {the} Gentiles, and not as do the Jews, why compellest thou the Gentiles to live as do the Jews?

Missionary Journeys and Activities

The faith and the patience of the Thessalonian converts

1 Thes. 2:13–16

[13]For this cause also thank we God without ceasing, because, when ye received the word of God which ye heard of us, ye received ~~it~~ not ~~as~~ the word of men, but as it is in truth, the word of God, which effectually worketh also in you ~~that~~ [who]

believe. [14]For ye, brethren, became followers /imitators/ of the
churches of God which in Judaea are in Christ Jesus: for ye also
have suffered like things of your own countrymen, even as they
~~have~~ of the /those particular/ Jews [15]Who both killed the Lord
Jesus, and their \own\ prophets, and have persecuted us; and
they please not God, and are contrary to all men: [16]Forbidding
us to speak to the Gentiles that they might be saved, to fill up
their sins alway /always/: for the wrath is ~~come~~ {coming} upon
them to the uttermost.

Paul's desire to visit the Saints in Thessalonica

1 Thes. [17]But we, brethren, being taken from you for a short time
2:17–20 in presence, not in heart, endeavoured the more abundantly to
see your face with great desire. [18]Wherefore we would have
come unto you, even I Paul, once and again; but Satan hindered us. [19]For what is our hope, or joy, or crown of rejoicing?
Are not even ye in the presence of our Lord Jesus Christ at his
coming? [20]For ye are our glory and joy.

Timothy's mission to Thessalonica

1 Thes. [1]Wherefore when we could no longer forbear, we thought
3:1–5 it good to be left at Athens alone; [2]And sent Timotheus, our
brother, and minister of God, and our fellowlabourer in the
gospel of Christ, to establish you, and to comfort you concerning your faith: [3]That no man should be moved /disturbed, per-
turbed/ by these afflictions: for yourselves know that we are
appointed thereunto [Acts 16:1–4]. [4]For verily, when we were
with you, we told you before that we should suffer tribulation;
even as it came to pass, and ye know. [5]For this cause, when I
could no longer forbear, I sent to know your faith, lest by some
means the tempter have tempted /put to trial, test/ you, and our
labour be in vain.

Paul thanks God for good reports of the Thessalonians

1 Thes. [6]But now when Timotheus came from you unto us, and
3:6–13 brought us good tidings of your faith and charity, and that ye
have good remembrance of us always, desiring greatly to see us,

as we also ~~to see~~ you: [7]Therefore, brethren, we were comforted
over you in all our affliction and distress by your faith: [8]For now
we live, if ye stand fast in the Lord. [9]For what thanks can we
render to God again for you, for all the joy wherewith we joy
for your sakes before our God; [10]Night and day praying exceedingly that we might see your face, and might perfect that which
is lacking in your faith? [11]Now God himself ~~and~~ our Father, and
our Lord Jesus Christ, direct our way unto you. [12]And the Lord
make you to increase and abound in love one toward another,
and toward all ~~men~~, even as we do toward you: [13]To the end he
may stablish /firmly fix/ your hearts unblameable in holiness
before God, even our Father, at the coming of our Lord Jesus
Christ with all his saints.

Plans for travel to Corinth

[5]Now I will come unto you, when I shall pass through 1 Cor.
Macedonia: for I do pass through Macedonia. [6]And it may be 16:5–9
that I will abide, yea, and winter with you, that ye may bring me
on my journey whithersoever I go. [7]For I will not see you now
by the way /in passing/; but I trust /hope/ to tarry a while with
you, if the Lord permit. [8]But I will tarry at Ephesus until Pente-
cost. [9]For a great door /opportunity/ and effectual /promising/ is
opened unto me, ~~and~~ {but} there are many adversaries.

On Timothy and Apollos coming to Corinth

[10]Now if Timotheus come, see that he may be with you 1 Cor.
without fear: for he worketh the work of the Lord, as I also ~~do~~. 16:10–12
[11]Let no man therefore despise him: but conduct him forth in
peace, that he may come unto me: for I look for him with the
brethren. [12]As touching /concerning/ our brother Apollos, I
greatly desired him to come unto you with the brethren: but his
will was not at all to come at this time; but he will come when he
shall have convenient time.

An appeal to accept Timothy

[14]I write not these things to shame you, but as my beloved 1 Cor.
sons I warn ~~you~~. [15]For though ye have ten thousand instructors 4:14–21

in Christ, yet have ye not many fathers: for in Christ Jesus I have begotten you through the gospel. [16]Wherefore I beseech you, be ye followers /imitators/ of me. [17]For this cause have I sent unto you Timotheus, who is my beloved son, and faithful in the Lord, who shall bring you into remembrance of my ways which be in Christ, as I teach every where in every church. [18]Now some are puffed up, as though I would not come to you. [19]But I will come to you shortly, if the Lord will, and will know, not the speech of them which are puffed up, but the power. [20]For the kingdom of God is not in word, but in power. [21]What will ye? shall I come unto you with a rod, or in love, and in the spirit of meekness /gentleness, kindness/?

Paul changed his plans to visit Corinth not due to fickleness

2 Cor. 1:12–2:4

[12]For our rejoicing is this, the testimony of our conscience, that in simplicity /plainness, singleness of heart/ \or holiness\ and godly sincerity /moral purity, gentleness, mercy/, not with fleshly wisdom, but by the grace of God, we have had our conversation in the world, and more abundantly to you-ward. [13]For we write none other things unto you, than what ye read or acknowledge; and I trust ye shall acknowledge even to the end; [14]As also ye have acknowledged us in part, that we are your rejoicing, even as ye also ~~are~~ ours in the day of the Lord Jesus. [15]And in this confidence I was minded to come unto you before, that ye might have a second benefit; [16]And to pass by you into Macedonia, and to come again out of Macedonia unto you, and of you to be brought on my way toward Judaea. [17]When I therefore was thus minded, did I use lightness /light-mindedness, levity/? or the things that I purpose /decide/, do I purpose according to the flesh, that with me there should be yea yea, and nay nay? [18]But ~~as~~ God ~~is~~ true, our word toward you was not yea and nay. [19]For the Son of God, Jesus Christ, who was preached among you by us, ~~even~~ by me and Silvanus and Timotheus, was not yea and nay, but in him was yea. [20]For all the promises of God in him are yea, and in him Amen, unto the glory of God by us. [21]Now he which stablisheth us with you in Christ, and hath anointed us, is God; [22]Who hath also sealed us, and given the earnest of the Spirit in our hearts. [23]Moreover I

call God for a record upon my soul, that to spare you I came not as yet unto Corinth. [24]Not for that we have dominion over your faith, but are helpers of your joy: for by faith ye stand. [1]But I determined this with myself, that I would not come again to you in heaviness. [2]For if I make you sorry, who is he then that maketh me glad, but the same which is made sorry by me? [3]And I wrote this same unto you, lest, when I came, I should have sorrow from them of whom I ought to rejoice; having confidence in you all, that my joy is ~~the joy~~ of you all. [4]For out of much affliction and anguish of heart I wrote unto you with many tears; not that ye should be grieved, but that ye might know the love which I have more abundantly unto you.

In Troas and Macedonia

[12]Furthermore, when I came to Troas to preach Christ's 2 Cor.
gospel, and a door was opened unto me of the Lord, [13]I had no 2:12–13
rest in my spirit, because I found not Titus my brother: but taking my leave of them, I went from thence into Macedonia.

Paul is joined by Titus in Macedonia

[5]For, when we were come into Macedonia, our flesh had 2 Cor.
no rest, but we were troubled on every side; without ~~were~~ fight- 7:5–7
ings, within ~~were~~ fears. [6]Nevertheless God, that comforteth those that are cast down, comforted us by the coming of Titus; [7]And not by his coming only, but by the consolation wherewith he was comforted in you, when he told us your earnest desire, your mourning, your fervent mind toward me; so that I rejoiced the more.

Paul beseeches the Galatians to remain zealous in righteousness

[12]Brethren, I beseech you, {to} be as {perfect as} I am Gal.
{perfect}; for I am {persuaded} as ye ~~are~~ {have a knowledge of 4:12–20
me}: ye have not injured me at all {by your sayings}. [13]Ye know how through infirmity /weakness, feebleness/ of the flesh I preached the gospel unto you at the first. [14]And my temptation /trial, test/ which was in my flesh ye despised not, nor rejected; but received me as an angel of God, even as Christ Jesus. [15]Where is then the blessedness ye spake of? for I bear you

record, that, if ~~it had been~~ possible, ye would have plucked out your own eyes, and have given them to me. 16Am I therefore become your enemy, because I tell you the truth? 17They [the Jewish-Christians] zealously affect you, but not well; yea, they would exclude you, that ye might affect them. 18But it is good to be zealously affected always in a good thing, and not only when I am present with you. 19My little children, of whom I travail in birth again until Christ be formed in you, 20I desire to be present with you now, and to change my voice; for I stand in doubt /am perplexed about/ of you.

Paul's desires to visit Rome and Spain

Rom. 15:22–33

22For which cause [in preaching the gospel in remote places] also I have been much hindered from coming to you. 23But now having no more place /opportunity/ in these parts, and having a great desire these many years to come unto you; 24When~~soever~~ I take my journey into Spain, I will come to you: for I trust to see you in my journey, and to be brought on my way thitherward by you, if first I be somewhat filled ~~with~~ {through} your ~~company~~ {prayers}. 25But now I go unto Jerusalem to minister unto the saints. 26For it hath pleased them of Macedonia and Achaia to make a certain contribution for the poor saints which are at Jerusalem. 27It hath pleased them ~~verily~~; and their debtors they are. For if the Gentiles have been made partakers of their spiritual things, their duty is also to minister unto them in carnal /material, temporal/ things. 28When therefore I have performed this, and have sealed to them this fruit, I will come by you into Spain. 29And I am sure that, when I come unto you, I shall come in the fulness of the blessing of \the gospel of\ Christ. 30Now I beseech you, brethren, for the Lord Jesus Christ's sake, and for the love of the Spirit, that ye strive together with me in ~~your~~ prayers to God for me; 31That I may be delivered from them that do not believe /refuse belief or obedience/ in Judaea; and that my service which I have for Jerusalem may be accepted of the saints; 32That I may come unto you with joy by the will of God, and may with you be refreshed. 33Now the God of peace be with you all. Amen.

The mission of Timothy and Epaphroditus

[19]But I trust in the Lord Jesus to send Timotheus shortly Philip.
unto you, that I also may be of good comfort, when I know your 2:19–30
state. [20]For I have no man likeminded, who will naturally care
for your state. [21]For all seek their own, not the things which are
Jesus Christ's. [22]But ye know the proof /trial/ of him, that, as a
son with the father, he hath served with me in the gospel. [23]Him
therefore I hope to send presently, so soon as I shall see how it
will go with me. [24]But I trust in the Lord that I also myself shall
come shortly. [25]Yet I supposed it necessary to send to you Epaphroditus, my brother, and companion in labour, and fellowsoldier, but your messenger, and he that ministered to my
wants. [26]For he longed after you all, and was full of heaviness,
because that ye had heard that he had been sick. [27]For indeed
he was sick nigh unto death: but God had mercy on him; and
not on him only, but on me also, lest I should have sorrow upon
sorrow. [28]I sent him therefore the more carefully, that, when ye
see him again, ye may rejoice, and that I may be the less sorrowful. [29]Receive him therefore in the Lord with all gladness;
and hold such in reputation /honor/: [30]Because for the work of
Christ he was nigh unto death, not regarding his life, to supply
your lack of service toward me.

Paul's concern for the Colossians' faith

[1]For I would that ye knew what great conflict /anguish/ I Col.
have for you, and ~~for~~ them at Laodicea, and ~~for~~ as many as have 2:1–5
not seen my face in the flesh; [2a]That their hearts might be comforted, being knit together in love, and unto all riches of the full
assurance of understanding, to the acknowledgement of the
mystery of God, and of {[2c]}~~and of~~ Christ, {who is of God, even
[2b]}~~and of~~ the Father. [3]In whom are hid all the treasures of wisdom and knowledge. [4]And this I say, lest any man should
beguile you with enticing words. [5]For though I be absent in the
flesh, yet am I with you in the spirit, joying and beholding your
order, and the stedfastness of your faith in Christ.

Autobiographical Statements of Testimony and Intent

Paul asserts the power of the gospel

Rom. 1:16–17 16For I am not ashamed of the gospel of Christ: for it is the power of God unto salvation to every one that believeth; to the Jew first, and also to the Greek. 17For therein is the righteousness of God revealed ~~from faith to faith~~ {through faith on his name}: as it is written, "The just shall live by faith" [Habakkuk 2:4].

Paul preaches the gospel of Christ

Rom. 15:14–21 14And I myself also am persuaded of you, my brethren, that ye also are full of goodness, filled with all knowledge, able also to admonish one another. 15Nevertheless, brethren, I have written the more boldly unto you in some sort /part/, as putting you in mind, because of the grace that is given to me of God, 16That I should be the minister /servant at one's own expense/ of Jesus Christ to the Gentiles, ministering the gospel of God, that the offering /sacrifice/ up of the Gentiles might be acceptable, being sanctified by the Holy Ghost. 17I have therefore whereof I may glory through Jesus Christ in those things which pertain to God. 18For I will not dare to speak of any of those things which Christ hath not wrought by me, to make the Gentiles obedient, by word and deed, 19Through mighty signs and wonders, by the power of the Spirit of God; so that from Jerusalem, and round about unto Illyricum, I have fully preached the gospel of Christ. 20Yea, so have I strived to preach the gospel, not where Christ was named, lest I should build upon another man's foundation: 21But as it is written, "To whom he was not spoken of, they shall see: and they that have not heard shall understand" [Isaiah 52:15].

Paul's labors in the service of the Gentiles

Col. 1:21–29 21And you, that were sometime /formerly/ alienated and enemies in ~~your~~ mind by wicked works, yet now hath he reconciled 22In the body of his flesh through death, to present you holy and unblameable and unreproveable in his sight: 23If ye continue in the faith grounded /established and steadfast/ and settled, and ~~be~~ not moved away from the hope of the gospel, which ye have heard, ~~and~~ which was preached to every creature which is under heaven; whereof I Paul am made a minister; [24]Who now rejoice in my sufferings for you, and fill up that which is behind of the afflictions of Christ in my flesh for his body's sake, which is the church: [25]Whereof I am made a minister, according to the dispensation of God which is given to me for you, to fulfil the word of God; [26]~~Even~~ the mystery which hath been hid from ages and from generations, but now is made manifest to his saints: [27]To whom God would make known what is the riches of the glory of this mystery among the Gentiles; which is Christ in you, the hope of glory: [28]Whom we preach, warning every man, and teaching every man in all wisdom; that we may present every man perfect in Christ Jesus: [29]Whereunto I also labour, striving according to his working, which worketh in me mightily.

Paul describes his preaching style

[1]For yourselves, brethren, know our entrance in unto you, 1 Thes. 2:1–12
that it was not in vain: [2]But even after that we had suffered before, and were shamefully entreated, as ye know, at Philippi, we were bold in our God to speak unto you the gospel of God with much contention /effort, struggle/. [3]For our exhortation ~~was~~ not of deceit, nor of uncleanness, nor in guile: [4]But as we were allowed /approved, found worthy, chosen/ of God to be put in trust /entrusted/ with the gospel, even so we speak; not as pleasing men, but God, which trieth /examines, proves by trial/ our hearts. [5]For neither at any time used we flattering words, as ye know, nor a cloke of covetousness; God ~~is~~ witness: [6]Nor of men sought we glory, neither of you, nor ~~yet~~ of others, when we might have been burdensome, as the apostles of Christ. [7]But we were \gentle, infants\ among you, even as a nurse cherisheth her children: [8]So being affectionately desirous of you, we were willing to have imparted unto you, not the gospel of God only, but also our own souls, because ye were dear unto us. [9]For ye remember, brethren, our labour and travail /toil/: for labouring night and day, because we would not be chargeable /burdensome/

unto any of you, we preached unto you the gospel of God. [10]Ye are witnesses, and God also, how holily and justly and unblameably we behaved ourselves among you that believe: [11]As ye know how we exhorted and comforted and charged every one of you, as a father ~~doth~~ his children, [12]That ye would walk worthy of God, who hath called you unto his kingdom and glory.

Paul explains his approach to missionary labors

1 Cor. 9:15–27

[15]But I have used none of these things [unrighteous dominion over others]: neither have I written these things, that it should be so done unto me: for it were better for me to die, than that any man should make my glorying void. [16]For though I preach the gospel, I have nothing to glory of: for necessity is laid upon me; yea, woe is unto me, if I preach not the gospel! [17]For if I do this thing willingly, I have a reward: but if against my will, a dispensation ~~of the gospel~~ is committed unto me. [18]What is my reward then? ~~Verily~~ that, when I preach the gospel, I may make the gospel of Christ without charge, that I abuse not my power in the gospel. [19]For though I be free from all ~~men~~, yet have I made myself servant unto all, that I might gain the more. [20]And unto the Jews I became as a Jew, that I might gain the Jews; to them that are under the law, as under the law, that I might gain them that are under the law; [21]To them that are without law, as without law, (being not without law to God, but under the law to Christ,) that I might gain them that are without law. [22]To the weak became I as weak, that I might gain the weak: I am made all things to all men, that I might by all means save some. [23]And this I do for the gospel's sake, that I might be partaker thereof with you. [24]Know ye not that they which run in a race ~~run~~ all {run}, but {only} one receiveth the prize? So run, that ye may obtain. [25]And every man that striveth for the mastery is temperate in all things. Now they do it to obtain a corruptible crown; but we an incorruptible. [26]I therefore so run, not as uncertainly; so fight I, not as one that beateth the air: [27]But I keep under /rigorously discipline/ my body, and bring it into subjection: lest that by any means, when I have preached to others, I myself should be a castaway.

Paul's reply to accusations of weakness and overbearing

1Now I Paul myself beseech you by the meekness and gen- 2 Cor.
tleness of Christ, who in presence am base among you, but 10:1–11
being absent am bold toward you: 2But I beseech you, that I
may not be bold when I am present with that confidence,
wherewith I think to be bold against some, which think of us as
if we walked according to the flesh. 3For though we walk in the
flesh, we do not war after the flesh: 4(For the weapons of our
warfare are not carnal, but mighty through God to the pulling
down of strong holds;) 5Casting down imaginations, and every
high thing that exalteth itself against the knowledge of God,
and bringing into captivity every thought to the obedience of
Christ; 6And having in a readiness to revenge all disobedience,
when your obedience is fulfilled. 7Do ye look on things after the
outward appearance? If any man trust to himself that he is
Christ's, let him of himself think this again, that, as he is
Christ's, even so are we Christ's. 8For though I should boast
somewhat more of our authority, which the Lord hath given us
for edification, and not for your destruction, I should not be
ashamed: 9That I may not seem as if I would terrify you by letters /epistles/. 10For his letters, say they, are weighty and powerful; but his bodily presence is weak, and his speech
contemptible. 11Let such an one think this, that, such as we are
in word by letters when we are absent, such will we be also in
deed when we are present.

Paul's aversion to ambition or self-commendation

12For we dare not make ourselves of the number, or com- 2 Cor.
pare ourselves with some that commend themselves: but they 10:12–18
measuring themselves by themselves, and comparing themselves among themselves, are not wise. 13But we will not boast of
things without our measure, but according to the measure of
the rule which God hath distributed to us, a measure to reach
even unto you. 14For we stretch not ourselves beyond our measure, as though we reached not unto you: for we are come as far
as to you also in preaching the gospel of Christ: 15Not boasting
of things without our measure, that is, of other men's labours;

but having hope, when your faith is increased, that we shall be enlarged by you according to our rule abundantly, 16To preach the gospel in the regions beyond you, and not to boast in another man's line of things made ready to our hand. 17"But he that glorieth, let him glory in the Lord" [Jeremiah 9:24]. 18For not he that commendeth himself is approved, but whom the Lord commendeth.

Paul sounds his own praises and rebukes false apostles

2 Cor. 11:1–15 1Would to God ye could bear with me a little in ~~my~~ folly: and indeed bear with me. 2For I am jealous over you with godly jealousy: for I have espoused you to one husband, that I may present ~~you as~~ a chaste virgin to Christ. 3But I fear, lest by any means, as the serpent beguiled Eve through his subtilty, so your minds should be corrupted from the simplicity that is in Christ. 4For if he that cometh preacheth another Jesus, whom we have not preached, or if ye receive another spirit, which ye have not received, or another gospel, which ye have not accepted, ye might well bear with ~~him~~ {me}. 5For I suppose I was not a whit behind the very chiefest apostles. 6But though ~~I be~~ rude in speech, yet not in knowledge; but we have been throughly made manifest among you in all things. 7Have I committed an offence in abasing myself that ye might be exalted, because I have preached to you the gospel of God freely? 8I robbed other churches /despoiled other churches, having taken provisions for you/, taking wages ~~of them~~, to do you service. 9And when I was present with you, and wanted, I was chargeable to no man: for that which was lacking to me the brethren which came from Macedonia supplied: and in all things I have kept myself from being burdensome unto you, and so will I keep myself. 10As the truth of Christ is in me, no man shall stop me of this boasting in the regions of Achaia. 11Wherefore? because I love you not? God knoweth. 12But what I do, that I will do, that I may cut off occasion from them which desire occasion; that wherein they glory /boast/, they may be found even as we. 13For such are false apostles, deceitful workers, transforming themselves into the apostles of Christ. 14And no marvel; for Satan himself is transformed into an angel of light. 15Therefore it is no great thing if

his ministers also be transformed as the ministers of righteousness; whose end shall be according to their works.

Paul's sufferings as an apostle

[16]I say again, Let no man think me a fool; if otherwise, yet 2 Cor.
as a fool receive /listen to, bear with, follow/ me, that I may boast 11:16–33
myself a little. [17]That which I speak, I speak ~~it~~ not after the Lord, but as it were foolishly, in this confidence of boasting. [18]Seeing that many glory /boast/ after the flesh, I will glory /boast/ also. [19]For ye suffer fools gladly, seeing ye ~~yourselves~~ are wise. [20]For ye suffer, if a man bring you into bondage, if a man devour ~~you~~, if a man take ~~of you~~, if a man exalt himself, if a man smite you on the face. [21]I speak as concerning reproach, as though we had been weak. Howbeit whereinsoever any is bold, (I speak foolishly,) I am bold also. [22]Are they Hebrews? so am I. Are they Israelites? so am I. Are they the seed of Abraham? so am I. [23]Are they ministers of Christ? (I speak as a fool) ~~I am~~ {so am I} ~~more;~~ in labours more abundant, in stripes above measure, in prisons more frequent, in deaths oft. [24]Of the Jews five times received I forty ~~stripes~~ save one. [25]Thrice was I beaten with rods, once was I stoned, thrice I suffered shipwreck, a night and a day I have been in the deep; [26]~~In~~ journeyings often, ~~in~~ perils of waters, ~~in~~ perils of robbers, ~~in~~ perils by ~~mine own~~ countrymen, ~~in~~ perils by the heathen, ~~in~~ perils in the city, ~~in~~ perils in the wilderness, ~~in~~ perils in the sea, ~~in~~ perils among false brethren; [27]In weariness /toil, trouble/ and painfulness, in watchings often, in hunger and thirst, in fastings often, in cold and nakedness. [28]Beside those things that are without, that which cometh upon me daily, the care of all the churches. [29]Who is weak, and I am not weak? who is offended, and I ~~burn~~ {anger} not? [30]If I must needs glory /boast/, I will glory /boast/ of the things which concern mine infirmities. [31]The God and Father of our Lord Jesus Christ, which is blessed for evermore, knoweth that I lie not. [32]In Damascus the governor under Aretas the king kept the city of the Damascenes with a garrison, desirous to apprehend me: [33]And through a window in a basket was I let down by the wall, and escaped his hands.

Paul gives thanks after affliction

2 Cor. 1:3–11 3Blessed ~~be~~ God, even the Father of our Lord Jesus Christ, the Father of mercies, and the God of all comfort; 4Who comforteth us in all our tribulation, that we may be able to comfort them which are in any trouble, by the comfort wherewith we ourselves are comforted of God. 5For as the sufferings of Christ abound in us, so our consolation also aboundeth by Christ. 6And whether we be afflicted, ~~it is~~ for your consolation and salvation, which is effectual /active, operative/ in the enduring of the same sufferings which we also suffer: or whether we be comforted, it is for your consolation and salvation. 7And our hope of you is stedfast, knowing, that as ye are partakers of the sufferings, so ~~shall ye be~~ also of the consolation. 8For we would not, brethren, have you ignorant of our trouble which came to us in Asia, that we were pressed out of measure, above strength, insomuch that we despaired even of life: 9But we had the sentence of death in ourselves, that we should not trust in ourselves, but in God which raiseth the dead: 10Who delivered us from so great a death, and doth deliver: in whom we trust that he will yet deliver ~~us~~; 11Ye also helping together by prayer for us, that for the gift bestowed upon us by the means of many persons thanks may be given by many on our behalf.

Paul's visions and revelations

2 Cor. 12:1–10 1It is not expedient for me doubtless to glory /boast/. I will come to visions and revelations of the Lord. 2I knew a man in Christ above fourteen years ago /I know a man in Christ who fourteen years ago/, (whether in the body, I cannot tell; or whether out of the body, I cannot tell: God knoweth;) such an one caught up to the third heaven. 3And I knew such a man, (whether in the body, or out of the body, I cannot tell: God knoweth;) 4How that he was caught up into paradise, and heard unspeakable /ineffable/ words, which it is not lawful /possible, permitted/ for a man to utter. 5Of such an one will I glory /boast/: yet of myself I will not glory /boast/, but in mine infirmities. 6For though I would desire to glory /boast/, I shall not be a fool; for I will say the truth: but now I forbear, lest any man

should think of me above that which he seeth {of} me ~~to be~~, or that he heareth of me. [7]And lest I should be exalted above measure through the abundance of the revelations, there was given to me a thorn in the flesh, the messenger of Satan to buffet me, lest I should be exalted above measure. [8]For this thing I besought the Lord thrice, that it might depart from me. [9]And he said unto me, My grace is sufficient for thee: for my strength is made perfect in weakness. Most gladly therefore will I rather glory /boast/ in my infirmities, that the power of Christ may rest upon me. [10]Therefore I take pleasure in infirmities, in reproaches, in necessities, in persecutions, in distresses for Christ's sake: for when I am weak, then am I strong.

Paul's own choice of life in Christ

Philip. 1:12–26

[12]But I would ye should understand, brethren, that the things which happened unto me have fallen /come/ out rather unto the furtherance of the gospel; [13]So that my bonds in Christ are manifest in all the palace, and in all other places; [14]And many of the brethren in the Lord, waxing confident by my bonds, are much more bold to speak the word without fear. [15]Some indeed preach Christ even of envy and strife; and some also of good will: [16]The one preach Christ of contention, not sincerely, supposing to add affliction to my bonds: [17]But the other of love, knowing that I am set for the defence of the gospel. [18]What then? notwithstanding, every way, whether in pretence, or in truth, Christ is preached; and I therein do rejoice, yea, and will rejoice. [19]For I know that this shall turn to my salvation through your prayer, and the supply of the Spirit of Jesus Christ, [20]According to my earnest expectation and ~~my~~ hope, that in nothing I shall be ashamed, but ~~that~~ with all boldness, as always, so now also Christ shall be magnified in my body, whether ~~it be~~ by life, or by death. [22]{[21]}But if I live in the flesh, ~~this is~~ {ye are} the fruit of my labour: yet what I shall choose I wot /know/ not. [21]{[22]}For to me to live is {to do the will of} Christ, and to die is {my} gain. [23]~~For~~ {Now} I am in a strait betwixt two /hard pressed to choose/, having a desire to depart, and to be with Christ; which is far better: [24]Nevertheless to abide in the flesh is more needful for you. [25]And having this

confidence, I know that I shall abide and continue with you all
for your furtherance and joy of faith; [26]That your rejoicing
{with me} may be more abundant in Jesus Christ for ~~me by~~ my
coming to you again.

Philip. 3:4–14 [4]Though I might also have confidence in the flesh. If any
other man thinketh that he hath whereof he might trust in the
flesh, I more: [5]Circumcised the eighth day, of the stock of Israel,
of the tribe of Benjamin, an Hebrew of the Hebrews; as touching the law, a Pharisee; [6]Concerning zeal, persecuting the
church; touching the righteousness which is in the law, blameless. [7]But what things were gain to me, those I counted loss for
Christ. [8]Yea doubtless, and I count all things but loss for the
excellency of the knowledge of Christ Jesus my Lord: for whom
I have suffered the loss of all things, and do count them but
dung /refuse/, that I may win /gain from/ Christ, [9]And be found
in him, not having mine own righteousness, which is of the law,
but that which is through the faith of Christ, the righteousness
which is of God by faith: [10]That I may know him, and the power
of his resurrection, and the fellowship of his sufferings, being
made conformable unto his death; [11]If by any means I might
attain unto the resurrection of the ~~dead~~ {just}. [12]Not as though
I had already attained \or had already been justified\, either
were already perfect: but I follow after /press forward/, if that I
may apprehend that for which also I am apprehended of Christ
Jesus. [13]Brethren, I count not myself to have apprehended: but
~~this~~ one thing I do, forgetting those things which are behind,
and reaching forth unto those things which are before, [14]I press
toward the mark for the prize of the high calling of God in
Christ Jesus.

Witnesses of Christ's glory from revelation and scripture

2 Pet. 1:16–21 [16]For we have not followed cunningly devised fables, when
we made known unto you the power and coming of our Lord
Jesus Christ, but were eyewitnesses of his majesty. [17]For he
received from God the Father honour and glory, when there
came such a voice to him from the excellent glory, "This is my
beloved Son, in whom I am well pleased" [Matthew 17:5]. [18]And
this voice which came from heaven we heard, when we were

with him in the holy mount. [19]We have ~~also~~ {therefore} a more
sure {knowledge of the} word of prophecy; ~~whereunto~~ {to
which word of prophecy} ye do well that ye take heed, as unto
a light that shineth in a dark place, until the day dawn, and the
day star arise in your hearts: [20]Knowing this first, that no
prophecy of the scripture is {given} of any private ~~interpreta-
tion~~ {will of man}. [21]For the prophecy came not in old time by
the will of man: but holy men /saints/ \of God\ spake as they
were moved by the Holy Ghost.

John's testimony of the Son of God

[1]{Brethren, this is the testimony which we give of} That 1 Jn.
which was from the beginning, which we have heard, which we 1:1–4
have seen with our eyes, which we have looked upon, and our
hands have handled the Word of life; [2](For the life was manifested, and we have seen ~~it~~, and bear witness, and shew
/declare, announce, bring tidings/ unto you that eternal life,
which was with the Father, and was manifested unto us;) [3]That
which we have seen and heard declare we unto you, that ye also
may have fellowship with us: and truly our fellowship is with
the Father, and with his Son Jesus Christ. [4]And these things
write we unto you, that your joy may be full.

Instructions and Recommendations Concerning Individuals

Recommendation of Tychicus and Onesimus

[7]All my state /circumstances/ shall Tychicus declare unto Col.
you, ~~who is~~ a beloved brother, and a faithful minister and fellow- 4:7–9
servant in the Lord: [8]Whom I have sent unto you for the same
purpose, that he might know your estate, and comfort your
hearts; [9]With Onesimus, a faithful and beloved brother, who is
~~one~~ of you. They shall make known unto you all things which
are ~~done~~ here.

Paul's recommendation of the delegates to the Corinthians

2 Cor. 8:16–9:5 [16]But thanks ~~be~~ to God, which put the same earnest care into the heart of Titus for you. [17]For indeed he accepted the exhortation; but being more forward, of his own accord he went unto you. [18]And we have sent with him the brother, whose praise is in the gospel throughout all the churches; [19]And not that only, but who was also chosen of the churches to travel with us with this grace, which is administered by us to the glory of the same Lord, and ~~declaration of~~ your ready mind: [20]Avoiding this, that no man should blame us in this abundance which is administered by us: [21]Providing for honest things, not only in the sight of the Lord, but also in the sight of men. [22]And we have sent with them our brother, whom we have ~~oftentimes~~ proved diligent in many things, but now much more diligent. {Therefore we send him unto you, in consequence of} ~~upon~~ the great confidence which ~~I~~ {we} have in you {that you will receive the things concerning you to [23b]}~~and~~ the glory of Christ, [23a]Whether {we send by the hand} ~~any do inquire~~ of Titus~~, he is~~ my partner and fellow~~helper~~ {laborer,} ~~concerning you:~~ or our brethren ~~be inquired of, they are~~ the messengers of the churches. [24]Wherefore shew ye to them, and before the churches, the proof of your love, and of our boasting /glorying/ on your behalf. [1]For as touching the ministering to the saints, it is superfluous for me to write to you: [2]For I know the forwardness /eagerness/ of your mind, for which I boast of you to them of Macedonia, that Achaia was ready a year ago; and your zeal hath provoked very many. [3]Yet have I sent the brethren, lest our boasting of you should be in vain in this behalf; that, as I said, ye may be ready: [4]Lest haply if they of Macedonia come with me, and find you unprepared, we (that we say not, ye) should be ashamed in this same confident boasting. [5]Therefore I thought it necessary to exhort the brethren, that they would go before unto you, and make up beforehand your bounty, whereof ye had notice before, that the same might be ready, as ~~a matter of~~ bounty /gift, blessing, benevolence/, and not as of covetousness.

Follow not a bad example

[9]I wrote unto the church: but Diotrephes, who loveth to 3 Jn.
have the preeminence among them, receiveth us not. [10]Where- 1:9–12
fore, if I come, I will remember his deeds which he doeth, prat-
ing /talking nonsense, bringing false accusations/ against us
with malicious words: and not content therewith, neither doth
he himself receive the brethren, and forbiddeth them that
would, and casteth them out of the church. [11]Beloved, follow
not that which is evil, but that which is good. He that doeth
good is of God: but he that doeth evil hath not seen God.
[12]Demetrius hath good report of all ~~men~~, and of the truth itself:
yea, and we ~~also~~ bear record; and ye know that our record /wit-
ness, testimony/ is true.

Timothy's responsibility

[18]This charge I commit unto thee, son Timothy, according 1 Tim.
to the prophecies which went before on thee, that thou by them 1:18–20
mightest war a good warfare; [19]Holding faith, and a good conscience; which some having put away concerning faith have
made shipwreck [ruined their lives]: [20]Of whom is Hymenaeus
and Alexander; whom I have delivered unto Satan, that they
may learn not to blaspheme.

Men forsake, but the Lord delivers

[9]Do thy diligence to come shortly unto me: [10]For Demas 2 Tim.
hath forsaken me, having loved this present world, and is 4:9–18
departed unto Thessalonica; Crescens to Galatia, Titus unto
Dalmatia. [11]Only Luke is with me. Take Mark, and bring him
with thee: for he is profitable to me for the ministry. [12]And
Tychicus have I sent to Ephesus. [13]The cloke that I left at Troas
with Carpus, when thou comest, bring ~~with thee~~, and the books,
but especially the parchments. [14]Alexander the coppersmith did
me much evil: the Lord reward him according to his works:
[15]Of whom be thou ware [beware] also; for he hath greatly withstood /opposed, resisted/ our words. [16]At my first answer
/defense/ no man stood with me, but all men forsook me: I pray
God that it may not be laid to their charge. [17]Notwithstanding

the Lord stood with me, and strengthened me; that by me the
preaching might be fully known, and ~~that~~ all the Gentiles might
hear: and I was delivered out of the mouth of the lion. 18And
the Lord shall deliver me from every evil work, and will pre-
serve /save, rescue/ me unto his heavenly kingdom: to whom be
glory for ever and ever. Amen.

Personal advice to Titus concerning his ministry

Titus 3:8–11 8This is a faithful saying, and these things I will that thou
affirm constantly, that they which have believed in God might
be careful to maintain good works. These things are good and
profitable unto men. 9But avoid foolish questions, and genealogies, and contentions, and strivings about the law; for they are
unprofitable and vain. 10A man that is an heretick after the first
and second admonition reject; 11Knowing that he that is such is
subverted /perverted, changed/, and sinneth, being condemned
of himself.

Paul beseeches Philemon to accept Onesimus

Philem. 1:8–21 8Wherefore, though I might be much bold in Christ to
enjoin thee that which is convenient, 9Yet for love's sake I rather
beseech ~~thee~~, being such an one as Paul the aged, and now also
a prisoner of Jesus Christ. 10I beseech thee for my son Onesimus, whom I have begotten in my bonds: 11Which in time past
was to thee unprofitable, but now profitable to thee and to me:
12Whom I have sent again: thou therefore receive him, that is,
mine own bowels: 13Whom I would have retained with me, that
in thy stead he might have ministered unto me in the bonds of
the gospel: 14But without thy mind /assent, suggestion/ would I
do nothing; that thy benefit should not be as it were of necessity,
but willingly. 15For perhaps he therefore departed for a season,
that thou shouldest receive him for ever; 16Not now as a servant,
but above a servant, a brother beloved, specially to me, but how
much more unto thee, both in the flesh, and in the Lord? 17If
thou count me therefore a partner, receive him as myself. 18If
he hath wronged thee, or oweth ~~thee~~ ought /something, any-
thing/, put that on mine account; 19I Paul have written ~~it~~ with
mine own hand, I will repay ~~it~~: albeit I do not say to thee how

thou owest unto me even thine own self besides. [20]Yea, brother,
let me have joy of thee in the Lord: refresh my bowels in the
Lord. [21]Having confidence in thy obedience I wrote unto thee,
knowing that thou wilt also do more than I say.

A personal request and good wishes

[22]But withal prepare me also a lodging: for I trust that Philem.
through your prayers I shall be given unto you. [23]There salute 1:22–25
thee Epaphras, my fellowprisoner in Christ Jesus; [24]Marcus,
Aristarchus, Demas, Lucas, my fellowlabourers. [25]The grace of
our Lord Jesus Christ be with you~~r spirit~~. Amen.

Comments on Onesiphorus and others in Asia

[15]This thou knowest, that all they which are in Asia 2 Tim.
[Turkey] be turned away from me; of whom are Phygellus and 1:15–18
Hermogenes. [16]The Lord give mercy unto the house of Onesiphorus; for he oft refreshed me, and was not ashamed of my
chain: [17]But, when he was in Rome, he sought me out very diligently, and found me. [18]The Lord grant unto him that he may
find mercy of the Lord in that day: and in how many things he
ministered unto me at Ephesus, thou knowest very well.

Paul's last charge to Timothy

[10]But thou hast fully known /followed closely, conformed 2 Tim.
to/ my doctrine, manner of life, purpose, faith, longsuffering, 3:10–4:8
charity, patience, [11]Persecutions, afflictions, which came unto
me at Antioch, at Iconium, at Lystra; what persecutions I
endured: but out of ~~them~~ all the Lord delivered me. [12]Yea, and
all that will live godly in Christ Jesus shall suffer persecution.
[13]~~But~~ {For} evil men and seducers /diviners, imposters, cheats/
shall wax worse and worse, deceiving, and being deceived.
[14]But continue thou in the things which thou hast learned and
hast been assured of, knowing of whom thou hast learned
~~them~~; [15]And that from a child thou hast known the holy scriptures, which are able to make thee wise unto salvation through
faith which is in Christ Jesus. [16]{And} All scripture ~~is~~ given by
inspiration of God, ~~and~~ is profitable /beneficial or useful for

instruction/ for doctrine, for reproof, for correction, for
instruction in righteousness: [17]That the man of God may be
perfect /suited, ready, complete/, throughly [thoroughly] fur-
nished unto all good works. [1]I charge thee therefore before
God, and the Lord Jesus Christ, who shall judge the quick and
the dead at his appearing ~~and~~ {in} his kingdom; [2]Preach the
word; be instant /urgent, earnest/ in season; {those who are}
out of season reprove, rebuke, exhort with all longsuffering
and doctrine. [3]For the time will come when they will not
endure sound doctrine; but after their own lusts shall they
heap to themselves teachers, having itching ears; [4]And they
shall turn away ~~their~~ ears from the truth, and shall be turned
unto fables. [5]But watch thou in all things, endure afflictions, do
the work of an evangelist, make full proof of /fulfill/ thy ministry. [6]For I am now ready to be offered, and the time of my
departure is at hand. [7]I have fought a good fight, I have finished my course, I have kept the faith: [8]Henceforth there is
laid up for me a crown of righteousness, which the Lord, the
righteous judge, shall give me at that day: and not to me only,
but unto all them also that love his appearing.

3

God, and Christ's Atonement

God's Fatherhood, Wisdom, and Love

We are children of God

[14]For as many as are led by the Spirit of God, they are Rom.
the sons of God. [15]For ye have not received the spirit of 8:14–17
bondage again to fear; but ye have received the Spirit of adoption, whereby we cry, Abba, Father. [16]The Spirit itself beareth
witness with our spirit, that we are the children of God: [17]And
if children, then heirs; heirs of God, and joint-heirs with
Christ; if so be that we suffer with him, that we may be also
glorified together.

We are God's heirs

[1]Now I say, ~~That~~ the heir, as long as he is a child, differeth Gal.
nothing from a servant, though he be lord of all; [2]But is under 4:1–11
tutors and governors until the time appointed of the father.
[3]Even so we, when we were children, were in bondage under
the elements of the world: [4]But when the fulness of the time was
come, God sent forth his Son, made /born/ of a woman, made
under the law, [5]To redeem them that were under the law, that
we might receive the adoption of sons. [6]And because ye are
sons, God hath sent forth the Spirit of his Son into your hearts,
crying, Abba, Father. [7]Wherefore thou art no more a servant
/slave/, but a son; and if a son, then an heir of God through
Christ. [8]Howbeit then, when ye knew not God, ye did service
/were slaves, were in bondage/ unto them which by nature are
no gods. [9]But now, after that ye have known God, or rather are
known of God, how turn ye again to the weak and beggarly elements, whereunto ye desire again to be in bondage? [10]Ye

observe days, and months, and times, and years. [11]I am afraid of /concerning/ you, lest I have bestowed upon you labour in vain.

God's fatherly instruction chastens in love

Heb. 12:5–17 [5]And ye have forgotten the exhortation which speaketh unto you as unto children, "My son, despise not thou the chastening of the Lord, nor faint when thou art rebuked of him: [6]For whom the Lord loveth he chasteneth, and scourgeth every son whom he receiveth" [Proverbs 3:11–12]. [7]If ye endure chastening /correction, instruction/, God dealeth with you as with sons; for what son is he whom the father chasteneth not? [8]But if ye be without chastisement, whereof all are partakers, then are ye bastards, and not sons. [9]Furthermore we have had fathers of our flesh which corrected ~~us~~, and we gave ~~them~~ reverence: shall we not much rather be in subjection unto the Father of spirits, and live? [10]For they verily for a few days chastened ~~us~~ after their own pleasure; but he for ~~our~~ profit, that we might be partakers of his holiness. [11]Now no chastening for the present seemeth to be joyous, but grievous: nevertheless afterward it yieldeth the peaceable fruit of righteousness unto them which are exercised /trained, disciplined/ thereby. [12]"Wherefore lift up the hands which hang down, and {strengthen} the feeble knees" [Isaiah 35:3]; [13]"And make straight paths for your feet, lest that which is lame be turned out of the way" [Proverbs 4:26 LXX]; but let it rather be healed. [14]Follow peace with all ~~men~~, and holiness, without which no man shall see the Lord: [15]Looking diligently lest any man fail /want, fall short of, lack/ of the grace of God; lest any root of bitterness springing up trouble you, and thereby many be defiled; [16]Lest there be any fornicator, or profane person, as Esau, who for one morsel of meat sold his birthright. [17]For ye know how that afterward, when he would have inherited the blessing, he was rejected: for he found no place of repentance, though he sought it carefully with tears.

God's power and knowledge

Heb. 4:12–13 [12]For the word of God is quick /living/, and powerful, and sharper than any two-edged sword, piercing even to the divid-

ing asunder of ~~soul~~ {body} and spirit, and of the joints and
marrow, and is a discerner of the thoughts and intents of the
heart. [13]Neither is there any creature that is not manifest in his
sight: but all things are naked and opened unto the eyes of him
with whom we have to do.

God judges the world in truth

[1]What advantage /preeminence/ then hath the Jew {over Rom.
the Gentile}? or what profit ~~is there~~ of circumcision {who is not 3:1–8
a Jew from the heart}? [2]{But he who is a Jew from the heart, I
say hath} Much every way: chiefly, because that unto them were
committed the oracles [words] of God. [3]For what if some did not
believe? shall their unbelief make the faith of God without
effect? [4]God forbid /May it not be!/: yea, let God be true, but
every man a liar; as it is written, "That thou mightest be justified in thy sayings, and mightest overcome when thou art
judged" [Psalm 51:4]. [5]But if {we remain in} our unrighteousness {and} commend /recommend/ the righteousness of God,
~~what shall~~ {how dare} we say~~? Is~~ God {is} unrighteous who
taketh vengeance? (I speak as a man {who fears God,}) [6]God
forbid /May it not be!/: for then how shall God judge the world?
[7a]For if the truth of God hath more abounded through /in, by,
because of/ my lie {(as is it called of the Jews,)} unto his glory;
why yet am I also judged as a sinner [8a]{[7a]}and not ~~rather~~
{received, because} (~~as~~ we ~~be~~ {are} slanderously reported?
[8b]and ~~as~~ some affirm that we say,) {[8c](whose damnation is just,)}
Let us do evil, that good may come? {But this is false.}

A hymn to God's wisdom

[33]O the depth of the riches both of the wisdom and knowl- Rom.
edge of God! how unsearchable ~~are~~ his judgments, and his ways 11:33–36
past finding out! [34]For who hath known the mind of the Lord?
or who hath been his counsellor? [35]Or who hath first given to
him, ~~and~~ it shall be recompensed unto him again? [36]For of him,
and through him, and to him, are all things: to whom be glory
for ever. Amen.

God freely gives wisdom to those who ask in faith

James 1:5–8 5If any of you lack wisdom, let him ask of God, that giveth to all ~~men~~ liberally, and upbraideth /reproacheth, censureth/ not; and it shall be given him. 6But let him ask in faith, nothing wavering /doubting, hesitating/. For he that wavereth is like a wave of the sea driven with the wind and tossed. 7For let not that man think that he shall receive any thing of the Lord. 8A double minded man is unstable in all his ways.

The word of God endures forever

1 Pet. 1:24–25 24"For all flesh is as grass, and all the glory of man as the flower of grass. The grass withereth, and the flower thereof falleth away: 25But the word of the Lord endureth for ever" [Isaiah 40:6–8]. And this is the word which by the gospel is preached unto you.

A hymn to God's love

Rom. 8:31–39 31What shall we then say to these things? If God be for us, who can ~~be~~ {prevail} against us? 32He that spared not his own Son, but delivered him up for us all, how shall he not with him also freely give us all things? 33Who shall lay /accuse/ any thing to the charge of God's elect? It is God that justifieth. 34Who is he that condemneth? It is Christ that died, yea rather, that is risen again, who is even at the right hand of God, who also maketh intercession for us. 35Who shall separate us from the love of Christ? shall tribulation, or distress, or persecution, or famine, or nakedness, or peril, or sword? 36As it is written, "For thy sake we are killed all the day long; we are accounted as sheep for the slaughter" [Psalm 44:22]. 37Nay, in all these things we are more than conquerors /abundantly victorious/ through him that loved us. 38For I am persuaded, that neither death, nor life, nor angels, nor principalities, nor powers, nor things present, nor things to come, 39Nor height, nor depth, nor any other creature, shall be able to separate us from the love of God, which is in Christ Jesus our Lord.

The Divine Greatness of the Lord Jesus Christ

Christ is the head of all creation[15]

Who is the image of the invisible /unseen/ God, the first- Col.
born of every creature /all creation/: [16]For by him were all things 1:15–20
created, that are in heaven, and that are in earth, visible and
invisible, whether ~~they be~~ thrones, or dominions, or principalities, or powers: all things were created by him, and for him:
[17]And he is before all things, and by him all things consist. [18]And
he is the head of the body, the church: who is the beginning, the
firstborn from the dead; that in all things he might have the
preeminence. [19]For it pleased the Father that in him should all
fulness dwell; [20]And, having made peace through the blood of
his cross, by him to reconcile all things unto himself; by him, ~~I
say,~~ whether ~~they be~~ things in earth, or things in heaven.

Prophets of old knew of Christ

[10a]~~Of~~ {Concerning} which salvation the prophets, {[10c]}who 1 Pet.
prophecied of the grace ~~that should come unto~~ {bestowed 1:10–12
upon} you, {[10b]}~~have~~ enquired and searched diligently.
[11]Searching what {time}, ~~or~~ {and} what manner of ~~time~~ {salva-
tion} the spirit of Christ which was in them did signify, when it
testified beforehand the sufferings of Christ, and the glory that
should follow. [12]Unto whom it was revealed, that not unto
themselves, but unto us they did minister the things, which are
now reported unto you by them that have preached the gospel
unto you with the Holy Ghost sent down from heaven; which
things the angels desire to look into.

The greatness of the incarnate Son of God

[1]God, who at sundry times and in divers manners /in Heb.
many locations and various ways/ spake in time past unto the 1:1–4
fathers by the prophets, [2]Hath in these last days spoken unto us
by his Son, whom he hath appointed heir of all things, by whom
also he made the worlds; [3]Who being the brightness of his glory,
and the express image of his person, and upholding all things
by the word of his power, when he had \by himself\ purged

/made purification, expiation for/ our sins, sat down on the right hand of the Majesty on high; [4]Being made so much better than the angels, as he hath by inheritance obtained a more excellent name than they.

The Son is greater than the angels

Heb. 1:5–14 [5]For unto which of the angels said he at any time, "Thou art my Son, this day have I begotten thee?" [Psalm 2:7] And again, "I will be to him a Father, and he shall be to me a Son?" [2 Samuel 7:14] [6a]And again, when he bringeth in the firstbegotten into the world, he saith, "And let all the angels of God worship him" [Deuteronomy 32:43 LXX] [7b]{[6b]}"who maketh {[7d]}his ministers {as} a flame of fire" [Psalm 104:4]. [7a]And of the angels he saith, {[7c]}~~his~~ Angels {are ministering} spirits. [8]But unto the Son ~~he saith~~, "Thy throne, O God, ~~is~~ for ever and ever: a sceptre of righteousness is the sceptre of thy kingdom. [9]Thou hast loved righteousness, and hated iniquity; therefore God, ~~even~~ thy God, hath anointed thee with the oil of gladness above thy fellows" [Psalm 45:6–7]. [10]And, "Thou, Lord, in the beginning hast laid the foundation of the earth; and the heavens are the works of thine hands: [11]They shall perish; but thou remainest; and they all shall wax old /grow old, become worn/ as doth a garment; [12]And as a vesture /cloak/ shalt thou fold them up, and they shall be changed: but thou art the same, and thy years shall not fail" [Psalm 102:25–27]. [13]But to which of the angels said he at any time, "Sit on my right hand, until I make thine enemies thy footstool?" [Psalm 110:1] [14]Are they not all ministering spirits, sent forth to minister /for service/ for them who shall be heirs of salvation?

The import of Christ's teachings

Heb. 2:1–4 [1]Therefore we ought to give the more earnest heed to the things which we have heard, lest at any time we should let them slip. [2]For if the word spoken by angels was stedfast, and every transgression and disobedience received a just recompence of reward; [3]How shall we escape, if we neglect so great salvation; which at the first began to be spoken by the Lord, and was confirmed unto us by them that heard him; [4]God also bearing ~~them~~ witness, both with signs and wonders, and with divers miracles, and gifts of the Holy Ghost, according to his own will?

Christ's greatness and condescension

5For unto the angels hath he not put in subjection the Heb.
world to come, whereof we speak. 6But one in a certain place 2:5–18
testified, saying, "What is man, that thou art mindful of him?
or the son of man, that thou visitest him? 7Thou madest him a
little lower than the angels; thou crownedst him with glory and
honour, \and didst set him over the works of thy hands\: 8Thou
hast put all things in subjection under his feet" [Psalm 8:5–7
LXX.] For in that he put all in subjection under him, he left
nothing that is not put under him. But now we see not yet all
things put under him. 9But we see Jesus, who was made a little
lower than the angels for /through/ the suffering of death,
crowned with glory and honour; that he \by the grace of God,
apart from God\ should taste death for every man. 10For it
became him /was fitting, suitable, proper for him/, for whom
are all things, and by whom are all things, in bringing many
sons unto glory, to make the captain of their salvation perfect
through sufferings. 11For both he that sanctifieth and they who
are sanctified are all of one: for which cause he is not ashamed
to call them brethren, 12Saying, "I will declare thy name unto
my brethren, in the midst of the church will I sing praise unto
thee" [Psalm 22:22]. 13And again, "I will put my trust in him"
[Isaiah 8:17 LXX]. And again, "Behold I and the children which
God hath given me" [Isaiah 8:18]. 14Forasmuch /Since/ then as
the children are partakers of flesh and blood, he also himself
likewise took part of the same; that through death he might
destroy him that had the power of death, that is, the devil;
15And deliver them who through fear of death were all their
lifetime subject to bondage. 16For verily he took not on him the
~~nature~~ {likeness} of angels; but he took on him the seed of
Abraham. 17Wherefore in all things it behoved [behooved] him
to be made like unto his brethren, that he might be a merciful
and faithful high priest in things pertaining to God, to make
reconciliation for the sins of the people. 18For in that he himself

hath suffered being tempted /tried, subjected to trial/, he is able to succour them that are tempted.

Witnesses of the Son

1 Jn. 5:6–12 [6]This is he that came by water and \blood, spirit\, ~~even~~ Jesus Christ; not by water only, but by water and blood. And it is the Spirit that beareth witness, because the Spirit is truth. [7]For there are three that bear record in heaven, the Father, the Word, and the Holy Ghost: and these three are one. [8]And there are three that bear witness in earth, the Spirit, and the water, and the blood: and these three agree in one. [9]If we receive the witness of men, the witness of God is greater: for this is the witness of God which he hath testified of his Son. [10]He that believeth on the Son of God hath the witness in himself: he that believeth not God hath made him a liar; because he believeth not the record /testimony, witness/ that God gave of his Son. [11]And this is the record, that God hath given to us eternal life, and this life is in his Son. [12]He that hath the Son hath life; ~~and~~ he that hath not the Son of God hath not life.

The Need for the Atonement

All have committed sins

1 Jn. 1:8–10 [8]If we say that we have no sin, we deceive ourselves, and the truth is not in us. [9]If we confess our sins, he is faithful and just to forgive us our sins, and to cleanse us from all unrighteousness. [10]If we say that we have not sinned, we make him a liar, and his word is not in us.

Wickedness alienates man from God

Rom. 1:18–32 [18]For the wrath of God is revealed from heaven against all ungodliness and unrighteousness of men, who ~~hold~~ {love not} the truth {but remain} in unrighteousness; [19a]~~Because~~ {after} that which may be known of God is manifest ~~in~~ {to} /among, within/ them; [19b]{[20a]}for God hath ~~shewed~~ {revealed} ~~it~~ unto them [20]{[20b]}~~For~~ the invisible things of him from the creation of the world, {which} are clearly seen, {things which are not seen,} being understood by the things that are made, ~~even~~

{through} his eternal power and Godhead; so that they are
without excuse: [21]Because that, when they knew God, they glorified him not as God, neither were {they} thankful; but
became vain in their imaginations /corrupt in their reasonings,
deliberations/, and their foolish heart{s} ~~was~~ {were} darkened.
[22]Professing themselves to be wise, they became fools, [23]And
changed the glory of the uncorruptible /incorruptible, immor-
tal/ God into an image made like to corruptible /perishable/
man, and to birds, and fourfooted beasts, and creeping things.
[24]Wherefore God also gave them up to uncleanness through the
lusts of their own hearts, to dishonour their own bodies
between themselves: [25]Who changed the truth of God into a lie,
and worshipped and served the creature more than the Creator, who is blessed for ever. Amen. [26]For this cause God gave
/abandoned, delivered/ them up unto vile affections /sufferings,
passions of dishonor/: for even their women did change the natural use into that which is against nature: [27]And likewise also the
men, leaving the natural use of the woman, burned in their lust
one toward another; men with men working that which is
unseemly, and receiving in themselves that recompence of their
error which was meet [appropriate]. [28]And even as they did not
like to retain /discern, choose/ God {according to some} in their
knowledge, God gave them over to a reprobate /worthless,
unable to stand test/ mind, to do those things which are not
convenient; [29]Being filled with all unrighteousness, fornication,
wickedness, covetousness, maliciousness; full of envy, murder,
debate /strife, discord/, deceit, malignity; whisperers, [30]Back-
biters /slanderers/, haters of God, despiteful /violent, overbear-
ing/, proud, boasters, inventors of evil things, disobedient to
parents, [31]Without understanding, covenantbreakers, without
natural affection, implacable, unmerciful: [32]{And some} Who
knowing the judgment of God, that they which commit such
things are worthy of death, {we are inexcusable} not only do
the same, but have pleasure in them /approve of them, sympathize with them/ that do them.

All, both Jew and Gentile, are guilty—there is none righteous

Rom. 3:9–20 [9]{If not so,} What then? \are we better than they?, do we have priority?, do we pray?, do we approach?\ No, in no wise: for we have before proved {before, that} ~~both~~ Jews and Gentiles, ~~that they~~ are all under sin; [10]As it is written, "There is none righteous, no, not one: [11]There is none that understandeth, there is none that seeketh after God. [12]They are all gone out of the way, they are together become unprofitable; there is none that doeth good, no, not one. [13]Their throat is an open sepulchre; with their tongues they have used deceit" [Psalm 5:9]; "the poison of asps is under their lips" [Psalm 140:3]: [14]"Whose mouth is full of cursing and bitterness" [Psalm 10:7]: [15]"Their feet are swift to shed blood: [16]Destruction and misery are in their ways: [17]And the way of peace have they not known" [Isaiah 59:7–8]: [18]"There is no fear of God before their eyes" [Psalm 36:1]. [19]Now we know that what things soever the law saith, it saith to them who are under the law: "that every mouth may be stopped, and all the world may become guilty before God" [Psalm 143:2]. {[20b]}For by /through/ the law is the knowledge of sin. {[20a]}"Therefore by the deeds of the law there shall no flesh be justified in his sight" [Psalm 143:2].

Christ atones for our sins

1 Cor. 6:9–11 [9]Know ye not that the unrighteous shall not inherit the kingdom of God? Be not deceived /led astray/: neither fornicators /sexually immoral persons, male prostitutes/, nor idolaters, nor adulterers, nor effeminate /catamites [boy kept for immoral purposes]/, nor abusers of themselves with mankind /male-bedders/, [10]Nor thieves, nor covetous, nor drunkards, nor revilers, nor extortioners, shall inherit the kingdom of God. [11]And such were some of you: but ye are washed, but ye are sanctified, but ye are justified in the name of the Lord Jesus, and by the Spirit of our God.

1 Jn. 2:1–2 [1]My little children, these things write I unto you, that ye sin not. ~~And~~ {But} if any man sin {and repent}, we have an advocate /intercessor, helper, comforter/ with the Father, Jesus

Christ the righteous: [2]And he is the propitiation for our sins: and not for ours only, but also for the sins of the whole world.

God, not man, will judge everyone for their deeds

[1]Therefore thou art inexcusable, O man, whosoever thou Rom.
art that {thus} judgest: for wherein thou judgest another, thou 2:1–11
condemnest thyself; for thou that judgest doest the same things. [2]But we are sure /know/ that the judgment of God is according to truth against them which commit such things. [3]And thinkest thou this, O man, that judgest them which do such things, and doest the same, that thou shalt escape the judgment of God? [4]Or despisest thou the riches of his goodness and forbearance and longsuffering; not knowing that the goodness of God leadeth thee to repentance? [5]But after /in accordance with/ thy hardness and impenitent heart treasurest up unto thyself wrath against the day of wrath and revelation of the righteous judgment of God; [6]Who will render /give back, recompense, restore/ to every man according to his deeds: [7]To them who by patient continuance in well doing seek for glory and honour and immortality, eternal life: [8]But unto them that are contentious, and do not obey the truth, but obey unrighteousness, indignation and wrath, [9]Tribulation and anguish, upon every soul of man that doeth evil, of the Jew first, and also of the Gentile /Greek/; [10]But glory, honour, and peace, to every man that worketh good, to the Jew first, and also to the Gentile /Greek/: [11]For there is no respect /partiality/ of persons with God.

Be circumcised of heart

[25]For circumcision verily profiteth, if thou keep the law: Rom.
but if thou be a breaker of the law, thy circumcision is made 2:25–29
uncircumcision. [26]Therefore if the uncircumcision keep the righteousness of the law, shall not his uncircumcision be counted for circumcision? [27]And shall not uncircumcision which is by nature, if it fulfil the law, judge thee, who by the letter and circumcision dost transgress the law? [28]For he is not a Jew, which is one outwardly; neither is that circumcision, which is outward in the flesh: [29]But he is a Jew, which is one inwardly;

and circumcision is that of the heart, in the spirit, and not in the letter; whose praise is not of men, but of God.

Christ greater than Moses

Heb. [1]Wherefore, holy brethren, partakers of the heavenly call-
3:1–6 ing, consider the Apostle and High Priest of our profession,
Christ Jesus; [2]Who was faithful to him that appointed him, as
also Moses ~~was faithful~~ in \all\ his house. [3]For ~~this man~~ {he} was
counted worthy of more glory than Moses, inasmuch as he who
hath builded the house hath more honour than the house. [4]For
every house is builded by some man; but he that built all things
is God. [5]And Moses verily was faithful in all his house, as a servant, for a testimony of those things which were to be spoken
after; [6]But Christ as a son over his own house; whose house are
we, if we hold fast the confidence and the rejoicing of the hope
firm unto the end.

The Fall and the Atonement: caused by one, but apply to all

Rom. [12]Wherefore, as by one man sin entered into the world,
5:12–21 and death by sin; and so \death\ passed upon /entered/ all men,
for that all have sinned: [13](For ~~until~~ {before} the law sin was in
the world: ~~but~~ {yet} sin is not imputed ~~when there is~~ {to those
who have} no law. [14]~~Nevertheless~~ {For I say that through the
offence,} death ~~reigned~~ {passed upon all} ~~from Adam to
Moses, even over them that had not sinned after the similitude
of Adam's transgression, who is the figure /type, pattern/ of him
that was to come~~. [15a]But {[15c]}the offence ~~so also~~ is {[15b]}not as
{[15d]}the free gift {for the gift aboundeth}. For if through the
offence of one many be dead, much more the grace of God, and
the gift by grace, ~~which is~~ {[15f]}hath abounded {[15e]}by one man,
Jesus Christ, [15g]unto many. [16]And not as it was by one that
sinned, so is the gift: for the judgment ~~was~~ {is} by one to condemnation, but the free gift is of many offences unto justification. [17]For if by one man's offence death reigned by one; much
more they which receive abundance of grace and of the gift of
righteousness shall reign in life by one, Jesus Christ.) [18]There-
fore as by the offence of one judgment came upon all men to
condemnation; even so by the righteousness of one the free gift

came upon all men unto justification of life. [19]For as by one
man's disobedience many were made sinners, so by the obedience of one shall many be made righteous. [20]Moreover the law
entered, that the offence might abound. But where sin
abounded, grace did much more abound: [21]That as sin hath
reigned unto death, even so might grace reign through righteousness unto eternal life by Jesus Christ our Lord.

Christ and His Priesthood

Jesus the compassionate high priest

[14]Seeing then that we have a great high priest, that is Heb.
passed into the heavens, Jesus the Son of God, let us hold fast 4:14–5:10
our profession. [15]For we have not an high priest which cannot
be touched /unable to sympathize with our frailties, imperfec-
tions/ with the feeling of our infirmities; but was in all points
tempted like as we are, yet without sin. [16]Let us therefore come
boldly unto the throne of grace, that we may obtain mercy, and
find grace to help in time of need. [1]For every high priest taken
from among men is ordained for men in things pertaining to
God, that he may offer both gifts and sacrifices for sins: [2]Who
can have compassion on the ignorant, and on them that are
out of the way /straying, wandering/; for that he himself also is
compassed with infirmity. [3]And by reason hereof he ought, as
for the people, so also for himself, to offer for sins. [4]And no
man taketh this honour unto himself, but he that is called of
God, as ~~was~~ Aaron. [5]So also Christ glorified not himself to be
made an high priest; but he that said unto him, "Thou art my
Son, to day have I begotten thee" [Psalm 110:1]. [6]As he saith
also in another place, "Thou art a priest for ever after the
order of Melchisedec" [Psalm 110:4]. [7]Who in the days of his
flesh, when he had offered up prayers and supplications with
strong crying /mighty, powerful supplication/ and tears unto
him that was able to save him from death, and was heard in
that he feared /because of his piety, reverence/; [8]Though he
were a Son, yet learned he obedience by the things which he
suffered; [9]And being made perfect, he became the author of

eternal salvation unto all them that obey him; 10Called of God
an high priest after the order of Melchisedec.

Melchizedek greater than Abraham

Heb. 7:1–10
1For this "Melchisedec, king of Salem, priest of the most
high God, who met Abraham returning from the slaughter of
the kings, and blessed him; 2To whom also Abraham gave a
tenth part of all" [Genesis 14:17–20]; first being by interpretation King of righteousness, and after that also King of Salem,
which is, King of peace; 3{For this Melchizedek was ordained a
priest after the order of the Son of God, which order was}
Without father, without mother, without descent, having neither beginning of days, nor end of life; ~~but~~ {and all those who
are ordained unto this priesthood are} made like unto the Son
of God; ~~abideth~~ {abiding} a priest continually. 4Now consider
how great this man was, unto whom even the patriarch Abraham gave the tenth of the spoils. 5And verily they that are of
the sons of Levi, who receive the office of the priesthood, have
a commandment to take tithes of the people according to the
law, that is, of their brethren, though they come out of the loins
of Abraham: 6But he whose descent is not counted from them
received tithes of Abraham, and blessed him that had the
promises. 7And without all contradiction the less is blessed of
the better. 8And here men that die receive tithes; but there he
receiveth them, of whom it is witnessed that he liveth. 9And as
I may so say, Levi also, who receiveth tithes, payed tithes in
Abraham. 10For he was yet in the loins of his father, when
Melchisedec met him.

Melchizedek priesthood greater than Levitical

Heb. 7:11–14
11If therefore perfection were by the Levitical priesthood, (for under it the people received the law,) what further
need ~~was there~~ that another priest should rise after the order
of Melchisedec, and not be called after the order of Aaron?
12For the priesthood being changed, there is made of necessity a change also of the law. 13For he of whom these things
are spoken pertaineth to another tribe, of which no man gave

attendance at the altar. [14]For it is evident that our Lord
sprang out of Juda; of which tribe Moses spake nothing concerning priesthood.

Melchizedek priesthood binds with an eternal oath

[15]And it is yet far more evident: for that after the simili- Heb.
tude of Melchisedec there ariseth another priest, [16]Who is 7:15–19
made, not after the law of a carnal commandment, but after the
power of an endless life. [17]For he testifieth, "Thou art a priest
for ever after the order of Melchisedec" [Psalm 110:4]. [18]For
there is verily a disannulling /setting aside, repealing/ of the
commandment going before for the weakness and unprof-
itableness thereof. [19]For the law {was administered without an
oath and} made nothing perfect, but {was only} the bringing in
of a better hope ~~did;~~ by the which we draw nigh unto God.

Christ's priesthood operates beyond death

[20]And inasmuch as {this high priest was} not without an Heb.
oath, ~~he was made priest:~~ [22]{[21]}By so much was Jesus made a 7:20–26
surety of a better testament. [21]{[22]}(For those priests were
made without an oath; but this with an oath by him that said
unto him, "The Lord sware and will not repent /change his
mind/, Thou art a priest for ever after the order of
Melchisedec" [Psalm 110:4]:) [23]And they truly were many
priests, because they were not suffered to continue by reason
of death: [24]But this man, because he continueth ever, hath an
unchangeable /incomparable/ priesthood. [25]Wherefore he is
able also to save them to the uttermost that come unto God by
him, seeing he ever liveth to make intercession for them.
[26]For such an high priest became us, who is holy, harmless,
undefiled, separate from sinners, and made ~~higher~~ {ruler}
~~than~~ {over} the heavens;

The perfection of Christ as the heavenly high priest

[27a]~~Who needeth~~ {And} not {[27c]}as those high priests ~~to~~ Heb.
{who} offer{ed} up sacrifice {[27b]}daily, {[27d]}first for ~~his~~ {their} 7:27–28
own sins, and then for the {sins of the} people~~'s~~; for {he

needeth not offer sacrifice for his own sins, for he knew no
sins; but for the sins of the people. And} 27e~~for~~ this he did once,
when he offered up himself. 28For the law maketh men high
priests which have infirmity; but the word of the oath, which
was since the law, maketh the Son, who is consecrated /per-
fected/ for evermore.

Christ officiates in the divine temple

Heb. 1Now of the things which we have spoken this is the sum:
8:1–5 We have such an high priest, who is set on the right hand of the
throne of the Majesty in the heavens; 2A minister of the sanctuary /holy things/, and of the true tabernacle, which the Lord
pitched, and not man. 3For every high priest is ordained to
offer gifts and sacrifices: wherefore it is of necessity that this
man have somewhat also to offer. 4{There}for{e while} ~~if~~ he
~~were~~ {was} on {the} earth, he ~~should not be a priest~~ {offered
for a sacrifice his own life for the sins of the people. Now every}
~~seeing that there are~~ priest~~s~~ {under the law,} ~~that~~ {must needs}
offer gifts, {or sacrifices} according to the law: 5Who serve unto
the example and shadow of heavenly things, as Moses was
admonished of God when he was about to make the tabernacle:
for, "See," saith he, "that thou make all things according to the
pattern shewed to thee in the mount" [Exodus 25:40].

Christ is the mediator of a better covenant

Heb. 6But now hath he obtained a more excellent ministry, by
8:6–13 how much also he is the mediator of a better covenant, which
was established upon better promises. 7For if that first ~~covenant~~
had been faultless, then should no place have been sought for
the second. 8For finding fault with them, he saith, "Behold, the
days come, saith the Lord, when I will make a new covenant
with the house of Israel and with the house of Judah: 9Not
according to the covenant that I made with their fathers in the
day when I took them by the hand to lead them out of the land
of Egypt; because they continued not in my covenant, and I
regarded them not, saith the Lord. 10For this is the covenant
that I will make with the house of Israel after those days, saith
the Lord; I will put my laws into their mind, and write them in

their hearts: and I will be to them a God, and they shall be to me a people: [11]And they shall not teach every man his neighbour, and every man his brother, saying, Know the Lord: for all shall know me, from the least to the greatest. [12]For I will be merciful to their unrighteousness, and their sins and their iniquities will I remember no more" [Jeremiah 31:31–34]. [13]In that he saith, A new covenant, he hath made the first old. Now that which decayeth and waxeth old is ready to vanish away.

Christ's Sacrifice

Herod's temple and the inadequacy of blood sacrifice

[1]Then verily the first covenant had also ordinances of divine service, and a worldly sanctuary. [2]For there was a tabernacle made; the first, wherein was the candlestick, and the table, and the shewbread; which is called the sanctuary. [3]And after the second veil, the tabernacle which is called the Holiest of all /Holy of holies/; [4]Which had the golden censer, and the ark of the covenant overlaid round about with gold, wherein was the golden pot that had manna, and Aaron's rod that budded, and the tables of the covenant; [5]And over it the cherubims of glory shadowing the mercyseat; of which we cannot now speak particularly. [6]Now when these things were thus ordained /prepared, built/, the priests went always into the first tabernacle, accomplishing the service ~~of God~~. [7]But into the second went the high priest alone once every year, not without blood, which he offered for himself, and ~~for~~ the errors of the people: [8]The Holy Ghost ~~this~~ signifying {this}, that the way into the holiest of all was not yet made manifest, while as {yet} the first tabernacle was ~~yet~~ standing: [9]Which was a figure /similitude, type, parable/ for the time then present, in which were offered both gifts and sacrifices, that could not make him that did the service perfect, as pertaining to the conscience; [10]Which ~~stood~~ {consisted} only in meats and drinks, and divers washings, and carnal ordinances, imposed on them until the time of reformation. Heb. 9:1–10

The efficacy of Christ's sacrifice

Heb. 9:11–14 [11]But Christ being come an high priest of good things to come, by a greater and more perfect tabernacle, not made with hands, that is to say, not of this building; [12]Neither by the blood of goats and calves, but by his own blood he entered in once into the holy place, having obtained eternal redemption ~~for us~~. [13]For if the blood of bulls and of goats, and the ashes of an heifer sprinkling the unclean, sanctifieth to the purifying of the flesh: [14]How much more shall the blood of Christ, who through the eternal Spirit offered himself without spot /blameless/ to God, purge your conscience from dead works to serve the living God?

Christ seals the new testament with his blood

Heb. 9:15–28 [15]And for this cause he is the mediator of the new ~~testament~~ {covenant}, that by means of death, for the redemption of the transgressions that were under the first ~~testament~~ {covenant}, they which are called might receive the promise of eternal inheritance. [16]For where a ~~testament~~ {covenant} is, there {also} must ~~also~~ of necessity be the death of the ~~testator~~ {victim}. [17]For a ~~testament~~ {covenant} is of force after {the} ~~men~~ {victim} ~~are~~ {is} dead: otherwise /since/ it is of no strength at all while the ~~testator~~ {victim} liveth. [18]Whereupon neither the first ~~testament~~ {covenant} was dedicated without blood. [19]For when Moses had spoken every precept to all the people according to the law, he took the blood of calves \and of goats\, with water, and scarlet wool, and hyssop, and sprinkled both the book, and all the people, [20]Saying, "This is the blood of the ~~testament~~ {covenant} which God hath enjoined unto you" [Exodus 24:8]. [21]Moreover he sprinkled with blood both the tabernacle, and all the vessels of the ministry. [22]And almost all things are by the law purged with blood; and without shedding of blood is no remission. [23]It was therefore necessary that the patterns of things in the heavens should be purified with these; but the heavenly things themselves with better sacrifices than these. [24]For Christ is not entered into the holy places made with hands, ~~which are~~ the figures of the true; but into heaven itself,

now to appear in the presence of God for us: [25]Nor yet that he
should offer himself often, as the high priest entereth into the
holy place every year with blood of others; [26]For then must he
often have suffered since the foundation of the world: but now
once in the ~~end~~ {meridian} of ~~the world~~ {time} /consummation
of the ages/ hath he appeared to put away sin by the sacrifice of
himself. [27]And as it is appointed unto men once to die, but after
this the judgment: [28a]So Christ was once offered to bear the sins
of many; and {[28c]he} shall ~~he~~ appear the second time, without
sin unto salvation [28b]unto them that look for him.

Christ's sacrifice superior to the sacrifices of the Mosaic law

[1]For the law having a shadow of good things to come, and Heb.
not the very image of the things, can never with those sacrifices 10:1–10
which they offered {continually} year by year ~~continually~~ make
the comers thereunto perfect. [2]For then would they not have
ceased to be offered? because that the worshippers once
purged should have had no more conscience of sins. [3]But in
those sacrifices there is a remembrance again made of sins
every year. [4]For it is not possible that the blood of bulls and of
goats should take away sins. [5]Wherefore when he cometh into
the world, he saith, "Sacrifice and offering thou wouldest not,
but a body hast thou prepared me: [6]In burnt offerings and sacrifices for sin thou hast had no pleasure. [7]Then said I, Lo, I
come (in the volume of the book it is written of me,) to do thy
will, O God" [Psalm 40:6–8]. [8]Above when he said, Sacrifice
and offering and burnt offerings and offering for sin thou
wouldest not, neither hadst pleasure therein; which are
offered by the law; [9]Then said he, Lo, I come to do thy will, O
God. He taketh away the first, that he may establish the second. [10]By ~~the~~ which will we are sanctified through the offering
{once} of the body of Jesus Christ ~~once~~ for all.

Christ's sacrifice brings remission of sins

[11]And every \high\ priest standeth daily ministering and Heb.
offering oftentimes the same sacrifices, which can never take 10:11–18
away sins: [12]But this man, after he had offered one sacrifice for

sins for ever, sat down on the right hand of God; [13]From henceforth ~~expecting till~~ {to reign until} his enemies be made his footstool. [14]For by one offering he hath perfected for ever them that are sanctified. [15]~~Whereof~~ the Holy Ghost also is a witness to us: for after that he had said before, [16]"This is the covenant that I will make with them after those days," saith the Lord, "I will put my laws into their hearts, and in their minds will I write them; [17]And their sins and iniquities will I remember no more" [Jeremiah 31:33–34]. [18]Now where remission of these is, there is no more offering for sin.

Christ died for the ungodly and sinners

Rom. 5:6–11 [6]For when we were yet without strength, in due time Christ died for the ungodly. [7]For scarcely for a righteous man will one die: yet peradventure for a good man some would even dare to die. [8]But God commendeth his love toward us, in that, while we were yet sinners, Christ died for us. [9]Much more then, being now justified by his blood, we shall be saved from wrath through him. [10]For if, when we were enemies, we were reconciled to God by the death of his Son, much more, being reconciled, we shall be saved by his life. [11]And not only so, but we also joy in God through our Lord Jesus Christ, by whom we have now received the atonement /reconciliation, restoration to favor/.

Revere God who has bought you back with Christ's blood

1 Pet. 1:17–21 [17]And if ye call on the Father, who without respect /favoritism/ of persons judgeth according to every man's work, pass the time of your sojourning /life/ ~~here~~ in fear /reverence/: [18]Forasmuch as ye know that ye were not redeemed with corruptible things, as silver and gold, from your vain /erroneous, fruitless/ conversation /conduct/ ~~received~~ by tradition from your fathers; [19]But with the precious blood of Christ, as of a lamb without blemish and without spot: [20]Who verily was foreordained before the foundation of the world /having been foreknown before the foundation/, but was manifest in these last times for you, [21]Who by him do believe in God, that raised him

up from the dead, and gave him glory; that your faith and hope might be in God.

4

Faith and Obedience to Divine Law

Faith

We are justified through faith in Christ

[21]But now the righteousness of God without /apart from, Rom.
without intervention of/ the law is manifested, being witnessed 3:21–26
by the law and the prophets; [22]Even the righteousness of God
~~which is~~ by faith of Jesus Christ unto all and upon all them that
believe: for there is no difference: [23]For all have sinned, and
come short of the glory of God; [24]{Therefore,} Being justified
~~freely~~ {only} by his grace through the redemption that is in
Christ Jesus: [25]Whom God hath set forth /purposed, designed
beforehand/ ~~to be~~ a propitiation /mercy seat/ through faith in
his blood, to declare his righteousness for the remission of sins
that are past, through the forbearance of God; [26]To declare, ~~I
say,~~ at this time his righteousness: that he might be just, and the
justifier of him which believeth in Jesus.

Jews, like Gentiles, are saved by faith in Christ

[15]We who are Jews by nature, and not sinners of the Gen- Gal.
tiles, [16]Knowing that a man is not justified by the works of the 2:15–21
law, but by the faith of Jesus Christ, even we have believed in
Jesus Christ, that we might be justified by the faith of Christ,
and not by the works of the law: for by the works of the law shall
no flesh be justified /vindicated, approved, guiltless/. [17]But if,
while we seek to be justified by Christ, we ourselves also are
found sinners, is therefore Christ the minister of sin? God forbid. [18]For if I build again the things which I destroyed, I make
myself a transgressor. [19]For I through the law am dead to the
law, that I might live unto God. [20]I am crucified with Christ:

nevertheless I live; yet not I, but Christ liveth in me: and the life which I now live in the flesh I live by the faith of the Son of God, who loved me, and gave himself for me. 21I do not frustrate the grace of God: for if righteousness come by the law, then Christ is dead in vain.

Salvation comes through faith

Rom. 10:5–13

5For Moses describeth the righteousness which is of the law, "That the man which doeth those things shall live by them" [Leviticus 18:5]. 6But the righteousness which is of faith speaketh on this wise, "Say not in thine heart, Who shall ascend into heaven?" [Deuteronomy 9:4; 30:12] (that is, to bring Christ down ~~from above~~:) 7Or, "Who shall descend into the deep?" [Deuteronomy 30:13] (that is, to bring up Christ again from the dead.) 8"But what saith it? The word is nigh thee, ~~even~~ in thy mouth, and in thy heart" [Deuteronomy 30:14]: that is, the word of faith, which we preach; 9That if thou shalt confess with thy mouth the Lord Jesus, and shalt believe in thine heart that God hath raised him from the dead, thou shalt be saved. 10For with the heart man believeth unto righteousness; and with the mouth confession is made unto salvation. 11For the scripture saith, "Whosoever believeth on him shall not be ashamed" [Isaiah 28:16]. 12For there is no difference between the Jew and the Greek: for the same Lord over all is rich /generous/ unto all that call upon him. 13"For whosoever shall call upon the name of the Lord shall be saved" [Joel 2:32].

The example of Abraham, who was justified by faith

Rom. 4:1–8

1What shall we say then that Abraham our father, as pertaining to the flesh, hath found? 2For if Abraham were justified by {the law of} works, he hath /ground, reason for boasting/ ~~whereof~~ to glory {in himself}; but not ~~before~~ {of} God. 3For what saith the scripture? "Abraham believed God, and it was counted unto him for righteousness" [Genesis 15:6]. 4aNow to him ~~that worketh~~ {who is justified by the law of works,} is the reward /wage, hire/ {4c}reckoned, /considered a favor but as his due/, {4b}not 4dof grace, but of debt. 5But to him that ~~worketh~~ {seeketh} not {to be justified by the law of works,} but believeth on him ~~that~~ {who} justifieth {not} the ungodly, his faith is counted for righteousness. [6]Even as David also describeth the blessedness of the man, unto whom God imputeth righteousness without {the law of} works, [7]Saying, "Blessed are they {through faith} whose iniquities are forgiven, and whose sins are covered. [8]Blessed is the man to whom the Lord will not impute sin" [Psalm 32:1–2].

Abraham was justified before he was circumcised

[9]Cometh this blessedness then upon the circumcision Rom.
only, or upon the uncircumcision also? for we say that "faith 4:9–12
was reckoned to Abraham for righteousness" [Genesis 15:6]. [10]How was it then reckoned? when he was in circumcision, or in uncircumcision? Not in circumcision, but in uncircumcision. [11]And he received the sign of circumcision, a seal of the righteousness of the faith which he had yet being uncircumcised: that he might be the father of all them that believe, though they be not circumcised; that righteousness might be imputed unto them also: [12]And the father of circumcision to them who are not of the circumcision only, but who also walk in the steps of that faith of our father Abraham, which he had being yet uncircumcised.

The promise to Abraham was based on faith

[13]For the promise, that he should be the heir of the world, Rom.
was not to Abraham, or to his seed, through the law, but 4:13–17
through the righteousness of faith. [14]For if they which are of the law be heirs, faith is made void, and the promise made of none effect: [15]Because the law worketh wrath: for where no law is, there is no transgression. [16]{And} Therefore ~~it is~~ {ye are justified} of faith {and works}, ~~that it might be by~~ {through} grace; to the end the promise might be sure to all the seed; not to ~~that~~ {them} only ~~which is~~ {who are} of the law, but to ~~that~~ {them} also ~~which is~~ {who are} of the faith of Abraham; who is the father of us all, [17](As it is written, "I have made thee a father of many nations") [Genesis 17:5] before him whom he believed, even God, who quickeneth the dead, and calleth those things which be not as though they were.

Abraham's faith, a model of Christian faith

Rom. 4:18–25

[18]Who against hope believed in hope, that he might become the father of many nations; according to that which was spoken, "So shall thy seed be" [Genesis 15:5]. [19]And being not weak in faith, he considered not his own body now dead, when he was about an hundred years old, neither yet the deadness of Sara's womb: [20]He staggered /doubted, hesitated/ not at the promise of God through unbelief; but was strong in faith, giving glory to God; [21]And being fully persuaded that, what he had promised, he was able also to perform. [22]And therefore it was imputed to him for righteousness. [23]Now it was not written for his sake alone, that it was imputed to him; [24]But for us also, to whom it shall be imputed, if we believe on him that raised up Jesus our Lord from the dead; [25]Who was delivered for our offences, and was raised again for our justification.

Justification by faith

Gal. 3:1–9

[1]O foolish Galatians, who hath bewitched you, that ye should not obey the truth, before whose eyes Jesus Christ hath been evidently set forth, crucified among you? [2]This only would I learn of you, Received ye the Spirit by the works of the law, or by the hearing of faith? [3]Are ye so foolish? having begun in the Spirit, are ye now made perfect by the flesh? [4]Have ye suffered so many things in vain? if it be yet in vain. [5]He therefore that ministereth /grants, furnishes/ to you the Spirit, and worketh miracles among you, doeth he it by the works of the law, or by the hearing of faith? [6]Even as "Abraham believed God, and it was accounted to him for righteousness" [Genesis 15:6]. [7]Know ye therefore that they which are of faith, the same are the children of Abraham. [8]And the scripture, foreseeing that God would justify the heathen through faith, preached before the gospel unto Abraham, saying, "In thee shall all nations be blessed" [Genesis 12:3]. [9]So then they which be of faith are blessed with faithful Abraham.

What we are like when we are justified by faith

[1]Therefore being justified by faith, \we have, let us have\ Rom.
peace with God through our Lord Jesus Christ: [2]By whom also 5:1–5
we have access by faith into this grace wherein we stand, and
rejoice in hope of the glory of God. [3]And not only ~~so~~ {this}, but
we glory in tribulations also: knowing that tribulation worketh
patience; [4]And patience, experience; and experience, hope:
[5]And hope maketh not ashamed; because the love of God is
shed abroad /flooded/ in our hearts by the Holy Ghost which is
given unto us.

Examples of Old Testament people who worked by faith

[1]Now faith is the ~~substance~~ {assurance} /basis, foundation/ Heb.
of things hoped for, the evidence /proof/ of things not seen. [2]For 11:1–40
by it the elders obtained a good report /received witness, testi-
mony/. [3]Through faith we understand that the worlds were
framed by the word of God, so that things which are seen were
not made of things which do appear. [4]By faith Abel offered unto
God a more excellent sacrifice than Cain, by which he obtained
witness that he was righteous, God testifying of his gifts: and by
it he being dead yet speaketh. [5]By faith Enoch was translated
that he should not see death; and "was not found, because God
had translated him" [Genesis 5:24]: for before his translation he
had this testimony, that he pleased God. [6]But without faith it is
impossible to please him: for he that cometh to God must
believe that he is, and that he is a rewarder of them that diligently seek him. [7]By faith Noah, being warned of God of things
not seen as yet, moved with fear /being cautious, reverent/, prepared an ark to the saving of his house; by ~~the~~ which he condemned the world, and became heir of the righteousness which
is by faith. [8]By faith Abraham, when he was called to go out into
a place which he should after receive for an inheritance,
obeyed; and he went out, not knowing whither he went. [9]By
faith he sojourned in the land of promise, as ~~in~~ a strange country, dwelling in tabernacles with Isaac and Jacob, the heirs with
him of the same promise: [10]For he looked for a city which hath
foundations, whose builder and maker is God. [11]Through faith

also Sara herself \being sterile\ received strength to conceive seed, and was delivered of a child when she was past age, because she judged him faithful who had promised. [12]Therefore sprang there even of one, and him as good as dead, ~~so~~ {as} many as the stars of the sky in multitude, and as the sand which is by the sea shore innumerable.

[13]These all died in faith, not having received the promises, but having seen them afar off, and were persuaded of them, and embraced them, and confessed that they were strangers and pilgrims on the earth. [14]For they that say such things declare plainly that they seek a country /homeland, native place/. [15]And truly, if they had been mindful of that ~~country~~ from whence they came out, they might have had opportunity to have returned. [16]But now they desire a better ~~country~~, that is, an heavenly: wherefore God is not ashamed to be called their God: for he hath prepared for them a city.

[17]By faith Abraham, when he was tried, offered up Isaac: and he that had received the promises offered up his only begotten ~~son~~, [18]Of whom it was said, That "in Isaac shall thy seed be called" [Genesis 21:12]: [19]Accounting /Considering/ that God was able to raise him up, even from the dead; from whence also he received him in a figure. [20]By faith Isaac blessed Jacob and Esau concerning things to come. [21]By faith Jacob, when he was ~~a~~ dying, blessed both the sons of Joseph; "and worshipped, ~~leaning~~ upon the top of his staff" [Genesis 47:31 LXX]. [22]By faith Joseph, when he died, made mention of the departing of the children of Israel; and gave commandment concerning his bones. [23]By faith Moses, when he was born, was hid three months of his parents, because they saw {that} he was a ~~proper~~ {peculiar} /handsome/ child; and they were not afraid of the king's commandment. [24]By faith Moses, when he was come to years {of discretion}, refused to be called the son of Pharaoh's daughter; [25]Choosing rather to suffer affliction with the people of God, than to enjoy the pleasures of sin for a season; [26]Esteeming the reproach of Christ greater riches than the treasures in Egypt: for he had respect /looked forward/ unto the recompence /payment/ of the reward. [27]By faith he forsook Egypt, not fearing the wrath of the king: for he endured, as seeing him

who is invisible /unseen/. 28Through faith he kept the passover, and the sprinkling of blood, lest he that destroyed the firstborn should touch them. 29By faith they passed through the Red sea as by dry land: which the Egyptians assaying to do were drowned. 30By faith the walls of Jericho fell down, after they were compassed about seven days. 31By faith the harlot Rahab perished not with them that believed not /those who were unbelieving, disobedient/, when she had received the spies with peace.

32And what shall I ~~more~~ say {more}? for the time would fail me to tell of Gedeon, and of Barak, and of Samson, and of Jephthae; of David also, and Samuel, and of the prophets: 33Who through faith subdued kingdoms, wrought righteousness, obtained promises, stopped the mouths of lions, 34Quenched the violence of fire, escaped the edge of the sword, out of weakness were made strong, waxed valiant in fight, turned to flight the armies of the aliens /enemies/. 35Women received their dead raised to life again: and others were tortured, not accepting deliverance; that they might obtain ~~a better~~ {the first} resurrection: 36And others had trial of ~~cruel~~ mockings and scourgings, yea, moreover of bonds and imprisonment: 37They were stoned, they were sawn asunder, were tempted, were slain with the sword: they wandered about in sheepskins and goatskins; being destitute, afflicted, tormented; 38(Of whom the world was not worthy:) they wandered in deserts, and ~~in~~ mountains, and ~~in~~ dens and caves of the earth. 39And these all, having obtained a good report /testimony, witness/ through faith, received not the promise{s}: 40God having provided /provided beforehand/ some better thing{s} for ~~us~~ {them through their sufferings,} ~~that they~~ {for} without ~~us~~ {sufferings they could} ~~should~~ not be made perfect.

Law

Faith justifies the law

27Where is boasting then? It is excluded. By what law? of Rom.
works? Nay: but by the law of faith. 28Therefore we conclude 3:27–31

that a man is justified by faith {alone} without /apart from,
without intervention of/ the deeds of the law. 29Is he the God of
the Jews only? is he not also of the Gentiles? Yes, of the Gentiles
also: 30Seeing ~~it~~ {that} ~~is one~~ God~~, which shall~~ {will} justify the
circumcision by faith, and uncircumcision through faith. 31Do
we then make void the law through faith? God forbid /May it
not be!/: yea /but/, we establish the law.

The law is made to help sinners

1 Tim. 8But we know that the law is good, if a man use it lawfully;
1:8–11 9Knowing this, that the law is not made for a righteous man, but
for the lawless and disobedient, for the ungodly and for sinners,
for unholy and profane, for murderers of fathers and murderers of mothers, for manslayers, 10For whoremongers, for them
that defile themselves with mankind /male-bedders/, for men-
stealers /kidnappers/, for liars, for perjured persons /oath
breakers/, and if there be any other thing that is contrary to
sound doctrine; 11According to the glorious gospel of the
blessed God, which was committed to my trust.

A curse brought by the law

Gal. 10For as many as are of the works of the law are under
3:10–14 the curse: for it is written, "Cursed is every one that continueth not in all things which are written in the book of the law
to do them" [Deuteronomy 27:26]. 11But that no man is justified by the law in the sight of God, it is evident: for, "The just
shall live by faith" [Habakkuk 2:4]. 12And the law is not of
faith: but, "The man that doeth them shall live in them"
[Leviticus 18:5]. 13Christ hath redeemed us from the curse of
the law, being made a curse for us: for it is written, "Cursed is
every one that hangeth on a tree" [Deuteronomy 21:23]:
14That the blessing of Abraham might come on the Gentiles
through Jesus Christ; that ~~we~~ {they} might receive the
promise of the Spirit through faith.

The law did not cancel the promise

Gal. 15Brethren, I speak after the manner of men; Though it be
3:15–18 but a man's covenant, yet ~~if~~ {when} it be confirmed, no man

disannulleth /set aside/, or addeth thereto. [16]Now to Abraham
and his seed were the promises made. He saith not, And to
seeds, as of many; but as of one, And to thy seed, which is
Christ. [17]And this I say, ~~that~~ the covenant, that was confirmed
before of God in Christ, the law, which was four hundred and
thirty years after, cannot disannul, that it should make the
promise of none effect. [18]For if the inheritance ~~be~~ {is} of the
law, {then} it is no more of promise: but God gave it to Abraham by promise.

The law was given looking toward Christ

[19a]Wherefore then, ~~serveth~~ the law~~? It~~ was added because Gal.
of transgressions, till the seed should come to whom the 3:19–22
promise was made {in the law given to Moses, who} ~~and it~~ was
ordained by {[19c]}~~in~~ the hand of [19b]angels {to be} a mediator {of
this first covenant, (the law)}. [20]Now ~~a~~ {this} mediator ~~is~~ {was}
not a mediator of ~~one~~ {the new covenant}; but ~~God~~ {there} is
one {mediator of the new covenant, who is Christ, as it is written in the law concerning the promises made to Abraham and
his seed. Now Christ is the mediator of life; for this is the
promise which God made unto Abraham.} [21]Is the law then
against the promises of God? God forbid: for if there had been
a law given which could have given life, verily righteousness
should have been by the law. [22]But the scripture hath concluded
all under sin, that the promise by faith of Jesus Christ might be
given to them that believe.

Analogy of marriage: Christians are loosed from the dead law

[1]Know ye not, brethren, (for I speak to them that know Rom.
the law,) how that the law hath dominion over a man {only} as 7:1–6
long as he liveth? [2]For the woman which hath an husband is
bound by the law to her husband ~~so~~ {only as} long as he liveth;
~~but~~ {for} if the husband be dead, she is loosed from the law of
her husband. [3]So then if, while her husband liveth, she be married to another man, she shall be called an adulteress: but if her
husband be dead, she is free from that law; so that she is no
adulteress, though she be married to another man. [4]Wherefore,

my brethren, ye also are become dead to the law by the body of Christ; that ye should be married to another, ~~even~~ to him who is raised from the dead, that we should bring forth fruit unto God. [5]For when we were in the flesh, the motions /sufferings, afflictions/ of sins, which were ~~by~~ {not according to} the law, did work in our members to bring forth fruit unto death. [6a]But now we are delivered /released, freed/ from the law {[6c]}wherein we were held, {[6b]}~~that~~ being dead {to the law,} [6d]that we should serve in newness of spirit, and not in the oldness of the letter.

The relationship between law and sin

Rom. 7:7–13

[7]What shall we say then? Is the law sin? God forbid /May it not be!/. Nay, I had not known sin, but by the law: for I had not known lust, except the law had said, "Thou shalt not covet" /lust for, set the heart upon/ [Exodus 20:17]. [8]But sin, taking occasion by the commandment, wrought in me all manner of concupiscence. For without the law sin was dead. [9]For {once} I was alive without {transgression of} the law ~~once~~: but when the commandment {of Christ} came, sin revived, and I died. [10]And {when I believed not} the commandment {of Christ which came}, which was ordained to life, I found {it condemned me} ~~to be~~ unto death. [11]For sin, taking occasion /having taken opportunity/ ~~by~~ {denied} the commandment, {and} deceived me, and by it ~~slew me~~ {I was slain}. [12]~~Wherefore~~ {Nevertheless I found} the law ~~is~~ {to be} holy, and the commandment {to be} holy, and just, and good. [13a]Was then that which is good made death unto me? God forbid /May it not be!/. But sin, that it might appear sin {[13c]}by that which is good, {[13b]}working death in me; [13d]that sin by the commandment might become exceeding sinful.

The law as a schoolmaster

Gal. 3:23–26

[23]But before faith came, we were kept under the law, shut up unto the faith which should afterwards be revealed. [24]~~Wherefore~~ the law was our schoolmaster /pedagogue, director, supervisor of children/ ~~to bring us unto~~ {until} Christ, that we might be justified by faith. [25]But after that faith is come, we are no longer under a schoolmaster. [26]For ye are all the children of God by faith in Christ Jesus.

Doing the Word

Doers of the law, not hearers only, are justified

Rom. 2:12–16

[12]For as many as have sinned without law shall also perish without law: and as many as have sinned in the law shall be judged by the law; [13](For not the hearers of the law are just before God, but the doers of the law shall be justified. [14]For when the Gentiles, which have not the law, do by nature the things contained in the law, these, having not the law, are a law unto themselves: [15]Which /who/ shew the work of the law written in their hearts, their conscience also bearing witness, and their thoughts the mean while accusing or else excusing one another;) [16]In the day when God shall judge the secrets of men by Jesus Christ according to ~~my~~ {the} gospel.

Doing the word that saves is pure religion

James 1:19–27

[19]Wherefore, my beloved brethren, let every man be swift to hear, slow to speak, slow to wrath: [20]For the wrath of man worketh not the righteousness of God. [21]Wherefore lay ~~apart~~ {aside} all filthiness and superfluity of naughtiness /overabundance of malice, trouble, evil/, and receive with meekness the engrafted /implanted/ word, which is able to save your souls. [22]But be ye doers of the word, and not hearers only, deceiving your own selves. [23]For if any be a hearer of the word, and not a doer, he is like unto a man beholding his natural face in a glass: [24]For he beholdeth himself, and goeth his way, and straightway forgetteth what manner of man he was. [25]But whoso looketh into the perfect law of liberty, and continueth therein, he being not a forgetful hearer, but a doer of the work, this man shall be blessed in his deed. [26]If any man among you seem to be religious, and bridleth not his tongue, but deceiveth his own heart, this man's religion is vain /useless, deceptive, erroneous/. [27]Pure religion and undefiled before God and the Father is this, To visit the fatherless and widows in their affliction, and to keep himself unspotted from the {vices of the} world.

Keep the whole law

James 2:10–11

[10]For whosoever shall, {save in one point,} keep the whole law, ~~and yet offend /stumble, err/ in one point,~~ he is guilty of all. [11]For he that said, "Do not commit adultery," said also, "Do not kill" [Exodus 20:13–14]. Now if thou commit no adultery, yet if thou kill, thou art become a transgressor of the law.

Faith without works is dead

James 2:14–26

[14]What ~~doth it~~ profit {is it}, my brethren, ~~though~~ {for} a man {to} say he hath faith, and have not works? can faith save him? [18]{[15]}Yea, a man may say, ~~thou hast~~ {I will show thee I have} faith ~~and I have~~ {without} works; {but I say,} shew me thy faith without works, and I will show thee my faith by my works. [15]{[18]For} If a brother or sister be naked, and destitute ~~of daily food~~, [16]And one of you say ~~unto them~~, Depart in peace, be ~~ye~~ warmed and filled; notwithstanding ~~ye~~ {he} give ~~them~~ not those things which are needful to the body; what ~~doth it~~ profit {is your faith unto such}? [17]Even so faith, if it hath not works, is dead, being alone. [20]{[18]Therefore} wilt thou know, O vain man, that faith without works is \dead, useless or idle\ {and cannot save you?} [19]Thou believest ~~that~~ there is one God; thou doest well: the devils also believe, and tremble; {thou hast made thyself like unto them, not being justified}. [21]{[20]}Was not Abraham our father justified by works, when he had offered Isaac his son upon the altar? [22]{[21]}Seest thou how ~~faith~~ {works} wrought with his ~~works~~ {faith}, and by works was faith made perfect? [23]And the scripture was fulfilled which saith, "Abraham believed God, and it was imputed /counted/ unto him for righteousness" [Genesis 15:6]: and he was called the Friend of God. [24]Ye see then that by works a man is justified, and not by faith only. [25]Likewise also, ~~was not~~ Rahab the harlot {was} justified by works, when she had received the messengers, and ~~had~~ sent them out another way? [26]For as the body without the spirit is dead, so faith without works is dead ~~also~~.

Keep the commandments

[3]And hereby we do know that we know him, if we keep his 1 Jn.
commandments. [4]He that saith, I know him, and keepeth not 2:3–11
his commandments, is a liar, and the truth is not in him. [5]But
whoso keepeth his word, in him verily is the love of God perfected: hereby know we that we are in him. [6]He that saith he
abideth in him ought himself also so to walk, even as he walked.
[7]Brethren, I write ~~no~~ {a} new commandment unto you, but ~~an~~
~~old~~ {it is the same} commandment which ye had from the
beginning. The old commandment is the word which ye have
heard from the beginning. [8]Again, a new commandment I write
unto you, which thing {was of old, ordained of God; and} is
true in him and in you: because the darkness is past /passing
away/ {in you}, and the true light now shineth. [9]He that saith
he is in the light, and hateth his brother, is in darkness even
until now. [10]He that loveth his brother abideth in the light, and
there is none occasion of stumbling in him. [11]But he that hateth
his brother is in darkness, and walketh in darkness, and
knoweth not whither he goeth, because that darkness hath
blinded his eyes.

5

Salvation's History and Future

God's Promises to Israel

The privileges of Israel

[1]I say the truth in Christ, I lie not, my conscience also Rom.
bearing me witness in the Holy Ghost, [2]That I have great heav- 9:1–5
iness and continual sorrow in my heart. [3]{(For once} I could
{have} wish{ed} that myself were accursed from {Christ,)} for
my brethren, my kinsmen according to the flesh: [4]Who are
Israelites; ~~to~~ {of} whom ~~pertaineth~~ {are} the adoption, and the
glory, and the covenants, and the giving of the law, and the service of God, and the promises; [5]~~Whose~~ are {made unto} the
fathers, and of whom, as concerning the flesh, Christ ~~came~~
{was}, who is {God} over all, ~~God~~ blessed for ever. Amen.

God has kept his promise to Israel

[6]Not as though the word of God hath taken none effect Rom.
/has been fruitless, ineffectual/. For they are not all Israel, which 9:6–13
are of Israel: [7]Neither, because they are {all} ~~seed~~ {children} of
Abraham, are they ~~all children~~ {the seed}: but, "In Isaac shall
thy seed be called" [Genesis 21:12]. [8]That is, "They which are
the children of the flesh, these are not the children of God: but
the children of the promise are counted for the seed" [Genesis
18:10, 14]. [9]For this is the word of promise, At this time will I
come, and Sara shall have a son. [10]And not only ~~this~~ {Sarah};
but when Rebecca also had conceived by one, ~~even by~~ our
father Isaac; [11](For the children being not yet born, neither having done any good or evil, that the purpose of God according to
election might stand, not of works, but of him that calleth;) [12]It
was said unto her, "The elder shall serve the younger" [Genesis

25:23]. [13]As it is written, "Jacob have I loved, but Esau have I hated" [Malachi 1:2–3].

God's will is not unjust

Rom. 9:14–24

[14]What shall we say then? Is there unrighteousness with God? God forbid /May it not be!/. [15]For he saith to Moses, "I will have mercy on whom I will have mercy, and I will have compassion on whom I will have compassion" [Exodus 33:19]. [16]So then it is not of him that willeth, nor of him that runneth, but of God that sheweth mercy. [17]For the scripture saith unto Pharaoh, "Even for this same purpose have I raised thee up, that I might shew my power in thee, and that my name might be declared throughout all the earth" [Exodus 9:16]. [18]Therefore hath he mercy on whom he will ~~have mercy~~, and whom he will he hardeneth /leaves to stubbornness, hardness/. [19]Thou wilt say then unto me, Why doth he yet find fault? For who hath resisted his will? [20]Nay but, O man, who art thou that repliest /contradictest, disputest/ against God? Shall the thing formed say to him that formed it, Why hast thou made me thus? [21]Hath not the potter power over the clay, of the same lump to make one vessel unto honour, and another unto dishonour? [22]~~What~~ if God, willing to shew his wrath, and to make his power known, endured with much longsuffering the vessels of wrath fitted to destruction: [23]And that he might make known the riches of his glory on the vessels of mercy, which he had ~~afore~~ {before} prepared unto glory, [24]Even us, whom he hath called, not of the Jews only, but also of the Gentiles?

Old Testament prophecies concerning Israel

Rom. 9:25–33

[25]As he saith also in ~~Osee~~ {Hosea}, "I will call them my people, which were not my people; and her beloved, which was not beloved" [Hosea 2:23]. [26]And it shall come to pass, that in the place where it was said unto them, "Ye are not my people; there shall they be called the children /sons/ of the living God" [Hosea 1:10]. [27]Esaias also crieth concerning Israel, "Though the number of the children of Israel be as the sand of the sea, a remnant shall be saved: [28]For he will finish the work, and cut it

short in righteousness: because a short work will the Lord make
upon the earth" [Isaiah 10:22–23]. [29]And as Esaias said before,
"Except the Lord of Sabaoth /Hebrew: hosts/ had left us a seed
/posterity/, we had been as Sodoma, and been made like unto
Gomorrha" [Isaiah 1:9]. [30]What shall we say then? That the
Gentiles, which followed not after righteousness, have attained
to righteousness, even the righteousness which is of faith. [31]But
Israel, which followed after the law of righteousness, hath not
attained to the law of righteousness. [32a]Wherefore /Why/?
~~Because for~~ {32c}they stumbled at that stumblingstone, {32b}~~they
sought it~~ not by faith, but as it were by the works \of the law\.
[33]As it is written, "Behold, I lay in Sion a stumblingstone and
rock of offence: and whosoever believeth on him shall not be
ashamed" [Isaiah 28:16].

Israel fails to see that God is the source of righteousness

[1]Brethren, my heart's desire and prayer to God for Rom.
Israel is, that they might be saved. [2]For I bear them record 10:1–4
that they have a zeal of God, but not according to knowledge.
[3]For they being ignorant of God's righteousness, and going
/desiring, endeavoring/ about to establish their own righteousness, have not submitted themselves unto the righteousness of God. [4]For Christ is the end of the law for righteousness
to every one that believeth.

Israel's unbelief

[14]How then shall they call on him in whom they have not Rom.
believed? and how shall they believe in him of whom they have 10:14–21
not heard? and how shall they hear without a preacher? [15]And
how shall they preach, except they be sent? as it is written,
"How beautiful are the feet of them that preach the gospel of
peace, and bring glad tidings of good things!" [Isaiah 52:7;
Nahum 1:15] [17]{16}So then faith cometh by hearing, and hearing by the word of \Christ, God\. [18]{17}But I say, "Have they not
heard? Yes verily, their sound went into all the earth, and their
words unto the ends of the world" [Psalm 19:4]. [16]{18}But they
have not all obeyed the gospel. For Esaias saith, "Lord, who
hath believed our report?" [Isaiah 53:1] [19]But I say, Did not

Israel know? ~~First~~ {Now} Moses saith, "I will provoke you to jealousy by them that are no people, and by a foolish nation I will anger you" [Deuteronomy 32:21]. [20]But Esaias is very bold, and saith, "I was found of them that sought me not; I was made manifest unto them that asked not after me" [Isaiah 65:1]. [21]But to Israel he saith, "All day long I have stretched forth my hands unto a disobedient and gainsaying /contradicting, opposing/ people" [Isaiah 65:2].

The remnant of Israel

Rom. 11:1–10 [1]I say then, Hath God cast away his \people, inheritance\? God forbid /May it not be!/. For I also am an Israelite, of the seed of Abraham, of the tribe of Benjamin. [2]God hath not cast away his people which he foreknew. ~~Wot~~ {Know} ye not what the scripture saith of Elias? how he maketh ~~intercession~~ {complaint} to God against Israel, saying, [3]"Lord, they have killed thy prophets, and digged down thine altars; and I am left alone, and they seek my life" [1 Kings 19:10, 14]. [4]But what saith the answer of God unto him? "I have reserved to myself seven thousand men, who have not bowed the knee to ~~the image of~~ Baal" [1 Kings 19:18]. [5]Even so then at this present time also there is a remnant according to the election of grace. [6]And if by grace, then ~~is it~~ no more of works: otherwise grace is no more grace. But if it be of works, then is it no more grace: \otherwise work is no more work\. [7]What then? Israel hath not obtained that which ~~he seeketh~~ {they seek} for; but the election /those selected/ hath obtained it, and the rest were blinded /became callous/ [8](According as it is written, "God hath given them the spirit of slumber /deep sleep, stupor/, eyes that they should not see, and ears that they should not hear" [Deuteronomy 29:4];) unto this day. [9]And David saith, "Let their table be made a snare, and a trap, and a stumbling block, and a recompence /retribution, requital/ unto them: [10]Let their eyes be darkened, that they may not see, and bow down their back alway" [Psalm 69:22–23].

The Jews to be restored in the future

[11]I say then, Have they [the Jews] stumbled that they Rom.
should fall? God forbid /May it not be!/: but rather through 11:11–15
their fall salvation is come unto the Gentiles, for to provoke
them to jealousy. [12]Now if the fall of them ~~be~~ {is} the riches of
the world, and the diminishing /default, failure/ of them the
riches of the Gentiles; how much more their fulness /fulfilment
of God's purposes/? [13]For I speak to you Gentiles, inasmuch as I
am the apostle of the Gentiles, I magnify mine office: [14]If by any
means I may provoke to emulation ~~them which are~~ my flesh,
and might save some of them. [15]For if the casting away of them
~~be~~ {is} the reconciling /atoning/ of the world, what shall the
~~receiving~~ {restoring} of them be, but life from the dead?

Gentiles should not boast; the Jews are still the chosen people

[16]For if the firstfruit ~~be~~ {is} holy, the lump is also holy: and Rom.
if the root be holy, so are the branches. [17]And if some of the 11:16–24
branches be broken off, and thou, being a wild olive tree, ~~wert~~
{wast} graffed in among them, and with them partakest of the
root and fatness of the olive tree; [18a]Boast not against the
branches, {[18c]}for thou bearest not the root, but the root thee.
[18b]{[19]}~~But~~ {For} if thou boast, [19]thou wilt say ~~then~~, The
branches were broken off, that ~~I~~ {we} might be ~~graffed~~
{grafted} in. [20]Well; because of unbelief they were broken off,
and thou standest by faith. Be not highminded /puffed up, con-
ceited/, but fear: [21]For if God spared not the natural branches,
take heed lest he also spare not thee. [22]Behold therefore the
goodness and severity of God: on them which fell, severity; but
toward thee, goodness, if thou continue in ~~his~~ goodness: otherwise thou also shalt be cut off. [23]And they also, if they abide not
still in unbelief, shall be graffed in: for God is able to graff them
in again. [24]For if thou ~~wert~~ {wast} cut out of the olive tree which
is wild by nature, and ~~wert~~ {wast} graffed contrary to nature
into a good olive tree: how much more shall these, which be the
natural branches, be graffed into their own olive tree?

The future conversion and restoration of the Jews

Rom. 11:25–32

25For I would not, brethren, that ye should be ignorant of this mystery, lest ye should be wise in your own conceits; that blindness /callousness/ in part is happened to Israel, until the fulness of the Gentiles be come in. 26And ~~so~~ {then} all Israel shall be saved: as it is written, "There shall come out of Sion the Deliverer, and shall turn away ungodliness from Jacob: 27For this is my covenant unto them, when I shall take away their sins" [Isaiah 59:20–21]. 28As concerning the gospel, they are enemies for your sakes: but as touching the election, they are beloved for the fathers' sakes. 29For the gifts and calling of God are without repentance. 30For as ye in times past have not believed /were disbelieving, disobedient to/ God, yet have now obtained mercy through their unbelief /disobedience, disbelief/: 31Even so have these also now not believed /obeyed/, that through your mercy they also may obtain mercy. 32For God hath concluded /closed up together/ them all in unbelief, that he might have mercy upon all.

Hagar and Sarah: an allegory for the Jews and Gentiles

Gal. 4:21–31

21Tell me, ye that desire to be under the law, do ye not hear the law? 22For it is written, that Abraham had two sons, the one by a bondmaid, the other by a freewoman. 23But he who was of the bondwoman was born after the flesh; but he of the freewoman was by promise. 24Which things are an allegory: for these are the two covenants; the one from the mount Sinai, which gendereth to bondage, which is Agar. 25For this Agar is mount Sinai in Arabia, and answereth to Jerusalem which now is, and is in bondage with her children. 26But Jerusalem which is above is free, which is the mother of us all. 27For it is written, "Rejoice, thou barren that bearest not; break forth and cry, thou that travailest not: for the desolate hath many more children than she which hath an husband" [Isaiah 54:1]. 28Now we, brethren, as Isaac was, are the children of promise. 29But as then he that was born after the flesh persecuted him that was born after the Spirit, even so it is now. 30Nevertheless what saith the scripture? "Cast out the bondwoman and her son: for the son of the bond-

woman shall not be heir with the son of the freewoman" [Gene-
sis 21:10]. [31]So then, brethren, we are not children of the bondwoman, but of the free.

The old covenants transcended by the new

[18]For ye are not come unto the mount [Sinai] that might be Heb.
touched, and that burned with fire, nor unto blackness, and 12:18–29
darkness, and tempest, [19]And the sound of a trumpet, and the
voice of words; which ~~voice~~ they that heard intreated that the
word should not be spoken to them any more: [20](For they could
not endure that which was commanded, And if so much as a
beast touch the mountain, it shall be stoned, or thrust through
with a dart: [21]And so terrible was the sight, ~~that~~ Moses said, I
exceedingly fear and quake:) [22]But ye are come unto mount
Sion, and unto the city of the living God, the heavenly
Jerusalem, and to an innumerable company of angels, [23]To the
general assembly and church of the firstborn /firstborns/, which
are written in heaven, and to God the Judge of all, and to the
spirits of just men made perfect, [24]And to Jesus the mediator of
the new covenant, and to the blood of sprinkling, that speaketh
better things than that of Abel. [25]See that ye refuse not him that
speaketh. For if they escaped not who refused him that spake
on earth, much more ~~shall not~~ we ~~escape~~, if we turn away from
him that speaketh from heaven: [26]Whose voice then shook the
earth: but now he hath promised, saying, Yet once more I shake
not the earth only, but also heaven. [27]And this ~~word~~, Yet once
more, signifieth the removing of those things that are shaken,
as of things that are made, that those things which cannot be
shaken may remain. [28]Wherefore we receiving a kingdom
which cannot be moved, ~~let us~~ {should} have grace, whereby
we may serve God acceptably with reverence and godly fear:
[29]For our God is a consuming fire.

Wickedness, False Teachers, and the Coming Apostasy

Prediction of wickedness

1 Tim. 4:1–5 1Now the Spirit speaketh expressly, that in the latter times
some shall depart from the faith, giving heed to seducing
/deceitful/ spirits, and doctrines of devils; 2Speaking lies in
hypocrisy; having their conscience seared {as} with a hot iron;
3Forbidding to marry, and commanding to abstain from meats,
which God hath created to be received with thanksgiving of
them which believe and know the truth. 4For every creature
/creation/ of God is good, and nothing to be refused, if it be
received with thanksgiving: 5For it is sanctified by the word of
God and prayer.

Apostolic prophecy of apostasy

Jude 1:17–19 17But, beloved, remember ye the words which were spoken before of the apostles of our Lord Jesus Christ; 18How that
they told you there should be mockers in the last time, who
should walk after their own ungodly lusts. 19These be they who
separate themselves /cause divisions/, sensual /worldly, unspiri-
tual/, having not the Spirit.

The character of people in the last days

2 Tim. 3:1–9 1This know also, that in the last days perilous times shall
come. 2For men shall be lovers of their own selves, covetous,
boasters, proud, blasphemers, disobedient to parents, unthank-
ful, unholy, 3Without natural affection, trucebreakers, false
accusers /slanderers/, incontinent /without self-control/, fierce,
despisers of those that are good, 4Traitors, heady /rash, reckless/,
highminded /puffed up, conceited/, lovers of pleasures more
than lovers of God; 5Having a form of godliness, but denying the
power thereof: from such turn away. 6For of this sort are they
which creep into houses, and lead captive silly women laden
with sins, led away with divers lusts, 7Ever learning, and never
able to come to the knowledge of the truth. 8Now as Jannes and
Jambres withstood Moses, so do these also resist the truth: men
of corrupt minds, reprobate concerning the faith. 9But they shall

proceed no further: for their folly shall be manifest unto all
men, as theirs also was.

The seriousness of personal apostasy

26For if we sin wilfully after that we have received the Heb.
knowledge of the truth, there remaineth no more sacrifice for 10:26–31
sins, 27But a certain fearful looking for of judgment and fiery
indignation, which shall devour the adversaries. 28He that
despised /rejected, violated/ Moses' law died without mercy
"under two or three witnesses" [Deuteronomy 17:6]: 29Of how
much sorer punishment /insult/, suppose ye, shall he be
thought worthy, who hath trodden under foot the Son of God,
and hath counted the blood of the covenant, wherewith he was
sanctified, an unholy thing, and hath done despite unto the
Spirit of grace? 30For we know him that hath said, "Vengeance
belongeth unto me, I will recompense" [Deuteronomy 32:35],
saith the Lord. And again, "The Lord shall judge his people"
[Deuteronomy 32:36]. 31~~It is~~ a fearful thing to fall into the
hands of the living God.

False prophets and the path of apostasy

1But there were false prophets also among the people, 2 Pet.
even as there shall be false teachers among you, who privily 2:1–22
shall bring in ~~damnable~~ {abominable} heresies, even denying
the Lord that bought them, and bring upon themselves swift
destruction. 2And many shall follow their pernicious /indecent,
licentious/ ways; by reason of whom the way of truth shall be
evil spoken of /blasphemed/. 3And through covetousness shall
they with feigned /phony, made up/ words make merchandise
of you: whose judgment now of a long time lingereth not, and
their ~~damnation~~ {destruction} slumbereth not. 4For if God
spared not the angels that sinned, but cast ~~them~~ down to hell,
and delivered ~~them~~ into \chains, pits\ of darkness, to be
reserved unto judgment; 5And spared not the old world, but
saved Noah the eighth ~~person~~, a preacher of righteousness,
bringing in the flood upon the world of the ungodly; 6And
turning the cities of Sodom and Gomorrha into ashes condemned ~~them~~ with an overthrow, making ~~them~~ an ensample

/token, example/ unto those that after should live ungodly;
7And delivered just Lot, vexed with the filthy conversation
[conduct] of the wicked /oppressed by the outrageous behavior
of the lawless/: 8(For that righteous man dwelling among them,
in seeing and hearing, vexed /oppressed, afflicted/ his righteous soul from day to day with ~~their~~ unlawful deeds;) 9The
Lord knoweth how to deliver the godly out of temptations,
and to reserve the unjust unto the day of judgment to be punished: 10But chiefly them that walk after the flesh in the lust of
uncleanness, and despise government /constituted authority/.
Presumptuous ~~are they~~, selfwilled, they are not afraid to speak
evil of dignities. 11Whereas angels, which are greater in power
and might, bring not railing accusation against them \before,
from\ the Lord. 12But these, as natural brute beasts, made to
be taken and destroyed, speak evil of the things that they
understand not; and shall utterly perish in their own corruption; 13And shall receive the reward of unrighteousness, ~~as~~
they that count it pleasure to riot in the day time. Spots ~~they
are~~ and blemishes, sporting themselves with their own deceiv-
ings while they feast with you; 14Having eyes full of adultery,
and that cannot cease from sin; beguiling unstable souls: an
heart they have exercised with covetous practices; cursed children: 15Which have forsaken the right way, and are gone
astray, following the way of Balaam ~~the son~~ of Bosor, who
loved the wages of unrighteousness; 16But was rebuked for his
iniquity: the dumb ass speaking with man's voice forbad the
madness of the prophet. 17These are wells without water,
clouds that are carried with a tempest; to whom the mist of
darkness is reserved for ever. 18For when they speak great
swelling words of vanity, they allure /entice, entrap/ through
the lusts of the flesh, ~~through much~~ wantonness, those that
were clean escaped from them who live in error. 19While they
promise them liberty, they themselves are the servants /slaves/
of corruption: for of whom a man is overcome, of the same is
he brought in{to} bondage. 20For if after they have escaped
the pollutions of the world through the knowledge of the Lord
and Saviour Jesus Christ, they are again entangled therein,
and overcome, the latter end is worse with them than the

beginning. [21]For it had been better for them not to have
known the way of righteousness, than, after they have known
~~it~~, to turn from the holy commandment delivered unto them.
[22]But it is happened unto them according to the true proverb,
"The dog ~~is~~ turned to his own vomit again; and the sow that
was washed to her wallowing in the mire" [Proverbs 26:11].

A warning: there is no other gospel

[6]I marvel that ye are so soon removed from him that Gal.
called you into the grace of Christ unto another gospel: [7]Which 1:6–10
is not another; but there be some that trouble /agitate, raise
doubts, perplex/ you, and would pervert the gospel of Christ.
[8]But though we, or an angel from heaven, preach any other
gospel unto you than that which we have preached unto you,
let him be accursed. [9]As we said before, so say I now again, If
any ~~man~~ preach any other gospel unto you than that ye have
received, let him be accursed. [10]For do I now ~~persuade~~
{please} /appease, aspire to the favor of/ men, or God? or do I
seek to please men? for if I yet pleased men, I should not be
the servant of Christ.

Walk in Christ; beware of tradition of men

[6]As ye have therefore received Christ Jesus the Lord, ~~so~~ Col.
walk ye in him: [7]Rooted and built up in him, and {e}stablished 2:6–8
in the faith, as ye have been taught, abounding therein with
thanksgiving. [8]Beware lest any man spoil you through philoso-
phy and vain deceit, after the tradition of men, after the rudiments of the world, and not after Christ.

Against false worship and false asceticism

[16]Let no man therefore judge you in meat, or in drink, or Col.
in respect of an holyday, or of the new moon, or of the sabbath 2:16–23
~~days~~: [17]Which are a shadow of things to come; but the body is of
Christ. [18]Let no man beguile you of your reward in a voluntary
humility and worshipping of angels, intruding into those things
which he hath not seen, vainly puffed up by his fleshly mind,
[19]And not holding the Head, from which all the body by joints

and bands having nourishment ministered, and knit together,
increaseth with the increase of God. [20]Wherefore if ye be dead
with Christ from the rudiments of the world, why, as though living in the world, are ye subject to ordinances, [21a]{Which are
after the doctrines and commandments of men, who teach you
to} Touch not; taste not; handle not; [22]{[21b]all those things which
are to perish with the using?} [23a]{[22]}Which things have indeed a
shew of wisdom in will worship, and humility, and neglecting ~~of~~
the body [23c]{as} to the satisfying of the flesh, [23b]not in any honor
{to God.}

Against evil practices

Philip. 3:1–3 [1]Finally, my brethren, rejoice in the Lord. To write the
same things to you, to me indeed is not grievous, ~~but~~ {and} for
you it is safe. [2]Beware of dogs, beware of evil workers, beware of
the concision /mutilation, [a wordplay on circumcision]/. [3]For
we are the circumcision, which worship God in the spirit, and
rejoice in Christ Jesus, and have no confidence in the flesh.

Warnings against false teachers

1 Tim. 1:3–7 [3]As I besought thee to abide still at Ephesus, when I went
into Macedonia, that thou mightest charge some that they teach
no other doctrine, [4]Neither give heed to fables and endless
genealogies, which minister /offer, present/ questions, rather
than godly edifying which is in faith~~: so do~~. [5]Now the end of the
commandment is charity out of a pure heart, and ~~of~~ a good
conscience, and ~~of~~ faith unfeigned: [6]From which some having
swerved /missed the mark/ have turned aside unto vain jangling
/idle, fruitless discussion/; [7]Desiring to be teachers of the law;
understanding neither what they say, nor whereof they affirm
/strongly assert/.

Jude 1:3–4 [3]Beloved, when I gave all diligence to write unto you of
the common /collective, shared/ salvation, it was needful for me
to write unto you, and exhort you that ye should earnestly con-
tend for the faith which was once delivered unto the saints. [4]For
there are certain men crept in unawares, who were before of
old ordained /publicly notified/ to this condemnation /judg-
ment, doom/, ungodly men, turning the grace of our God into

lasciviousness /licentiousness/, and denying the only Lord God,
and our Lord Jesus Christ.

Opposing the false teachers

10For there are many unruly and vain talkers /idle speak- Titus
ers, disputers/ and deceivers, specially they of the circumcision: 1:10–16
11Whose mouths must be stopped, who subvert whole houses,
teaching things which they ought not, for filthy lucre's sake.
12One of themselves, ~~even~~ a prophet of their own, said, The
Cretians are alway liars, evil beasts, slow bellies /lazy gluttons/.
13This witness is true. Wherefore rebuke them sharply, that they
may be sound in the faith; 14Not giving heed to Jewish fables,
and commandments /who reject, repudiate the truth/ of men,
that turn from the truth. 15Unto the pure {let} all things ~~are~~
{be} pure: but unto them that are defiled and unbelieving ~~is~~
nothing {is} pure; but even their mind and conscience is
defiled. 16They profess that they know God; but in works they
deny him, being abominable, and disobedient, and unto every
good work reprobate /unfit, worthless/.

God punishes apostates

5I will therefore put you in remembrance, though ye once Jude
knew this, how that the \Lord, Jesus, God, Christ God\, having 1:5–16
saved the people out of the land of Egypt, afterward destroyed
them that believed not. 6And the angels which kept not their
first estate, but left their own habitation, he hath reserved in
everlasting chains under darkness unto the judgment of the
great day. 7Even as Sodom and Gomorrha, and the cities about
them in like manner, giving themselves over to fornication, and
going after strange flesh, are set forth for an example, suffering
the vengeance of eternal fire. 8Likewise also these ~~filthy~~ dream-
ers defile the flesh, despise /set aside/ dominion /lordship/, and
speak evil of dignities /glories/. 9Yet Michael the archangel,
when contending with the devil he disputed /talked/ about the
body of Moses, durst not bring against him a railing /reviling/
accusation, but said, "The Lord rebuke thee" [Zechariah 3:2].
10But these speak evil of those things which they know not: but
what they know naturally, as brute beasts, in those things they

corrupt themselves. [11]Woe unto them! for they have gone in the way of Cain, and ran greedily after the error of Balaam for reward, and ~~perished~~ {shall perish} in the gainsaying /rebellion/ of Core. [12]These are spots /stains, hidden reefs/ in your feasts of charity, when they feast with you, feeding themselves without fear: clouds ~~they are~~ without water, carried about of winds; trees whose fruit withereth, without fruit, twice dead, plucked up by the roots; [13]Raging waves of the sea, foaming out their own shame; wandering stars, to whom is reserved the blackness of darkness for ever. [14]And Enoch also, the seventh from Adam, prophesied of these, saying, Behold, the Lord cometh with ten thousands of his saints, [15]To execute judgment upon all, and to convince all that are ungodly among them of all their ungodly deeds which they have ungodly committed, and of all their hard speeches which ungodly sinners have spoken against him. [16]These are murmurers, complainers, walking after their own lusts; and their mouth speaketh great swelling words, having men's persons in admiration because of advantage /profit, gain/ [playing favorites to get gain].

The Second Coming

Watch for the coming of the Lord

1 Thes. 5:1–11 [1]But of the times and the seasons, brethren, ye have no need that I write unto you. [2]For yourselves know perfectly that the day of the Lord so cometh as a thief in the night. [3]For when they shall say, Peace and safety; then sudden destruction cometh upon them, as travail upon a woman with child; and they shall not escape. [4]But ye, brethren, are not in darkness, that that day should overtake you as a thief. [5]Ye are all the children /sons/ of light, and the children of the day: we are not of the night, nor of darkness. [6]Therefore let us not sleep, as ~~do~~ others; but let us watch and be sober /vigilant, circumspect/. [7]For they that sleep sleep in the night; and they that be drunken are drunken in the night. [8]But let us, who are of the day, be sober, putting on the breastplate of faith and love; and for an helmet, the hope of salvation. [9]For God hath not appointed us

to wrath, but to obtain salvation by our Lord Jesus Christ, [10]Who died for us, that, whether we wake or sleep, we should live together with him. [11]Wherefore comfort /exhort, console, encourage/ yourselves together, and edify one another, even as also ye do.

Conditions at the time of the Lord's coming

[1]This second epistle, beloved, I now write unto you; in 2 Pet. 3:1–10
~~both~~ which I stir up your pure minds by way of remembrance: [2]That ye may be mindful of the words which were spoken before by the holy prophets, and of the commandment{s} of us the apostles of the Lord and Saviour: [3a]Knowing this first, that {[3c]}in the last days {[3b]}there shall come [3d]scoffers, walking after their own lusts, [4]{Denying the Lord and Jesus Christ} And saying, Where is the promise of ~~his~~ {Christ's} coming? for since the fathers fell asleep /died, passed away/, all things {must} continue as they ~~were~~ {are} and have continued as they are from the beginning of the creation. [5a]For this they willingly are ignorant of, that {[5d]}of old {[5c]}the heavens {[5e]}and the earth standing out of the water and in the water {were created [5b]}by the word of God: [6]~~Whereby~~ {and by the word of God,} the world that then was, being overflowed with water, perished: [7a]But the heavens and the earth, which are now, {[7c]}are kept in store, {[7b]}by the same word [7d]reserved unto fire against the day of judgment and perdition of ungodly men. [8]But {concerning the coming of the Lord}, beloved, ~~be~~ {I would} not {have you} ignorant of this one thing, that one day is with the Lord as a thousand years, and a thousand years as one day. [9]The Lord is not slack concerning his promise{s and coming}, as some men count slackness; but ~~is~~ longsuffering ~~to us ward~~ {toward us}, not willing that any should perish, but that all should come to repentance. [10]But the day of the Lord will come as a thief in the night; in the which the heavens shall {shake, and the earth also shall tremble, and the mountains shall melt and} pass away with a great noise, and the elements shall be filled with fervent heat, the earth also {shall be filled,} and the {corruptible} works that are therein shall be burned up.

Prepare for Christ's promised coming

2 Pet. [11]~~Seeing~~ {If} then that all these [worldly] things shall be
3:11–18 ~~dissolved~~ {destroyed}, what manner of persons ought ye to be
in ~~all~~ holy ~~conversation~~ {conduct} and godliness, [12]Looking
{unto and preparing} for ~~and hastening unto~~ the day of {the
coming of the} ~~God~~ {Lord}, wherein the {corruptible things of
the} heavens being on fire shall be dissolved, and the ~~elements~~
{mountains} shall melt with fervent heat? [13]Nevertheless {if}
we {shall endure we shall be kept} according to his promise,
{and we} look for {a} new heavens and a new earth, wherein
dwelleth righteousness. [14]Wherefore, beloved, seeing that ye
look for such things, be diligent that ye may be found of him in
peace, without spot, and blameless. [15a]And account /count,
regard/ {[15c]}even as our beloved brother Paul also, according to
the wisdom given unto him hath written unto you, [15b]~~that~~ the
longsuffering /patience/ {and waiting} of our Lord ~~is~~ {for} salvation; [16]As also in all his epistles, speaking in them of these
things; in which are some things hard to be understood, which
they ~~that~~ {who} are unlearned and unstable wrest /twist, dis-
tort/, as they do also the other scriptures, unto their own
destruction. [17a]Ye therefore, beloved, seeing ye know
{[17c]}before, {[17b]}~~these~~ {the} things {which are coming,} [17d]be-
ware lest ye also, being led away with the error of the wicked,
fall from your own stedfastness. [18]But grow in grace, and ~~in~~ the
knowledge of our Lord and Saviour Jesus Christ. To him be
glory both now and for ever. Amen.

Prepare for the Second Coming by living righteously

Rom. [11]And that [the fulness of Christ's law of love], knowing the
13:11–14 time, that now it is high time to awake out of sleep: for now is
our salvation nearer than when we believed. [12]The night is far
spent, the day is at hand: let us therefore cast off the works of
darkness, and let us put on the armour of light. [13]Let us walk
honestly /with propriety, decently, gracefully/, as in the day; not
in rioting and drunkenness, not in chambering /lewdness,
whoredoms/ and wantonness, not in strife and envying. [14]But

put ye on the Lord Jesus Christ, and make not provision for the
flesh, to ~~fulfil~~ {gratify} the lusts thereof.

The prelude to the coming of the Lord

[1]Now we beseech you, brethren, by /concerning/ the com- 2 Thes.
ing of our Lord Jesus Christ, and ~~by~~ our gathering together 2:1–12
unto him, [2a]That ye be not soon shaken in mind, or be troubled
{[2c]}~~nor~~ by {the} ~~letter~~ {latter, except ye receive it} from us,
{[2b]}neither by spirit, nor by word, [2d]as that the day of Christ is
at hand. [3]Let no man deceive you by any means: for ~~that day~~
{there shall} ~~not~~ {come} ~~except there come~~ {a falling} /apos-
tasy, defection/ away first, and that man of \sin, lawlessness\ be
revealed, the son of perdition; [4]Who opposeth and exalteth
himself above all that is called God, or that is worshipped; so
that he \as God\ sitteth in the temple of God, shewing himself
that he is God. [5]Remember ye not, that, when I was yet with
you, I told you these things? [6]And now ye know what withhold-
eth /the one who possesses, holds in firm grasp, restrains/ that
he might be revealed /disclosed, discovered, manifested/ in his
time. [7]For the mystery of iniquity /lawlessness/ doth already
work: ~~only~~ {and} he {it is} who now {worketh, and Christ suffereth him to work}, until {the time is fulfilled that he shall} be
taken out of the way. [8]And then shall that Wicked /lawless/
{one} be revealed, whom the Lord shall consume with the
spirit of his mouth, and shall destroy with the brightness of his
coming: [9]{Yea, the Lord,} Even ~~him~~ {Jesus}, whose coming is
{not until} after {there cometh a falling away, by} the working
of Satan with all power and signs and lying wonders, [10]And with
all deceivableness of unrighteousness in them that perish;
because they received not the love of the truth, that they might
be saved. [11]And for this cause God shall send them strong delu-
sion, that they should believe a lie: [12]That they all might be
damned /brought to account, trial/ who believed not the truth,
but had pleasure in unrighteousness.

Avoid the antichrist by heeding truth through the anointing

[18]Little children, it is the last time: and as ye have heard 1 Jn.
that antichrist shall come, even now are there many antichrists; 2:18–27

whereby we know that it is the last time. [19]They went out from us, but they were not of us; for if they had been of us, they would ~~no doubt~~ have continued with us: but ~~they went out~~, that they might be made manifest that they were not all of us. [20]But ye have an unction /anointing/ from the Holy One, and ye know all things. [21]I have not written unto you because ye know not the truth, but because ye know it, and that no lie is of the truth. [22]Who is a liar but he that denieth that Jesus is the Christ? He is antichrist, that denieth the Father and the Son. [23]Whosoever denieth the Son, the same hath not the Father~~: (but) he that acknowledgeth the Son hath the Father also~~. [24]Let that therefore abide in you, which ye have heard from the beginning. If that which ye have heard from the beginning shall remain in you, ye also shall continue in the Son, and in the Father. [25]And this is the promise that he hath promised us, ~~even~~ eternal life. [26]These ~~things~~ have I written unto you concerning them that seduce /deceive, lead astray, cause to wander/ you. [27]But the anointing which ye have received of him abideth in you, and ye need not that any man teach you: but as the same anointing teacheth you of all things, and is truth, and is no lie, and even as it hath taught you, ye shall abide in him.

Justice at the last judgment

2 Thes. 1:3–12 [3]We are bound to thank God always for you, brethren, as it is meet, because that your faith groweth exceedingly, and the charity of every one of you all toward each other aboundeth; [4]So that we ourselves glory in you in the churches of God for your patience /endurance/ and faith in all your persecutions and tribulations that ye endure: [5]Which is a manifest token of the righteous judgment of God, that ye may be counted worthy of the kingdom of God, for which ye also suffer: [6]Seeing it is a righteous thing with God to recompense tribulation to them that trouble you; [7]And to you who are troubled rest with us, when the Lord Jesus shall be revealed from heaven with his mighty angels, [8]In flaming fire taking vengeance on them that know not God, and that obey not the gospel of our Lord Jesus Christ: [9a]Who shall be punished with {[9c]}destruction from the

presence of the Lord, and from the glory of his {[9b]}everlasting [9d]power; [10]When he shall come to be glorified in his saints, and to be admired in all them that believe (because our testimony among you was believed) in that day. [11]Wherefore also we pray always for you, that our God would count you worthy of this calling, and fulfil all the good pleasure of his goodness, and the work of faith with power: [12]That the name of our Lord Jesus Christ may be glorified in you, and ye in him, according to the grace of our God and the Lord Jesus Christ.

The Resurrection

Witness of the resurrected Christ

[1]Moreover, brethren, I declare unto you the gospel which 1 Cor.
I preached unto you, which also ye have received, and wherein 15:1–8
ye stand; [2]By which also ye are saved, if ye keep /hold fast to,
retain/ in memory what I preached unto you, unless ye have
believed in vain. [3]For I delivered unto you first of all that which
I also received, how that Christ died for our sins according to
the scriptures; [4]And that he was buried, and that he rose again
the third day according to the scriptures: [5]And that he was
seen of Cephas, then of the twelve: [6]After that, he was seen of
above /more than, over/ five hundred brethren at once; of
whom the greater part remain unto this present, but some are
fallen asleep. [7]After that, he was seen of James; then of all the
apostles. [8]And last of all he was seen of me also, as of one born
out of due time.

Christ preached to the spirits in the spirit prison

[19]~~By~~ {For} which {cause} also, he [Christ] went and 1 Pet.
preached unto the spirits in prison; [20a]~~Which sometime~~ {Some 3:19–22
of whom} were disobedient {[20c]}in the days of Noah, {[20b]}~~when
once~~ {while} the long-suffering of God waited [20d]while the ark
was a preparing, wherein few, that is, eight souls were saved by
water. [21]The like figure /foreshadowing/ whereunto even baptism doth also now save us (not the putting away of the filth of
the flesh, but the answer of a good conscience toward God,) by

the resurrection of Jesus Christ: 22Who is gone into heaven, and is on the right hand of God; angels and authorities and powers being made subject unto him.

Importance of belief in the resurrection

1 Cor. 15:12–19

12Now if Christ be preached that he rose from the dead, how say some among you that there is no resurrection of the dead? 13But if there be no resurrection of the dead, then is Christ not risen: 14And if Christ be not risen, then is our preaching vain, and your faith is also vain. 15Yea, and we are found false witnesses of God; because we have testified of God that he raised up Christ: whom he raised not up, if so be that the dead rise not. 16For if the dead rise not, then is not Christ raised: 17And if Christ be not raised, your faith is vain /useless, empty, ineffective/; ye are yet in your sins. 18Then they also which are fallen asleep /died/ in Christ are perished /lost, destroyed/. 19If in this life only we have hope in Christ, we are of all men most miserable.

The resurrection of the righteous dead

1 Thes. 4:13–18

13But I would not have you to be ignorant, brethren, concerning them which are asleep /dead/, that ye sorrow not, even as others which have no hope. 14For if we believe that Jesus died and rose again, even so them also which sleep in Jesus will God bring with him. 15For this we say unto you by the word of the Lord, that ~~we~~ {they} ~~which~~ {who} are alive ~~and remain unto~~ {at} the coming of the Lord shall not prevent /precede, make progress over/ them ~~which~~ {who remain unto the coming of the Lord, who} are asleep. 16For the Lord himself shall descend from heaven with a shout /a cry of command, a cheer/, with the voice of the archangel, and with the trump of God: and the dead in Christ shall rise first: 17Then ~~we~~ {they} ~~which~~ {who} are alive, ~~and remain~~ shall be caught up together ~~with them~~ in{to} the clouds {with them who remain}, to meet the Lord in the air: and so shall we ever be with the Lord. 18Wherefore comfort one another with these words.

Adam and death; Christ and life

20But now is Christ risen from the dead, and become the 1 Cor.
firstfruits /firstling/ of them that slept. 21For since by man came 15:20–23
death, by man came also the resurrection of the dead. 22For as
in Adam all die, even so in Christ shall all be made alive. 23But
every man in his own order /rank/: Christ the firstfruits
/firstling/; afterward they that are Christ's at his coming.

Baptism for the dead as evidence of resurrection

29Else what shall they do which are baptized for /in behalf 1 Cor.
of, for the sake of/ the dead, if the dead rise not at all? why are 15:29
they then baptized for the dead?

Daily life as a reflection of belief in the resurrection

30And why stand we in jeopardy /danger, peril/ every 1 Cor.
hour? 31aI protest {unto you the resurrection of the dead;} ~~by~~ 15:30–34
~~your~~ {and this is my} rejoicing which I have in Christ Jesus our
Lord {31c}daily, {though} 31bI die. 32If after the manner of men I
have fought with beasts at Ephesus, what advantageth it me, if
the dead rise not? "let us eat and drink; for to morrow we die"
[Isaiah 22:13]. 33Be not deceived: evil communications /conver-
sations, associations/ corrupt good manners. 34Awake to righteousness, and sin not; for some have not the knowledge of God:
I speak ~~this~~ to your shame.

The manner of the resurrection, various glories

35But some ~~man~~ will say, How are the dead raised up? and 1 Cor.
with what body do they come? 36~~Thou~~ fool, that which thou 15:35–53
sowest is not quickened, except it die: 37And that which thou
sowest, thou sowest not that body that shall be, but ~~bare~~ grain, it
may ~~chance~~ {be} of wheat, or ~~of~~ some other grain: 38But God
giveth it a body as it hath pleased him, and to every seed his
own body. 39All flesh is not the same flesh: but ~~there is~~ one ~~kind~~
~~of~~ flesh of men, another flesh of beasts, another of fishes, ~~and~~
another of birds. 40~~There are~~ Also celestial bodies, and bodies
terrestrial {and bodies telestial}: but the glory of the celestial, ~~is~~
one, and ~~the glory of~~ the terrestrial, ~~is~~ another, {and the telestial,

another}. [41]~~There is~~ one glory of the sun, and another glory of the moon, and another glory of the stars: for ~~one~~ star differeth from ~~another~~ star in glory. [42]So also ~~is~~ the resurrection of the dead. It is sown in corruption; it is raised in incorruption: [43]It is sown in dishonour; it is raised in glory: it is sown in weakness; it is raised in power: [44]It is sown a natural body; it is raised a spiritual body. There is a natural body, and there is a spiritual body. [45]And so it is written, "The first man Adam was made a living soul; the last Adam was made a quickening spirit" [Genesis 2:7]. [46a]Howbeit that ~~was~~ {[46e]}which is natural {[46c]}first, {[46b]and} not {that [46d]}which is spiritual, but [46f]~~and~~ afterward that which is spiritual. [47]The first man ~~is~~ of the earth, earthy: the second man \~~is~~ the Lord\ from heaven. [48]As ~~is~~ the earthy, such ~~are~~ they also that are earthy: and as ~~is~~ the heavenly, such ~~are~~ they also that are heavenly. [49]And as we have borne the image of the earthy, we shall also bear the image of the heavenly. [50]Now this I say, brethren, that flesh and blood cannot inherit the kingdom of God; neither doth corruption inherit incorruption. [51]Behold, I shew you a mystery; We shall not all sleep /die, sleep in death/, but we shall all be changed, [52]In a moment, in the twinkling of an eye, at the {sound of the} last trump: for the trumpet shall sound, and the dead shall be raised incorruptible, and we shall be changed. [53]For this corruptible must put on incorruption, and this mortal ~~must~~ put on immortality.

After the resurrection

1 Cor. 15:24–28 [24]~~Then~~ {Afterward} cometh the end, when he shall have delivered up the kingdom to God, even the Father; when he shall have put down /brought to an end, abolished/ all rule and all authority and power. [25]For he must reign, till he hath put all enemies under his feet. [26a]The last enemy, {[26c]}~~is~~ death, [26b]~~that~~ shall be destroyed. [27a]For {he saith, when [27d]}it is manifest /clear, plain, evident/ that {[27b]}"he hath put all things under his feet" [Psalm 8:6] {[27c]}~~But~~ {and} ~~when he saith~~ {that} all things are put under ~~him~~, [27e]he is excepted /made an exception/ {of the father}, ~~which~~ {who} did put all things under him. [28]And when all things shall be subdued unto him, then shall the Son also

himself be subject unto him that put all things under him, that God may be all in all.

A concluding hymn of triumph

[54]So when this corruptible shall have put on incorruption, 1 Cor.
and this mortal shall have put on immortality, then shall be 15:54–58
brought to pass the saying that is written, "Death is swallowed
up in victory" [Isaiah 25:8]. [55]"O death /Hades, hell/, where ~~is~~
thy sting? O grave, where ~~is~~ thy victory?" [Hosea 13:14] [56]The
sting of death, ~~is~~ sin; and the strength /power/ of sin, ~~is~~ the law.
[57]But thanks ~~be~~ to God, which giveth us the victory through our
Lord Jesus Christ. [58]Therefore, my beloved brethren, be ye
stedfast, unmoveable, always abounding in the work of the
Lord, forasmuch as ye know that your labour is not in vain in
the Lord.

6

Leadership Instructions

Apostles of Jesus Christ

Pray for the apostles; speak always with grace

[2]Continue in prayer, and watch in the same with thanks- Col.
giving; [3]Withal praying also for us, that God would open unto 4:2–6
us a door of utterance, to speak the mystery of Christ, for which
I am also in bonds: [4]That I may make it manifest, as I ought to
speak. [5]Walk in wisdom toward them that are without /outside/,
redeeming /making the most of/ the time. [6]Let your speech be
alway with grace, seasoned with salt, that ye may know how ye
ought to answer every man.

Apostles make manifest the sweet fragrance of knowing Christ

[14]Now thanks ~~be~~ unto God, which always causeth us to tri- 2 Cor.
umph in Christ, and maketh manifest the savour /fragrance/ of 2:14–17
his knowledge by us in every place. [15]For we are unto God a
sweet savour of Christ, in them that are saved, and in them that
perish: [16]To the one ~~we are the~~ savour /smell/ of death unto
death; and to the other the savour /smell/ of life unto life. And
who is sufficient /fit, qualified/ for these things? [17]For we are not
as many, which corrupt the word of God: but as of sincerity, but
as of God, in the sight of God speak we in Christ.

Ministers of the new covenant

[1]Do we begin again to commend ourselves? or need we, as 2 Cor.
some ~~others~~, epistles of commendation to you, or ~~letters~~ of com- 3:1–18
mendation from you? [2]Ye are our epistle written in our hearts,
known and read of all men: [3]~~Forasmuch as ye are~~ manifestly
declared to be the epistle of Christ ministered by us, written not

with ink, but with the Spirit of the living God; not in tables of stone, but in fleshy tables of the heart. 4And such trust have we through Christ to God-ward: 5Not that we are sufficient of ourselves to think any thing as of ourselves; but our sufficiency is of God; 6Who also hath made us able ministers of the new testament [covenant]; not of the letter, but of the spirit: for the letter killeth, but the spirit giveth life. 7But if the ministration of death, written ~~and~~ engraven in stones, was glorious, so that the children of Israel could not stedfastly behold the face of Moses for the glory of his countenance; which glory was to be done away: 8How shall not the ministration of the spirit be rather glorious? 9For if the ministration of condemnation be glory, much more doth the ministration of righteousness exceed in glory. 10For even that which was made glorious had no glory in this respect, by reason of the glory that excelleth. 11For if that which is done away was glorious, much more that which remaineth is glorious. 12Seeing then that we have such hope, we use great plainness /boldness, frankness/ of speech: 13And not as Moses, ~~which~~ [who] put a vail over his face, that the children of Israel could not stedfastly look to the end of that which is abolished: 14But their minds were blinded: for until this day remaineth the same vail untaken away in the reading of the old testament; which ~~vail~~ is done away in Christ. 15But even unto this day, when Moses is read, the vail is upon their heart. 16Nevertheless when ~~it~~ {their heart} shall turn to the Lord, the vail shall be taken away. 17Now the Lord is that /the/ Spirit: and where the Spirit of the Lord is, there is liberty. 18But we all, with open face beholding as in a glass the glory of the Lord, are changed into the same image from glory to glory, even as by the Spirit of the Lord.

Apostles spread awareness of the light of Christ

2 Cor. 4:1–6

1Therefore seeing we have this ministry, as we have received mercy, we faint not; 2But have renounced the hidden things of dishonesty /shame, disgrace/, not walking in craftiness, nor handling the word of God deceitfully; but by manifestation of the truth commending ourselves to every man's conscience in the sight of God. 3But if our gospel be hid, it is hid to them that are lost: [4]In whom the god of this world hath blinded the minds of them which believe not, lest the light of the glorious gospel of Christ, who is the image of God, should shine unto them. [5]For we preach not ourselves, but Christ Jesus the Lord; and ourselves your servants for Jesus' sake. [6]For God, who commanded the light to shine out of darkness, hath shined in our hearts, to give the light of the knowledge of the glory of God in the face of Jesus Christ.

Apostles bring life in Christ

2 Cor. 4:7–5:10

[7]But we have this treasure in earthen vessels, that the excellency of the power may be of God, and not of us. [8]~~We are~~ troubled on every side, yet not distressed; ~~we are~~ perplexed, but not in despair; [9]Persecuted, but not forsaken; cast down, but not destroyed; [10]Always bearing about in the body the dying of the Lord Jesus, that the life also of Jesus might be made manifest in our body. [11]For we which live are alway delivered unto death for Jesus' sake, that the life also of Jesus might be made manifest in our mortal flesh. [12a]So then {it [12c]}worketh {[12b]}death [12d]~~in~~ {unto} us, but life ~~in~~ {unto} you. [13]We having the same spirit of faith, according as it is written, I believed, and therefore have I spoken; we also believe, and therefore speak; [14]Knowing that he which raised up the Lord Jesus shall raise up us also by Jesus, and shall present us with you. [15]For {we bear} all things ~~are~~ for your sakes, that the abundant grace might through the thanksgiving of many redound /abound/ to the glory of God. [16]For which cause we faint not; but though our outward man perish, yet the inward man is renewed day by day. [17]For our light affliction, which is but for a moment, worketh for us a far more exceeding and eternal weight of glory; [18]While we look not at the things which are seen, but at the things which are not seen: for the things which are seen are temporal; but the things which are not seen are eternal. [1]For we know that if our earthly house of this tabernacle were dissolved, we have a building of God, an house not made with hands, eternal in the heavens. [2]For in this we groan, earnestly desiring to be clothed upon with our house which is from heaven: [3]~~If so be~~ that being

clothed we shall not be found naked. 4For we that are in this tabernacle do groan, being burdened: not for that we would be unclothed, but clothed upon, that mortality might be swallowed up of life. 5Now he that hath wrought us for the selfsame thing is God, who also hath given unto us the earnest of the Spirit. 6Therefore ~~we are~~ always confident /of good courage, of good cheer/, knowing that, whilst we are at home in the body, we are absent from the Lord: 7(For we walk by faith, not by sight:) 8We are confident, ~~I say,~~ and willing rather to be absent from the body, and to be present with the Lord. 9Wherefore we labour, that, whether present or absent, we may be accepted of him. 10For we must all appear before the judgment seat of Christ; that every one may receive {a reward of} the ~~things~~ {deeds} done in ~~his~~ {the} body, {things} according to ~~that~~ {what} he hath done, whether ~~it be~~ good or bad.

Apostles have the ministry of reconciling the world to God

2 Cor. 5:11–6:2 11Knowing therefore the terror of the Lord, we persuade men; but we are made manifest unto God; and I trust also are made manifest in your consciences. 12For we commend not ourselves again unto you, but give you occasion to glory on our behalf, that ye may have somewhat to answer them which glory in appearance, and not in heart. 13For {we bear record} ~~whether~~ {that} we ~~be~~ {are not} beside ourselves, {for whether we glory,} it is to God: or whether we be sober, it is for your ~~cause~~ {sakes}. 14For the love of Christ constraineth us; because we thus judge, that if one died for all, then ~~were~~ {are} all dead: 15And ~~that~~ he died for all, that they which live should not henceforth live unto themselves, but unto him which died for them, and rose again. 16aWherefore henceforth ~~know~~ {live} we no ~~man~~ {more} after the flesh: yea, though {we once lived after the flesh, yet since} we have known Christ, {16c}~~yet~~ now henceforth ~~know~~ {live we} ~~him~~ {16dno more} 16bafter the flesh. 17Therefore if any man ~~be~~ {live} in Christ, he is a new creature: old things are passed away; behold, all things are become new. 18And {receiveth} all {the} things ~~are~~ of God, who hath reconciled us to himself by Jesus Christ, and hath given to us the min-

istry of reconciliation; [19]To wit, that God ~~was~~ {is} in Christ, reconciling the world unto himself, not imputing their trespasses unto them; and hath committed unto us the word of reconciliation. [20]Now then we are ambassadors for Christ, as though God did beseech ~~you~~ by us: we pray ~~you~~ in Christ's stead, be ye reconciled to God. [21]For he hath made him ~~to be~~ sin for us, who knew no sin; that we might be made the righteousness of God in him. [1]We then, as workers together with ~~him~~ {Christ}, beseech you also that ye receive not the grace of God in vain. [2](For he saith, "I have heard thee in a time accepted, and in the day of salvation have I succoured thee: behold, now is the accepted time; behold, now is the day of salvation" [Isaiah 49:8].)

Apostles suffer afflictions, yet always rejoice

[3]Giving no offence in any thing, that the ministry be not 2 Cor.
blamed: [4]But in all ~~things~~ approving ourselves as the ministers 6:3–10
of God, in much patience, in afflictions, in necessities, in distresses, [5]In stripes, in imprisonments, in tumults, in labours, in watchings, in fastings; [6]By pureness, by knowledge, by longsuffering, by kindness, by the Holy Ghost, by love unfeigned, [7]By the word of truth, by the power of God, by the armour of righteousness on the right hand and on the left, [8]By honour and dishonour, by evil report and good report: as deceivers, and ~~yet~~ true; [9]As unknown, and ~~yet~~ well known; as dying, and, behold, we live; as chastened, and not killed; [10]As sorrowful, yet alway rejoicing; as poor, yet making many rich; as having nothing, and ~~yet~~ possessing all things.

The stewardship of the apostles over the mysteries of God

[1]Let a man so account of us, as of the ministers of Christ, 1 Cor.
and stewards of the mysteries of God. [2]Moreover it is required 4:1–13
~~in~~ {of} stewards, that a man be found faithful. [3]But with me it is a very small thing that I should be judged of you, or of man's judgment: yea, I judge not mine own self. [4]For {though} I know nothing ~~by~~ {against} myself; yet ~~am~~ I {am} not hereby justified: but he ~~that~~ {who} judgeth me is the Lord. [5]Therefore

{I} judge nothing before the time, until the Lord come, who both will bring to light the hidden things of darkness, and will make manifest the counsels of the hearts: and then shall every man have praise of God. 6And these things, brethren, I have in a figure transferred to myself and to Apollos for your sakes; that ye might learn in us not to think ~~of men~~ above that which is written, that no one of you be puffed up /proud, arrogant/ for one against another. 7For who maketh thee to differ /different from, superior to/ ~~from another~~? and what hast thou that thou didst not receive? now if thou didst receive it, why dost thou glory, as if thou hadst not received it? 8Now ye are full, now ye are rich, ye have reigned as kings without us: and I would to God ye did reign, that we also might reign with you. 9For I think that God hath set forth us the apostles last /last apostles/, as it were appointed to death: for we are made a spectacle unto the world, and to angels, and to men. 10We are fools for Christ's sake, but ye are wise in Christ; we are weak, but ye are strong; ye are honourable, but we are despised. 11Even unto this present hour we both hunger, and thirst, and are naked, and are buffeted /roughly treated, afflicted/, and have no certain dwellingplace; 12And labour, working with our own hands: being reviled, we bless; being persecuted, we suffer /endure patiently/ it: 13Being defamed, we intreat: we are made as the filth of the world, ~~and are~~ the offscouring of all things unto this day.

Apostles set an example; he who will not work should not eat

2 Thes. 3:6–15 6Now we command you, brethren, in the name of our Lord Jesus Christ, that ye withdraw yourselves from every brother that walketh disorderly, and not after the tradition which he received of us. 7For yourselves know how ye ought to follow /imitate/ us: for we behaved not ourselves disorderly among you; 8Neither did we eat any man's bread for nought /undeservedly, gratuitously/; but wrought with labour and travail night and day, that we might not be chargeable to any of you: 9Not because we have not power /authority/, but to make ourselves an ensample unto you to follow us. 10For even when we were with you, this we commanded you, that if any would

not work, neither should he eat. [11]For we hear that there are some which walk among you disorderly, working not at all, but are busybodies. [12]Now them that are such we command and exhort by our Lord Jesus Christ, that with quietness they work, and eat their own bread. [13]But ye, brethren, be not weary in well doing. [14]And if any man obey not our word by this epistle, note that man, and have no company with him, that he may be ashamed. [15]Yet count him not as an enemy, but admonish ~~him~~ as a brother.

Temporal support of the apostles

[1]Am I not an apostle? am I not free /independent/? have I not seen Jesus Christ our Lord? are not ye my work in the Lord? [2]If I be not an apostle unto others, yet doubtless I am to you: for the seal /certification, proof, token/ of mine apostleship are ye in the Lord. [3]Mine answer /defense/ to them that do examine /question, call into account, judge/ me is this, [4]Have we not power to eat and to drink? [5]Have we not power to lead about a sister, a wife, as well as other apostles, and as the brethren of the Lord, and Cephas? [6]Or I only and Barnabas, have not we power to forbear working? [7]Who goeth a warfare any time at his own charges? who planteth a vineyard, and eateth not of the fruit thereof? or who feedeth a flock, and eateth not of the milk of the flock? [8]Say I these things as a man? or saith not the law the same also? [9]For it is written in the law of Moses, "Thou shalt not muzzle the mouth of the ox that treadeth out the corn" [Deuteronomy 25:4]. Doth God take care for oxen? [10]Or saith he it altogether for our sakes? For our sakes, no doubt, this is written: that he that ploweth should plow in hope; and that he that thresheth in hope should be partaker of his hope. [11]If we have sown unto you spiritual things, is it a great thing if we shall reap your carnal /temporal/ things? [12]If others be partakers of ~~this~~ power /authority/ over you, ~~are~~ [do] not we rather [have a greater right]? Nevertheless we have not used this power; but suffer all things, lest we should hinder the gospel of Christ. [13]Do ye not know that they which minister about holy things live /eat/ ~~of the things~~ of the temple? and they

1 Cor. 9:1–14

which wait at the altar are partakers with the altar? 14Even so
hath the Lord ordained that they which preach the gospel
should live of the gospel.

Instructions to Church Leaders

Qualifications to be a bishop or local leader

1 Tim. 1This is a true saying, If a man desire the office of a bishop,
3:1–7 he desireth a good work. 2A bishop then must be blameless, the
husband of one wife, vigilant, sober /temperate, circumspect/, of
good behaviour, given to hospitality, apt to teach; 3Not given to
wine, no striker /bully, violent person/, not greedy of filthy
lucre; but patient, not a brawler, not covetous; 4One that ruleth
well his own house, having his children in subjection with all
gravity; 5(For if a man know not how to rule his own house, how
shall he take care of the church of God?) 6Not a novice /recent
convert/, lest being lifted up with pride he fall into the condemnation of the devil. 7Moreover he must have a good report of
them which are without /outside the faith/; lest he fall into
reproach and the snare of the devil.

Titus 5For this cause left I thee in Crete, that thou shouldest set
1:5–9 in order the things that are wanting, and ordain elders in every
city, as I had appointed /directed, ordered/ thee: 6If any be
blameless, the husband of one wife, having faithful children not
accused of riot /debauchery or insubordination/ or unruly. 7For
a bishop must be blameless, as the steward of God; not selfwilled /obstinate, arrogant/, not soon angry, not given to wine,
no striker, not given to filthy lucre; 8But a lover of hospitality, a
lover of good /what is good/ men, sober, just, holy, temperate
/self-controlled/; 9Holding fast the faithful word as he hath been
taught, that he may be able by sound doctrine both to exhort
and to convince the gainsayers /those who deny, contradict/.

Instructions concerning elders

1 Tim. 17Let the elders that rule well be counted worthy of double
5:17–25 honour, especially they who labour in the word and doctrine.
18For the scripture saith, "Thou shalt not muzzle the ox that

treadeth out the corn" [Deuteronomy 25:4]. And, The labourer
is worthy of his reward /wage/. [19]Against an elder receive not an
accusation, but before "two or three witnesses" [Deuteronomy
17:6]. [20]Them that sin rebuke before all, that others also may
fear. [21]I charge thee before God, and the Lord Jesus Christ, and
the elect angels, that thou observe these things without preferring one before another /apart from prejudice/, doing nothing
by partiality. [22]Lay hands suddenly on no man, neither be partaker of other men's sins: keep thyself pure. [24]{[23]}Some men's
sins are open beforehand, going before to judgment; and some
men they follow after /appear later/. [25]{[24]}Likewise also the
good works of some are manifest beforehand; and they that are
otherwise cannot be hid. [23]{[25]}Drink no longer water, but use a
little wine for thy stomach's sake and thine often infirmities.

Advice to the elders: feed the sheep of God

[1]The elders which are among you I exhort, who am also 1 Pet.
an elder, and a witness of the sufferings of Christ, and also a 5:1–4
partaker of the glory that shall be revealed: [2]Feed /tend, super-
intend/ the flock of God which is among you, taking the over-
sight ~~thereof~~ /overseeing, guarding, watching/, not by
constraint, but willingly; not for filthy lucre, but of a ready
mind; [3]Neither as being lords over God's heritage, but being
ensamples to the flock. [4]And when the chief Shepherd shall
appear, ye shall receive a crown of glory that fadeth not away.

Being a good minister of Jesus Christ

[6]If thou put the brethren in remembrance of these things, 1 Tim.
thou shalt be a good minister of Jesus Christ, nourished up in 4:6–16
the words of faith and of good doctrine, whereunto thou hast
attained /which thou hast followed closely/. [7]But refuse profane
and old wives' fables, and exercise thyself ~~rather~~ unto godliness.
[8]For bodily exercise profiteth little /a little while/: but godliness
is profitable unto all things, having promise of the life that now
is, and of that which is to come. [9]This is a faithful saying and
worthy of all acceptation /approval/. [10]For therefore we both
labour and \struggle, suffer reproach\, because we trust in the
living God, who is the Saviour of all men, specially of those that

believe. 11These things command and teach. 12Let no man
despise thy youth; but be thou an example of the believers, in
word, in conversation /conduct, behavior/, in charity, in spirit,
in faith, in purity. 13Till I come, give attendance to reading, to
exhortation, to doctrine. 14Neglect not the gift that is in thee,
which was given thee by prophecy, with the laying on of the
hands of the presbytery /elders/. 15Meditate upon these things;
give thyself wholly to them; that thy profiting /progress,
advancement/ may appear to all /be manifest in all/. 16Take heed
unto thyself, and unto the doctrine; continue in them: for in
doing this thou shalt both save thyself, and them that hear thee.

Healing the sick by faith, prayer, and anointing

James 14Is any sick among you? let him call for the elders of the
5:14–18 church; and let them pray over him, anointing him with oil in
the name of the Lord: 15And the prayer of faith shall save the
sick, and the Lord shall raise him up; and if he have committed
sins, they shall be forgiven him. 16Confess your faults one to
another, and pray one for another, that ye may be healed. The
effectual fervent prayer of a righteous man availeth much.
17Elias was a man subject to like passions as we are, and he
prayed earnestly that it might not rain: and it rained not on the
earth by the space of three years and six months. 18And he
prayed again, and the heaven gave rain, and the earth brought
forth her fruit.

Qualifications to be a deacon

1 Tim. 8aLikewise {8c}the deacons {8b}must 8dbe grave /honorable,
3:8–13 dignified/, not doubletongued /deceitful/, not given to much
wine, not greedy of filthy lucre; 9Holding the mystery of the
faith in a pure conscience. 10And let these also first be proved;
then let them use the office of a deacon, being ~~found~~ blameless.
11Even so must their wives /women in like manner/ be grave
/honorable, dignified/, not slanderers, sober /temperate, vigilant, circumspect/, faithful in all things. 12Let the deacons be the
husbands of one wife, ruling their children and their own
houses well. 13For they that have used the office of a deacon well

purchase /earn, acquire for themselves good standing rank/ to themselves a good degree, and great boldness in the faith which is in Christ Jesus.

Instructions and Encouragement to Fellow Laborers

Obey and pray for religious leaders

[17]Obey them that have the rule over you, and submit your- Heb.
selves: for they watch for your souls, as they that must give 13:17–19
account, that they may do it with joy, and not with grief: for that
is unprofitable for you. [18]Pray for us: for we trust we have a
good conscience, in all things willing to live honestly. [19]But I
beseech ~~you the~~ rather to do this, that I may be restored to you
the sooner.

Church members are to follow the elders in humility

[5]Likewise, ye younger, submit yourselves unto the elder. 1 Pet.
Yea, all ~~of you~~ be subject one to another, and be clothed with 5:5–10
humility: "for God resisteth /opposes, is adverse to/ the proud,
and giveth grace to the humble" [Proverbs 3:34 LXX]. [6]Humble
yourselves therefore under the mighty hand of God, that he
may exalt you in due time: [7]Casting all your care upon him; for
he careth for you. [8]Be sober, be vigilant; because your adversary
the devil, as a roaring lion, walketh about, seeking whom he
may devour: [9]Whom resist stedfast in the faith, knowing that
the same afflictions are accomplished /laid upon, endured by/ in
your brethren that are in the world. [10]But the God of all grace,
who hath called us unto his eternal glory by Christ Jesus, after
that ye have suffered a while, make you perfect /restored to former condition, fully trained/, stablish /confirm, support/,
strengthen, settle you.

Help those who promote the truth

[5]Beloved, thou doest faithfully whatsoever thou doest to 3 Jn.
the brethren, and to strangers; [6]Which have borne witness of 1:5–8
thy charity before the church: whom if thou bring forward on
their journey after a godly sort /worthy of God/, thou shalt do

well: [7]Because that for his name's sake they went forth, taking nothing of the Gentiles. [8]We therefore ought to receive such, that we might be fellowhelpers to the truth.

The blessings of converting a sinner

James [19]Brethren, if any of you do err from the truth, and one
5:19–20 convert him; [20]Let him know, that he which converteth the sinner from the error of his way shall save a soul from death, and
shall hide /cover, remove from sight/ a multitude of sins.

Become the people of God

1 Pet. [4]To whom coming, ~~as unto~~ a living stone, disallowed
2:4–10 indeed of men, but chosen of God, ~~and~~ precious, [5]Ye also, as
lively /living/ stones, are built up a spiritual house, an holy
priesthood {nation}, to offer up spiritual sacrifices, acceptable
to God by Jesus Christ. [6]Wherefore also it is contained in the
scripture, "Behold, I lay in Sion a chief corner stone, elect, precious: and he that believeth on him shall not be confounded
/ashamed, disappointed/" [Isaiah 28:16]. [7a]Unto you therefore
~~which~~ {who} believe, he is precious: but unto them ~~which be~~
{who are} disobedient, {[8b]}~~Which~~ {who} stumble at the word
through disobedience whereunto they were appointed, {[8a]}"a
stone of stumbling and a rock of offense" [Isaiah 8:14]. [7b]"{For}
the stone which the builders disallowed /rejected as useless/, ~~the~~
~~same~~ is ~~made~~ {become} the head of the corner" [Psalm 118:22].
[9]"But ye are a chosen generation" [Isaiah 43:20], "a royal priesthood, "an holy nation" [Exodus 19:6], "a peculiar /purchased,
preserved, personally owned/ people" [Isaiah 43:21]; that ye
should shew forth the praises of him who hath called you out of
darkness into his marvellous light: [10]Which in time past were
not a people, but are now the people of God: which had not
obtained mercy, but now have obtained mercy.

Be not ashamed of the gospel and of spiritual gifts received

2 Tim. [6]Wherefore I put thee in remembrance that thou stir up
1:6–14 /rekindle, revive/ the gift of God, which is in thee by the putting
on of my hands. [7]For God hath not given us the spirit of fear;

but of power, and of love, and of a sound mind. [8]Be not thou
therefore ashamed of the testimony of our Lord, nor of me his
prisoner: but be thou partaker of the afflictions of the gospel
according to the power of God; [9]Who hath saved us, and called
us with an holy calling, not according to our works, but according to his own purpose and grace, which was given us in Christ
Jesus before the world began, [10]But is now made manifest by
the appearing of our Saviour Jesus Christ, who hath abolished
death, and hath brought life and immortality to light through
the gospel: [11]Whereunto I am appointed a preacher, and an
apostle, and a teacher \of the Gentiles\. [12]For the which cause I
also suffer these things: nevertheless I am not ashamed: for I
know whom I have believed, and am persuaded that he is able
to keep that which I have committed unto him against that day.
[13]Hold fast the form /sketch, model, example/ of sound /uncor-
rupted/ words, which thou hast heard of me, in faith and love
which is in Christ Jesus. [14]That good thing which was committed unto thee keep by the Holy Ghost which dwelleth in us.

Be not afraid to testify of Christ

[13]And who is he that will harm you, if ye be followers of 1 Pet.
that which is good? [14]But ~~and~~ if ye suffer for righteousness' 3:13–18
sake, happy are ye: "and be not afraid of their terror, neither be
troubled; [15a]But sanctify /reverence as holy/ the Lord God in
your hearts" [Isaiah 8:12–13]: and be ready always to give an
answer /a defense/ {[15c]}with meekness and fear /reverence, awe/
[15b]to every man that asketh {of} you a reason ~~of~~ {for} the hope
that is in you: [16]Having a good conscience; that, whereas they
speak evil \of you\, \as of evildoers\, they may be ashamed that
falsely accuse your good ~~conversation~~ {conduct} in Christ.
[17]For it is better, if the will of God be so, that ye suffer for well
doing, than for evil doing. [18a]For Christ also ~~hath~~ once \suf-
fered, died\ for sins, the just for the unjust, {[18c]}being put to
death in the flesh, but quickened by the Spirit {[18b]}that he
might bring us to God:

A good soldier of Christ Jesus faces hardships

2 Tim. 2:1–13

1Thou therefore, my son, be strong in the grace that is in Christ Jesus. 2And the things that thou hast heard of me among many witnesses, the same commit thou to faithful men, who shall be able to teach others also. 3Thou therefore endure hardness /afflictions, vexations/, as a good soldier of Jesus Christ. 4No man that warreth entangleth himself with the affairs of ~~this~~ life; that he may please him who hath chosen him to be a soldier. 5And if a man also strive /compete in a contest/ for masteries, ~~yet~~ {he} is ~~he~~ not crowned, except he strive lawfully. 6The husbandman that laboureth must be ~~first~~ partaker of the fruits. 7Consider what I say; and the Lord give thee understanding in all things. 8Remember that Jesus Christ of the seed of David was raised from the dead according to ~~my~~ {the} gospel: 9Wherein I suffer trouble, as an evil doer, ~~even~~ unto bonds; but the word of God is not bound. 10Therefore I endure all things for the elect's sakes, that they may also obtain the salvation which is in Christ Jesus with eternal glory. 11~~It~~ {For this} is a faithful saying: For if we be dead with him, we shall also live with him: 12If we suffer, /endure, remain constant/ we shall also reign with him: if we deny him, he also will deny us: 13If we believe not /are unfaithful/, ~~yet~~ he abideth faithful: he cannot deny himself.

Suffer as a Christian

1 Pet. 4:12–19

12Beloved, think it not strange concerning the fiery trial which is to try you, as though some strange thing happened unto you: 13But rejoice, inasmuch as ye are partakers of Christ's sufferings; that, when his glory shall be revealed, ye may be glad also with exceeding joy. 14If ye be reproached for the name of Christ, happy are ye; for the spirit of glory and of God resteth upon you: \on their part he is evil spoken of /blasphemed/, but on your part he is glorified\. 15But let none of you suffer as a murderer, or as a thief, or as an evildoer, or as a busybody in other men's matters. 16Yet if any ~~man~~ suffer as a Christian, let him not be ashamed; but let him glorify God on this behalf. 17For the time is come that judgment must begin at the house of God: and if it first begin at us, what shall the end be of

them that obey not the gospel of God? 18“And if the righteous
scarcely be saved, where shall the ungodly and the sinner
appear?” [Proverbs 11:31 LXX] 19Wherefore let them that suffer
according to the will of God commit the keeping of their souls
to him in well doing, as unto a faithful Creator.

Be an approved workman against false teachings

14Of these things put them in remembrance, charging 2 Tim.
them before the Lord that they strive not about words /dispute 2:14–26
not about words, or trivialities/ to no profit, ~~but~~ to the subvert-
ing of the hearers. 15Study to shew thyself approved unto God,
a workman that needeth not to be ashamed, rightly dividing
the word of truth /setting forth without perversion, distortion/.
16But shun profane and vain babblings /disputations/: for they
will increase unto more ungodliness. 17And their word will eat
as doth a canker /teaching will spread like gangrene/: of whom
is Hymenaeus and Philetus; 18Who concerning the truth have
erred, saying that the resurrection is past already; and overthrow the faith of some. 19Nevertheless the foundation of God
standeth sure, having this seal, “The Lord knoweth them that
are his” [Numbers 16:5]. And, Let every one that nameth the
name of Christ depart from iniquity. 20But in a great house
there are not only vessels of gold and of silver, but also of wood
and of earth /clay, earthenware/; and some to honour, and some
to dishonour. 21If a man therefore purge himself from these, he
shall be a vessel unto honour, sanctified, and meet /useful, prof-
itable/ for the master’s use, ~~and~~ prepared unto every good
work. 22Flee also youthful lusts /impure, violent desires/: but follow righteousness, faith, charity, peace, with them that call on
the Lord out of a pure heart. 23But foolish and unlearned questions avoid, knowing that they do gender strifes. 24And the servant of the Lord must not strive; but be gentle unto all ~~men~~, apt
to teach, patient, 25In meekness instructing those that oppose
themselves; if God peradventure /perchance/ will give them
repentance to the acknowledging of the truth; 26And ~~that~~ they
may recover themselves out of the snare of the devil, who are
taken captive by him at his will.

7

Church Policies and Practices

Prayer and Worship

Pray for everyone

[1]I exhort therefore, that, first of all, supplications, 1 Tim.
prayers, intercessions, ~~and~~ giving of thanks, be made for all 2:1–8
men; [2]For kings, and ~~for~~ all that are in authority; that we may
lead a quiet and peaceable life in all godliness and honesty
/dignity, gravity/. [3]For this is good and acceptable in the sight of
God our Saviour; [4]Who {is} will{ing to} /desires to/ have all
men to be saved, and to come unto the knowledge of the truth
{which is in Christ Jesus, who is the Only Begotten Son of God,
and ordained to be a Mediator between God and man; who is
one God, and hath power over all men.} [5]For there is one God,
and one mediator between God and men, the man Christ
Jesus; [6]Who gave himself a ransom for all, to be testified in due
time. [7]Whereunto I am ordained a preacher, and an apostle, (I
speak the truth in Christ, and lie not;) a teacher of the Gentiles
in faith and verity /truth/. [8]I will /desire/ therefore that men
pray every where, lifting up holy hands, without wrath and
doubting /dispute, contention/.

Women in the assembly

[9]In like manner also, that women adorn themselves in 1 Tim.
modest apparel, with shamefacedness /modesty, dignity, rever- 2:9–15
ence/ and sobriety /prudence/; not with broided /plaited,
braided/ hair, or gold, or pearls, or costly array; [10]But (which
becometh women professing godliness) with good works. [11]Let
the woman learn in silence /serenity, without anxiety/ with all
subjection /due submission/. [12]~~But~~ {For} I suffer not a woman

to teach, nor to usurp authority /excercise dominion, be auto-
cratic, domineer/ over the man, but to be in silence /quietness,
tranquility/. [13]For Adam was first formed, then Eve. [14]And Adam
was not deceived /led astray/, but the woman being deceived
was in the transgression. [15]Notwithstanding ~~she~~ {they} shall be
saved in childbearing, if they continue in faith and charity and
holiness with sobriety /modesty/.

Head coverings of men and women

1 Cor. [2]Now I praise you, brethren, that /because/ ye remember
11:2–16 me in all things, and keep the ordinances /precepts, doctrines,
traditions/, as I delivered ~~them~~ to you. [3]But I would have you
know, that the head of every man is Christ; and the head of the
woman, ~~is~~ the man; and the head of Christ, ~~is~~ God. [4]Every man
praying or prophesying, having his head covered, dishonoureth his head [Christ]. [5]But every woman that prayeth or
prophesieth with her head uncovered [unveiled] dishonoureth
her head [her husband]: for that is even all one as /one and the
same as/ if she were shaven. [6]For if the woman be not covered
[veiled], let her also be shorn: but if it be a shame for a woman
to be shorn or shaven, let her be covered. [7]For a man indeed
ought not to cover his head, forasmuch as he is the image and
glory of God: but the woman [wife] is the glory of the man. [8]For
the man is not of the woman; but the woman of the man. [9]Nei-
ther was the man created for [because of] the woman; but the
woman for [because of] the man. [10]For this cause ought the
woman to have ~~power~~ {a covering} on her head because of the
angels. [11]Nevertheless neither is the man without the woman,
neither the woman without the man, in the Lord. [12]For as the
woman is of the man, even so is the man also by the woman; but
all things of God. [13]Judge in yourselves: is it comely /proper, fitting, becoming/ that a woman pray unto God uncovered?
[14]Doth not even nature itself teach you, that, if a man have long
hair, it is a shame unto him? [15]But if a woman have long hair, it
is a glory to her: for her hair is given her for a covering. [16]But if
any man seem to be contentious, we have no such custom /we
do not act that way/, neither the churches of God.

Pray and sing

[13]Is any among you afflicted? let him pray. Is any merry? James
let him sing psalms. 5:13

The Sacrament

The Last Supper

[23]For I have received of the Lord that which also I deliv- 1 Cor.
ered unto you, That the Lord Jesus the ~~same~~ night in which he 11:23–26
was betrayed took bread: [24]And when he had given thanks, he
brake ~~it~~, and said, Take, eat: this is my body, which is broken for
you: this do in remembrance of me. [25]After the same manner
also ~~he took~~ the cup, when he had supped, saying, This cup is
the new testament in my blood: this do ye, as oft as ye drink it,
in remembrance of me. [26]For as often as ye eat this bread, and
drink this cup, ye do shew /proclaim, announce/ the Lord's
death till he come.

Avoid abuses in observing the Lord's Supper

[17]Now in this that I declare ~~unto you~~ I praise ~~you~~ not, that 1 Cor.
ye come together not for the better, but for the worse. [18]For first 11:17–22
of all, when ye come together in the church, I hear that there be
divisions /dissensions, schisms/ among you; and I partly believe
it. [19]For there must be also ~~heresies~~ {divisions} /sects, factions/
among you, that they which are approved may be made manifest among you. [20]When ye come together ~~therefore~~ into one
place, ~~this~~ is {it} not to eat the Lord's supper{?}. [21]~~For~~ {But} in
eating every one taketh before other his own supper: and one is
hungry, and another is drunken. [22]What? have ye not houses to
eat and to drink in? or despise ye the church of God, and shame
them that have not? What shall I say to you? shall I praise you
in this? I praise ~~you~~ not.

Do not partake of the Sacrament unworthily

[27]Wherefore whosoever shall eat this bread, and drink this 1 Cor.
cup of the Lord, unworthily, shall be guilty of /offend against/ 11:27–34
the body and blood of the Lord. [28]But let a man examine himself,

and so let him eat of that bread, and drink of that cup. [29]For he
that eateth and drinketh unworthily, eateth and drinketh
~~damnation~~ {condemnation} /judgment/ to himself, not discerning the Lord's body. [30]For this cause many are weak and sickly
among you, and many sleep. [31]For if we would judge /scruti-
nize, examine/ ourselves, we should not be judged. [32]But when
we are judged, we are chastened of the Lord, that we should
not be condemned with the world. [33]Wherefore, my brethren,
when ye come together to eat, tarry one for another. [34]And if
any man hunger, let him eat at home; that ye come not together
unto condemnation. And the rest will I set in order when I
come.

Making Donations

Instructions on gathering contributions

1 Cor. 16:1–4 [1]Now concerning the collection for the saints, as I have
given /directed, arranged/ order to the churches of Galatia,
even so do ye. [2]Upon the first ~~day~~ of the week let every one of
you lay by him in store, as God hath prospered him, that there
be no gatherings when I come. [3]And when I come, whomsoever
ye shall approve by your letters, them will I send to bring your
liberality /gift/ unto Jerusalem. [4]And if it be meet /suitable,
worthwhile/ that I go also, they shall go with me.

Be generous

2 Cor. 8:1–9 [1]Moreover, brethren, we ~~do~~ {would have} you to ~~wit~~
{know} /we make known (or declare) to you/ of the grace of
God bestowed on the churches of Macedonia; [2]How that in a
great trial of affliction the abundance of their joy and their deep
poverty abounded unto the riches of their liberality /sincerity,
purity of mind/. [3]For to their power, I bear record, yea, and
beyond their power they were willing of themselves; [4]Praying
us with much intreaty that we would receive the gift, and ~~take
upon us~~ the fellowship of the ministering to the saints. [5]And this
they did, not as we ~~hoped~~ {required}, but first gave their own
selves to the Lord, and unto us by the will of God. [6]Insomuch

that we desired Titus, that as he had begun, so he would also finish in you the same grace also. 7Therefore, as ye abound in every thing, in faith, and utterance, and knowledge, and in all diligence, and in your love to us, see that ye abound in this grace also. 8I speak not by commandment, but by occasion of the forwardness of others, and to prove the sincerity of your love. 9For ye know the grace of our Lord Jesus Christ, that, though he was rich, yet for your sakes he became poor, that ye through his poverty might be rich.

Guidance on giving 2 Cor. 8:10–15

10And herein I give ~~my~~ advice: for this is expedient for you, who have begun before, not only to do, but also to be forward a year ago. 11Now therefore perform the doing ~~of it~~; that as ~~there was~~ a readiness to will, so ~~there may be~~ a performance also out of that which ye have. 12For if there be first a willing mind, it is accepted according to that a man hath, and not according to that he hath not. 13For I mean not that other men be eased, and ye burdened: 14But by an equality, that now at this time your abundance may be a supply for their want, that their abundance also may be a supply for your want: that there may be equality: 15As it is written, "He that had gathered much had nothing over; and he that had gathered little had no lack" [Exodus 16:18].

Blessings come from giving 2 Cor. 9:6–15

6But this I say, He which soweth sparingly shall reap also sparingly; and he which soweth bountifully shall reap also bountifully. 7Every man according as he purposeth in his heart, ~~so let him give~~; not grudgingly, or of necessity: for God loveth a cheerful giver. 8And God is able to make all grace abound toward you; that ye, always having all sufficiency in all things, may abound to every good work: 9(As it is written, "He hath dispersed abroad; he hath given to the poor: his righteousness remaineth for ever" [Psalm 112:9]. 10Now he that ministereth seed to the sower both minister bread for ~~your~~ food, and multiply your seed sown, and increase the fruits of your righteousness;) 11Being enriched in every thing to all bountifulness,

which causeth through us thanksgiving to God. [12]For the
administration of this service not only supplieth the want of the
saints, but is abundant also by many thanksgivings unto God;
[13]Whiles by the experiment of this ministration they glorify
God for your professed subjection unto the gospel of Christ,
and for ~~your~~ liberal distribution unto them, and unto all ~~men~~;
[14]And by their prayer for you, which long after you for the
exceeding grace of God in you. [15]Thanks ~~be~~ unto God for his
unspeakable gift.

Combine godliness and material contentment

1 Tim. [3]If any man teach otherwise, and consent not to whole-
6:3–10 some words, ~~even~~ the words of our Lord Jesus Christ, and to
the doctrine which is according to godliness; [4]He is proud,
knowing nothing, but doting about questions /obsessed with
questions/ and strifes of words, whereof cometh envy, strife,
railings, evil surmisings /wicked suspicions/, [5]Perverse disputings of men of corrupt minds, and destitute of the truth, supposing that gain is godliness: \from such withdraw thyself\. [6]But
godliness with contentment is great gain. [7]For we brought nothing into this world, and ~~it is~~ certain we can carry nothing out.
[8]And having food and raiment let us be therewith content. [9]But
they that will be rich /those desiring to be rich/ fall into temptation and a snare, and ~~into~~ many foolish and hurtful lusts, which
drown men in destruction and perdition. [10]For the love of
money is the root of all evil: which while some coveted after,
they have erred /wandered, apostatized/ from the faith, and
pierced themselves through with many sorrows.

Worldly Wisdom Versus Spiritual Knowledge

Love not the world

1 Jn. [15]Love not the world, neither the things that are ~~in~~ {of}
2:15–17 the world. If any man love the world, the love of the Father is
not in him. [16]For all ~~that is~~ in the world {that is of the lusts} of
the flesh, and the lust of the eyes, and the pride /haughtiness,
ostentation/ of life, is not of the Father, but is of the world. [17]And

the world passeth away, and the lust thereof: but he that doeth
the will of God abideth for ever.

Worldliness is the enemy of God

[1]From whence come wars and fightings among you? come James
they not hence, even of your lusts /pleasures, gratifications, pas- 4:1–5
sions/ that war in your members? [2]Ye lust, and have not: ye kill,
and desire to have, and cannot obtain: ye fight and war, yet ye
have not, because ye ask not. [3]Ye ask, and receive not, because
ye ask amiss /wickedly, wrongly/, that ye may consume /waste,
expend/ it upon your lusts. [4]Ye \adulterers and\ adulteresses,
know ye not that the friendship of the world is enmity with
God? whosoever therefore will be a friend of the world is the
enemy of God. [5]Do ye think that the scripture saith in vain, The
spirit that dwelleth in us lusteth to envy?

Cease from sin and have fervent charity

[1a]Forasmuch then as Christ hath suffered for us in the 1 Pet.
flesh, arm yourselves likewise with the same mind /intent, idea, 4:1–11
thought/: [1b]{[2a]}for ~~he~~ {you} ~~that hath~~ {who have} suffered \in
the flesh\ ~~hath~~ {should} cease~~d~~ from sin; [2]~~That~~ {for} ~~he~~ {you}
no longer {[2c]}the rest of ~~his~~ {your} time in the flesh {[2c]}should
live [2d]to the lusts of men, but to the will of God. [3]For the time
past of ~~our~~ life may suffice ~~us~~ to have wrought the will of the
Gentiles, when ~~we~~ {ye} walked in lasciviousness, lusts, excess of
wine, revellings, banquetings, and abominable idolatries:
[4a]Wherein they, {[4c]}speak~~ing~~ evil of you, {[4b]}think{ing} it
strange that ~~ye~~ {you} run not with them to the same excess of
riot [debauchery, insubordination]: [5]Who shall give account to
him that is ready to judge the quick and the dead. [6a]~~For for~~
{Because of} this cause ~~was~~ {is} the gospel preached ~~also~~ to
them ~~that~~ {who} are dead, that they might be judged according
to men in the flesh, but live {[6c]}in the spirit [6b]according to {the
will of} God. [7]But {to you} the end of all things is at hand: be ye
therefore sober, and watch unto prayer. [8]And above all things
have fervent charity among yourselves: for charity ~~shall cover~~
{preventeth} a multitude of sins. [9]Use hospitality one to
another without grudging. [10]As every man hath received the

gift, ~~even so~~ minister the same one to another, as good stewards of the manifold /multifaceted, diversified/ grace of God. [11]If any man speak, let him speak as {an} oracle~~s~~ of God; if any man minister, let him do it as of the ability which God giveth: that God in all things may be glorified through Jesus Christ, to whom be praise and dominion for ever and ever. Amen.

God's wisdom is greater than the world's

1 Cor. 1:17–25 [17]For Christ sent me not to baptize, but to preach the gospel: not with wisdom of words, lest the cross of Christ should be made of none effect. [18]For the preaching of the cross is to them that perish foolishness; but unto us which are saved it is the power of God. [19]For it is written, "I will destroy the wisdom of the wise, and will bring to nothing the understanding of the prudent" [Isaiah 29:14]. [20]Where is the wise? where is the scribe? where is the disputer of this world /age/? hath not God made foolish the wisdom of this world? [21]For after that in the wisdom of God the world by /by means of, through/ wisdom knew not God, it pleased God by the foolishness of preaching to save them that believe. [22]For the Jews require a sign, and the Greeks seek after wisdom: [23]But we preach Christ crucified, unto the Jews a stumblingblock, and unto the Greeks foolishness; [24]But unto them {who believe} which are called, both Jews and Greeks, Christ the power of God, and the wisdom of God. [25]Because the foolishness of God is wiser than men; and the weakness of God is stronger than men.

God chooses the foolish to confound the wise

1 Cor. 1:26–31 [26]For ye see your calling, brethren, how that not many wise men after the flesh, not many mighty, not many noble, are ~~called~~ {chosen}: [27]~~But~~ {For} God hath chosen the foolish things of the world to confound /shame, frustrate/ the wise; and God hath chosen the weak things of the world to confound the things which are mighty; [28]And base things of the world, and things which are despised, hath God chosen, yea, and things which are not, to bring to nought things that are {mighty}: [29]That no flesh should glory in his presence. [30]But of him are ye in Christ Jesus, who of God is made unto us wis-

dom, and righteousness, and sanctification, and redemption:
31That, according as it is written, "He that glorieth, let him
glory in the Lord" [Jeremiah 9:24].

Paul preaches not with wisdom, but the Spirit

1And I, brethren, when I came to you, came not with 1 Cor.
excellency of speech or of wisdom, declaring unto you the \tes- 2:1–5
timony, mystery, gospel, salvation\ of God. 2For I determined
not to know any thing among you, save /except/ Jesus Christ,
and him crucified. 3And I was with you in weakness, and in
fear, and in much trembling. 4And my speech and my preaching was not with enticing /persuasive/ words of \man's\ wisdom,
but in demonstration of the Spirit and of power: 5That your
faith should not stand in the wisdom of men, but in the power
of God.

Revelation through God's Spirit

6Howbeit we speak wisdom among them that are perfect: 1 Cor.
yet not the wisdom of this world, nor of the princes of this 2:6–16
world, that come to nought: 7But we speak the wisdom of God
in a mystery, even the hidden wisdom, which God ordained
/foreordained/ before the world unto our glory: 8Which none of
the princes of this world knew: for had they known it, they
would not have crucified the Lord of glory. 9But as it is written,
"Eye hath not seen, nor ear heard, neither have entered into
the heart of man, the things which God hath prepared for them
that love him" [Isaiah 64:4; 52:15]. 10But God hath revealed
them unto us by his Spirit: for the Spirit searcheth /explores,
investigates/ all things, yea, the deep things of God. 11For what
man knoweth the things of a man, save the spirit of man which
is in him? even so the things of God knoweth no man, ~~but~~
{except he has} the Spirit of God. 12Now we have received, not
the spirit of the world, but the spirit which is of God; that we
might know the things that are freely given to us of God.
13Which things also we speak, not in the words which man's wisdom teacheth, but which the Holy Ghost teacheth; comparing
spiritual things with spiritual. 14But the natural man receiveth
not the things of the Spirit of God: for they are foolishness unto

him: neither can he know them, because they are spiritually dis-
cerned /examined, tried, judged/. 15But he that is spiritual judgeth /examines, tries/ all things, yet he himself is judged of no
man. 16"For who hath known the mind of the Lord, that he may
instruct him?" [Isaiah 40:13] But we have the mind of Christ.

The Wrongful Worship of Idols

There is none other God but one

1 Cor. 1Now as touching /concerning/ things offered unto idols,
8:1–6 we know that we all have knowledge. Knowledge puffeth up,
but charity /love/ edifieth /builds up, strengthens, establishes,
repairs/. 2And if any man think that he knoweth anything, he
knoweth nothing yet as he ought to know. 3But if any man love
God, the same is known of him. 4aAs concerning therefore the
eating of those things that are {4c}in the world {4b}offered in
sacrifice unto idols, 4dwe know that an idol is nothing and that
there is none other God but one. 5For though there be that are
called gods, whether in heaven or in earth, (as there be gods
many, and lords many,) 6But to us ~~there is but~~ one God, the
Father, of whom are all things, and we in him; and one Lord
Jesus Christ, by whom are all things, and we by him.

Do not partake of the table of devils

1 Cor. 14Wherefore, my dearly beloved, flee from idolatry. 15I
10:14–22 speak as to wise men; judge ye what I say. 16The cup of blessing
which we bless, is it not the communion /aid, fellowship, part-
nership/ of the blood of Christ? The bread which we break, is it
not the communion of the body of Christ? 17For we ~~being~~ many
are one bread, ~~and~~ one body: for we are all partakers /sharers,
partners/ of that one bread. 18Behold Israel after the flesh: are
not they which eat of the sacrifices partakers of the altar?
19What say I then? that the idol is any thing, or that which is
offered in sacrifice to idols is any thing? 20But ~~I say, that~~ the
things which the Gentiles sacrifice, they sacrifice to devils, and
not to God: and I would not that ye should have fellowship with
devils. 21Ye cannot drink the cup of the Lord, and the cup of
devils: ye cannot be partakers of the Lord's table, and of the

table of devils. [22]Do we provoke the Lord to jealousy? are we stronger than he?

Be an example; do not give others an excuse to sin

[7]Howbeit there is not in every man that knowledge: for 1 Cor.
some with \conscience, custom\ of the idol unto this hour eat ~~it~~ 8:7–13
as a thing offered unto an idol; and their conscience being weak is defiled. [8]But meat commendeth us not to God: for neither, if we eat, are we the better; neither, if we eat not, are we the worse. [9]But take heed lest by any means this liberty of yours become a stumblingblock to them that are weak. [10]For if any man see thee which hast knowledge sit at meat in the idol's temple, shall not the conscience of him which is weak be emboldened to eat those things which are offered to idols; [11]And through thy knowledge shall the weak brother perish, for whom Christ died? [12]~~But~~ when ye sin so against the brethren, and wound their \weak\ conscience, ye sin against Christ. [13]Wherefore, if meat make my brother to offend /cause my brother to stumble, falter/, I will eat no flesh while the world standeth, lest I make my brother to offend.

If you know it is wrong, do not do it

[23]All things are {not} lawful for me, ~~but~~ {for} all things are 1 Cor.
not expedient /advantageous, appropriate, beneficial/: all 10:23–11:1
things are {not} lawful, for ~~me, but~~ all things edify not. [24]Let no man seek {therefore} his own, but every man another's ~~wealth~~ {good}. [25]Whatsoever is sold in the shambles /market/, ~~that~~ eat, asking no question for conscience sake: [26]"For the earth is the Lord's, and the fulness thereof" [Psalm 24:1]. [27]If any of them that believe not bid you to a feast, and ye be disposed to ~~go~~ {eat}; whatsoever is set before you, eat, asking no question for conscience sake. [28]But if any man say unto you, This is offered in sacrifice unto idols, eat not for his sake that shewed it, and for conscience sake: \for the earth is the Lord's, and the fulness thereof\: [29]Conscience, I say, not thine own, but of the other: for why is my liberty judged of another man's conscience? [30]For if I by grace /with gratitude, graciousness/ be a partaker, why am I

evil spoken of for that for which I give thanks? [31]Whether therefore ye eat, or drink, or whatsoever ye do, do all to the glory of
God. [32]Give none offence, neither to the Jews, nor to the Gentiles, nor to the church of God: [33]Even as I please all men in all
things, not seeking mine own profit /benefit, advantage/, but
~~the profit~~ of {the} many, that they may be saved. [1]Be ye followers /imitators/ of me, even as I also ~~am~~ of Christ.

Do not be a stumblingblock to another

Rom. 14:13–23 [13]Let us not therefore judge one another any more: but
judge this rather, that no man put a stumblingblock or an occasion to fall in his brother's way. [14]I know, and am persuaded by
the Lord Jesus, that there is nothing unclean /ceremonially
unclean/ of itself: but to him that esteemeth any thing to be
unclean, to him it is unclean. [15]But if thy brother be grieved
with thy meat, ~~now~~ {thou} walkest ~~thou~~ not charitably /accord-
ing to love/ {if thou eatest, therefore,} Destroy not him with thy
meat /on account of food/, for whom Christ died. [16]Let not then
your good be evil spoken of: [17]For the kingdom of God is not
meat /food/ and drink; but righteousness, and peace, and joy in
the Holy Ghost. [18]For he that in these things serveth Christ is
acceptable to God, and approved of men. [19]Let us therefore follow after the things which make for peace, and things wherewith one may edify another. [20]For meat /because of food/
destroy not the work of God. All things indeed are pure; but it
is evil for that man who eateth with offence. [21]It is good neither
to eat flesh, nor to drink wine, nor any thing whereby thy
brother stumbleth, or is offended, or is made weak. [22]Hast thou
faith? have it to thyself before God. Happy is he that condemneth not himself in that thing which he alloweth /by what he
tries, approves/. [23]And he that doubteth is ~~damned~~ {con-
demned} if he eat, because ~~he eateth~~ {it is} not of faith: for
whatsoever is not of faith is sin.

Morality

Incest and other immorality in Corinth

[1]It is reported commonly ~~that there is~~ fornication /sexual 1 Cor.
immorality/ among you, and such fornication as is not so much 5:1–13
as named among the Gentiles, that one should have his father's
wife. [2]And ye are puffed up, and have not rather mourned, that
he that hath done this deed might be taken away from among
you. [3a]For I verily, as /as it were/ absent in body, but present in
spirit, {I} have judged already {[3c]}him ~~that~~ {who} hath so done
this deed, [3a]as though I were present. [4]In the name of our Lord
Jesus Christ, when ye are gathered together, and {have} ~~my~~
{the} spirit, with the power of our Lord Jesus Christ, [5]To
deliver such an one unto Satan for the destruction of the flesh,
that the spirit may be saved in the day of the Lord Jesus. [6]Your
glorying /boasting/ is not good. Know ye not that a little leaven
leaveneth the whole lump? [7]Purge out therefore the old leaven,
that ye may be a new lump, as ye are unleavened. For even
Christ our passover is sacrificed for us: [8]Therefore let us keep
the feast, not with old leaven, neither with the leaven of malice
and wickedness; but with the unleavened ~~bread~~ of sincerity and
truth. [9]I wrote unto you in an epistle not to company with fornicators /sexually immoral persons, male prostitutes/: [10]Yet not
altogether with the fornicators of this world, or with the covetous, or extortioners /swindlers, robbers/, or with idolaters; for
then must ye needs go out of the world. [11]But now I have written unto you not to keep company, if any man that is called a
brother be a fornicator, or covetous, or an idolater, or a railer,
or a drunkard, or an extortioner; with such an one no not /not
even/ to eat. [12]For what have I to do to judge them also that are
without /outside, foreign, not belonging/? do not ~~ye~~ {they}
judge them that are within? [13]But them that are without God
judgeth. "Therefore put away from among yourselves that
wicked person" [Deuteronomy 17:7].

Avoid fornication; glorify God in your body

[12]All {these} things are {not} lawful unto me, ~~but~~ {and} 1 Cor.
all {these} things are not expedient /beneficial, advantageous/: 6:12–20

all things are {not} lawful for me, ~~but~~ {therefore} I will not be brought under the power of any. [13]Meats for the belly, and the belly for meats: but God shall destroy both it and them. Now the body is not for fornication /sexual immoriality/, but for the Lord; and the Lord for the body. [14]And God hath both raised up the Lord, and will also raise up us by his own power. [15]Know ye not that your bodies are the members of Christ? shall I then take the members of Christ, and make them the members of an harlot? God forbid [may it not be so]. [16]What? know ye not that he which is joined to an harlot is one body? for "two," saith he, "shall be one flesh" [Genesis 2:24]. [17]But he that is joined unto the Lord is one spirit. [18]Flee fornication. Every sin that a man ~~doeth~~ {committeth} is ~~without~~ {against} the body {of Christ}; ~~but~~ {and} he ~~that~~ {who} committeth fornication sinneth against his own body. [19]What? know ye not that your body is the temple of the Holy Ghost which is in you, which ye have of God, and ye are not your own? [20]For ye are bought with a price: therefore glorify God in your body, \and in your spirit which are God's\.

Marriage is good

1 Cor. 7:1–11 [1]Now concerning the things whereof ye wrote unto me {saying}: It is good for a man not to touch a woman. [2]Nevertheless, {I say} to avoid fornication, let every man have his own wife, and let every woman have her own husband. [3]Let the husband render unto the wife due benevolence: and likewise also the wife unto the husband. [4]The wife hath not power of her own body, but the husband: and likewise also the husband hath not power of his own body, but the wife. [5]~~Defraud~~ {Depart} ye not one {from} the other, except it be with consent for a time, that ye may give yourselves to \fasting and\ prayer; and come together again, that Satan tempt you not for your incontinency. [6]~~But~~ {And now what} I speak ~~this~~ {is} by permission, and not ~~of~~ {by} commandment. [7]For I would that all men were even as I myself. But every man hath his proper /own/ gift of God, one after this manner, and another after that. [8]I say therefore to the unmarried and widows, It is good for them if they abide even as I. [9]But if they cannot ~~contain~~ {abide} /use self-control/, let them marry: for it is

better to marry than ~~to burn~~ {that any should commit sin} /burn with lust/. [10]And unto the married I command, ~~yet~~ not I, but the Lord, Let not the wife depart from her husband: [11]But ~~and~~ if she depart, let her remain unmarried, or be reconciled to her husband: and let not the husband put away his wife.

Marriage of a believer to an unbeliever

1 Cor. 7:12–16

[12]But to the rest speak I, not the Lord: If any brother hath a wife that believeth not, and she be pleased to dwell with him, let him not put her away. [13]And the woman which hath an husband that believeth not, and if he be pleased to dwell with her, let her not leave him. [14]For the unbelieving \husband, brother\ is sanctified by /in/ the \believing\ wife, and the unbelieving wife is sanctified /cleansed/ by /in/ the \believing\ husband: else were your children unclean; but now are they holy. [15]But if the unbelieving depart, let him depart. A brother or a sister is not under bondage in such cases: but God hath called us to peace. [16]For what knowest thou, O wife, whether thou shalt save thy husband? or how knowest thou, O man, whether thou shalt save thy wife?

Keeping God's commandments takes priority over one's status

1 Cor. 7:17–24

[17]But as God hath distributed to every man, as the Lord hath called every one, so let him walk. And so ordain /order, prescribe/ I in all churches. [18]Is any man called being circumcised? let him not become uncircumcised /conceal, obliterate circumcision/. Is any called in uncircumcision? let him not be circumcised. [19]Circumcision is nothing, and uncircumcision is nothing, but the keeping of the commandments of God. [20]Let every man abide in the same calling wherein he was called. [21]Art thou called ~~being~~ a servant? care not for it: but if thou mayest be made free, use it rather. [22]For he that is called in the Lord, ~~being~~ a servant, is the Lord's freeman: likewise also he that is called, ~~being~~ free, is Christ's servant. [23]Ye are bought with a price; be not ye the servants /slaves/ of men. [24]Brethren, let every man, wherein he is called, therein abide with God.

When to marry

1 Cor. 7:25–40

25 Now concerning virgins I have no commandment of the
Lord: yet I give my judgment, as one that hath obtained mercy
of the Lord to be faithful. 26 I suppose therefore that this is good
for the present distress /trial, affliction/, ~~I say, that it is good~~ for
a man so to ~~be~~ {remain that he may do greater good}. 27 Art
thou bound unto a wife? seek not to be loosed. Art thou loosed
from a wife? seek not a wife. 28 But ~~and~~ if thou marry, thou hast
not sinned; and if a virgin marry, she hath not sinned. Nevertheless such shall have trouble in the flesh: ~~but~~ {for} I spare you
{not}. 29 But {I speak unto you, who are called unto the ministry, for} this I say, brethren, the time {that remaineth} is
{but} short {that ye shall be sent forth unto the ministry. Even}
~~it remaineth, that both~~ they ~~that~~ {who} have wives {shall} be as
though they had none; {for ye are called and chosen to do the
Lord's work.} 30 And {it shall be with} ~~they~~ {them} ~~that~~ {who}
weep, as though they wept not; and ~~they~~ {them} ~~that~~ {who}
rejoice, as though they rejoiced not; and ~~they~~ {them} ~~that~~
{who} buy, as though they possessed not; 31 And ~~they~~ {them}
~~that~~ {who} use this world, as not ~~abusing~~ {using} it: for the
fashion of this world passeth away. 32 But {I would, brethren,
that ye magnify your calling.} I would have you without carefulness /cares/. {For} He ~~that~~ {who} is unmarried careth for the
things that belong to the Lord, how he may please the Lord;
{therefore he prevaileth.} 33 But he ~~that~~ {who} is married
careth for the things that are of the world, how he may please
his wife; {therefore there is a difference, for he is hindered.}
34 There is {a} difference also between a wife and a virgin. The
unmarried woman careth for the things of the Lord, that she
may be holy both in body and in spirit: but she that is married
careth for the things of the world, how she may please her husband. 35 And this I speak for your own profit; not that I may cast
a snare upon you, but for that which is comely /proper, well
arranged/, and that ye may attend upon the Lord without dis-
traction. 36 But if any man think that he behaveth himself
uncomely toward his virgin {whom he hath espoused}, if she
pass the flower of ~~her~~ age, and need so require, let him do what

he ~~will~~ {hath promised}, he sinneth not: let them marry. 37Nev-
ertheless he that standeth stedfast in his heart, having no necessity, but hath power over his own will, and hath so decreed in
his heart that he will keep his virgin, doeth well. 38So then he
that giveth ~~her~~ {himself} in marriage doeth well; but he that
giveth ~~her~~ {himself} not in marriage doeth better. 39The wife is
bound by the law as long as her husband liveth; but if her husband be dead, she is at liberty to be married to whom she will;
only in the Lord. 40But she is happier if she so abide, after my
judgment: and I think also that I have the Spirit of God.

8

Domestic Guidance

Spouses

Wives and husbands

22Wives, \be, submit yourselves\ unto your own husbands, Eph.
as /in the same way as/ unto the Lord. 23For the husband is the 5:22–33
head of the wife, even as Christ is the head of the church: and
he is the saviour of the body. 24Therefore as the church is subject unto /arranged under, submissive to/ Christ, so let the wives
be to their own husbands in every thing. 25Husbands, love /have
the pure love of God toward/ your wives, even as Christ also
loved the church, and gave himself for it; 26That he might sanctify and cleanse it with the washing of water by the word, 27That
he might present it to himself a glorious church, not having
spot, or wrinkle, or any such thing; but that it should be holy
and without blemish. 28So ought men to love their wives as their
own bodies. He that loveth his wife loveth himself. 29For no man
ever yet hated his own flesh; but nourisheth and cherisheth it,
even as the Lord the church: 30For we are members of his body,
of his flesh, and of his bones. 31"For this cause shall a man leave
his father and mother, and shall be joined unto his wife, and
they two shall be one flesh" [Genesis 2:24]. 32This is a great mystery: but I speak concerning Christ and the church. 33Neverthe-
less let every one of you in particular so love his wife even as
himself; and the wife see that she reverence her husband.

Advice to wives: adorn your relationship with righteousness

1Likewise, ye wives, be in subjection to your own hus- 1 Pet.
bands; that, if any obey not the word, they also may without the 3:1–6
word be won by the ~~conversation~~ {conduct} of the wives;

2While they behold your chaste ~~conversation~~ {conduct} coupled
with fear /respect/. 3{Let your} adorning ~~not~~ be {not} that outward adorning of plaiting the hair, and of wearing of gold, or of
putting on of apparel; 4But ~~let it be~~ the hidden man of the
heart, in that which is not corruptible, ~~even the ornament~~ of a
meek /gentle, mild, forgiving/ and quiet spirit, which is in the
sight of God of great price. 5For after this manner in the old
time{s} the holy women ~~also~~, who trusted in God, adorned
themselves, being in subjection unto /obedient, submissive to/
their own husbands: 6Even as Sara obeyed Abraham, calling
him lord: whose daughters ye are, as long as ye do well, and are
not afraid with any amazement /dismay, consternation/.

Advice to husbands: inherit life with your wife

1 Pet. 3:7 7Likewise, ye husbands, dwell with them [the daughters of
God] according to knowledge /revealed truth/, giving honour
unto the wife, as unto the weaker /more frail/ vessel /instru-
ment/, and as being heirs together of the grace of life; that your
prayers be not hindered.

Other Family Members

Caring for widows

1 Tim. 5:3–16 3Honour widows that are widows indeed. 4But if any
widow have children or nephews /grandchildren, descendants/,
let them learn first to shew piety /godly devotion/ at home, and
to requite /pay back/ their parents: for that is good and acceptable before God. 5Now she that is a widow indeed, and desolate
/left alone/, trusteth in God, and continueth in supplications
and prayers night and day. 6But she that liveth in pleasure
/wantonly/ is dead while she liveth. 7And these things give in
charge /instruct, command/, that they may be blameless. 8But if
any provide not for his own, and specially for those of his own
house, he hath denied the faith, and is worse than an infidel.
9Let not a widow be taken into the number under threescore
[sixty] years old, having been the wife of one man, 10Well
reported of for good works; if she have brought up children, if

she have lodged strangers, if she have washed the saints' ~~feet~~ {clothes}, if she have relieved the afflicted, if she have diligently followed every good work. 11But the younger widows refuse: for when they have begun to wax wanton /restive/ against Christ, they will marry; 12Having damnation /judgment/, because they have cast off /set aside/ their first faith [Christ]. 13And withal they learn to be idle, wandering about from house to house; and not only idle, but tattlers also and busybodies, speaking things which they ought not. 14I will /desire/ therefore that the younger women marry, bear children, guide the house, give none occasion to the adversary to speak reproachfully. 15For some are already turned aside after Satan. 16If any man or woman that believeth have widows, let them relieve them, and let not the church be charged /burdened down, troubled/; that it may relieve them that are widows indeed.

Children and parents

Eph. 6:1–4

1Children, obey your parents \in the Lord\: for this is right. 2"Honour thy father and mother" [Exodus 20:12]; (which is the first commandment with promise;) 3"That it may be well with thee, and thou mayest live long on the earth" [Exodus 20:12]. 4And, ye fathers, provoke not your children to wrath: but bring them up in the nurture and admonition of the Lord.

Instructions to various age groups

Titus 2:1–10

1But speak thou the things which become sound doctrine: 2That the aged men be sober /circumspect/, grave, temperate, sound in faith, in charity, in patience. 3The aged women likewise, that they be in behaviour as becometh holiness, not false /slanderers, traitors, devils/ accusers, not given to much wine, teachers of good things; 4That they may teach the young women to be sober, to love their husbands, to love their children, 5~~To be~~ discreet, chaste, keepers at home /housekeepers, guards/, good, obedient to their own husbands, that the word of God be not blasphemed. 6Young men likewise exhort to be sober minded. 7In all things shewing thyself a pattern of good works: in doctrine ~~shewing~~ uncorruptness, gravity /dignity, respectfulness/, sincerity, 8Sound speech, that cannot be condemned;

that he that is of the contrary part /an opponent, enemy/ may
be ashamed, having no evil thing to say of you. 9~~Exhort~~ servants
to be obedient unto their own masters, ~~and~~ to please them
well in all ~~things~~; not answering again /arguing against,
opposing, contradicting/; 10Not purloining /misappropriating,
stealing/, but shewing all good fidelity; that they may adorn
/honor, put in order/ the doctrine of God our Saviour in all
things.

Christian Conduct in All Relationships

Slaves and masters

Eph. 6:5–9 5Servants, be obedient to them that are ~~your~~ masters
according to the flesh, with fear and trembling, in singleness of
~~your~~ heart, as unto Christ; 6Not with eyeservice, as menpleasers; but as the servants of Christ, doing the will of God
from the heart; 7With good will doing service, as to the Lord,
and not to men: 8Knowing that whatsoever good thing any man
doeth, the same shall he receive of the Lord, whether ~~he be~~
bond or free. 9And, ye masters, do the same things unto them,
forbearing threatening: knowing that your Master also is in
heaven; neither is there respect of persons with him.

Instructions to slaves

1 Tim. 6:1–2 1Let as many servants /slaves/ as are under the yoke
count their own masters worthy of all honour, that the name
of God and his doctrine be not blasphemed. 2And they that
have believing masters, let them not despise ~~them~~, because
they are brethren; but rather do ~~them~~ service, because they
are faithful and beloved, partakers of the benefit. These things
teach and exhort.

Advice to servants: follow the example of Christ's suffering

1 Pet. 2:18–25 18Servants /slaves/, be subject to your masters with all fear
/respect/; not only to the good and gentle, but also to the
froward /crooked, wicked/. 19For this is thankworthy /pleasing,
gracious/, if a man for conscience toward God endure grief, suffering wrongfully. 20For what glory is it, if, when ye be buffeted

for your faults, ye shall take it patiently? but if, when ye do well, and suffer for it, ye take it patiently, this is acceptable /pleasing, gracious/ with God. [21]For even hereunto were ye called: because Christ also \suffered, died\ for us, leaving us an example, that ye should follow his steps: [22]"Who did no sin, neither was guile found in his mouth" [Isaiah 53:9]: [23]Who, when he was reviled, reviled not again; when he suffered, he threatened not; but committed himself to him that judgeth righteously: [24]"Who his own self bare our sins in his own body on the tree" [Isaiah 53:4], that we, being dead to sins, should live unto righteousness: by whose stripes ye were healed. [25]"For ye were as sheep going astray" [Isaiah 53:6]; but are now returned unto the Shepherd and Bishop of your souls.

Morals and duties in household relationships

[18]Wives, submit yourselves unto your own husbands, as it is fit in the Lord. [19]Husbands, love ~~your~~ wives, and be not bitter against them. [20]Children, obey ~~your~~ parents in all things: for this is well pleasing unto the Lord. [21]Fathers, provoke not your children ~~to anger~~, lest they be discouraged. [22]Servants, obey in all things ~~your~~ masters according to the flesh; not with eyeservice, as menpleasers; but in singleness of heart, fearing God: [23]And whatsoever ye do, do ~~it~~ heartily, as to the Lord, and not unto men; [24]Knowing that of the Lord ye shall receive the reward of the inheritance: for ye serve the Lord Christ. [25]But he that doeth wrong shall receive for the wrong which he hath done: and there is no respect of persons. [1]Masters, give unto ~~your~~ servants that which is just and equal; knowing that ye also have a Master in heaven.

Col. 3:18–4:1

9

Christian Living

The Christian's Divine Nature and Destiny

God has reserved an eternal inheritance for you

[3]Blessed be the God and Father of our Lord Jesus Christ, 1 Pet.
which according to his abundant mercy hath begotten us again 1:3–6a
unto a lively /living/ hope by the resurrection of Jesus Christ
from the dead, [4]To an inheritance incorruptible, and undefiled, and that fadeth not away, reserved in heaven for you,
[5]Who are kept by the power of God through faith unto salvation ready /prepared/ to be revealed in the last time. [6a]Wherein
ye greatly rejoice.

[3]Blessed be the God and Father of our Lord Jesus Christ, Eph.
who hath blessed us with all spiritual blessings in heavenly 1:3–14
places in Christ: [4]According as he hath chosen us in him before
the foundation of the world, that we should be holy and without blame before him in love: [5]Having predestinated /foreor-
dained/ us unto the adoption of children by Jesus Christ to
himself, according to the good pleasure of his will, [6]To the
praise of the glory of his grace, wherein he hath made us
accepted in the beloved. [7]In whom we have redemption
through his blood, the forgiveness of sins, according to the
riches of his grace; [8]Wherein he hath abounded toward us in all
wisdom and prudence; [9]Having made known unto us the mystery of his will, according to his good pleasure which he hath
purposed in himself: [10]That in the dispensation of the fulness of
times he might gather together in one all things in Christ, both
which are in heaven, and which are on earth; ~~even~~ in him: [11]In
whom also we have obtained an inheritance, being predestinated according to the purpose of him who worketh all things

after the counsel of his own will: 12That we should be to the
praise of his glory, who first trusted /hoped beforehand/ in
Christ. 13In whom ye also trusted, after that ye heard the word
of truth, the gospel of your salvation: in whom also after that ye
believed, ye were sealed with that holy Spirit of promise,
14Which is the earnest of our inheritance until the redemption
of the purchased possession, unto the praise of his glory.

The promise and election to partake of the divine nature

2 Pet. 3According as his divine power hath given unto us all
1:3–11 things that pertain unto life and godliness, through the knowledge of him that hath called us to glory and /through, by/
virtue: 4Whereby are given unto us exceeding great and precious promises: that by these ye might be partakers of the
divine nature, having escaped the corruption that is in the
world through lust. 5And beside this, giving all diligence, add to
your faith virtue; and to virtue knowledge; 6And to knowledge
temperance /self-control/; and to temperance patience; and to
patience godliness /reverence, piety, godliness/; 7And to godliness brotherly kindness; and to brotherly kindness charity. 8For
if these things be in you, and abound, they make you that ye
shall neither be barren /idle, unprofitable, injurious/ nor
unfruitful in the knowledge of our Lord Jesus Christ. 9But he
that lacketh these things is blind, and cannot see afar off, and
hath forgotten that he was purged from his old sins. 10Where-
fore the rather, brethren, give diligence \through your good
works\ to make your calling and election sure: for if ye do these
things, ye shall never fall: 11For so an entrance shall be ministered unto you abundantly into the everlasting kingdom of our
Lord and Saviour Jesus Christ.

Children of God become like God

1 Jn. 28And now, little children, abide in him; that, when he
2:28–3:10 shall appear, we may have confidence, and not be ashamed
before him at his coming. 29If ye know that he is righteous, ye
know that every one that doeth righteousness is born of him.
1Behold, what manner of love the Father hath bestowed upon

us, that we should be called the sons /children, people/ of God: therefore the world knoweth us not, because it knew him not. [2]Beloved, now are we the sons /children, people/ of God, and it doth not yet appear what we shall be: but we know that, when he shall appear, we shall be like /of the same nature as/ him; for we shall see him as he is. [3]And every man that hath this hope in him purifieth himself, even as he is pure. [4]Whosoever committeth sin transgresseth also the law: for sin is the transgression of the law. [5]And ye know that he was manifested to take away \our\ sins; and in him is no sin. [6]Whosoever abideth in him sinneth not: whosoever ~~sinneth~~ {continueth in sin} hath not seen him, neither known him. [7]Little children, let no man deceive you: he that doeth righteousness is righteous, even as he is righteous. [8]He that ~~committeth~~ {continueth in} sin is of the devil; for the devil sinneth from the beginning. For this purpose the Son of God was manifested, that he might destroy the works of the devil. [9]Whosoever is born of God doth not ~~commit~~ {continue in} sin; for ~~his seed~~ {the spirit of God} remaineth in him; and he cannot {continue in} sin, because he is born of God {having received that holy spirit of promise}. [10]In this the children of God are manifest /conspicuous, apparent/, and the children of the devil: whosoever doeth not righteousness is not of God, neither he that loveth not his brother.

Glory is the destiny of sons of God

Rom. 8:18–27

[18]For I reckon that the sufferings of this present time are not worthy to be ~~compared~~ {named} with the glory which shall be revealed in /to/ us. [19]For the earnest expectation /eager hope/ of the creature /creation, material universe/ waiteth for the manifestation /revelation/ of the sons of God. [20]For the creature was made subject to ~~vanity~~ {tribulation}, not willingly, but by reason of him who hath subjected ~~the same~~ {it} in hope, [21]Because the creature /creation, material universe/ itself also shall be delivered from the bondage of corruption into the glorious liberty of the children of God. [22]For we know that the whole creation groaneth and travaileth in pain together until now. [23]And not only they, but ourselves also, which /who/ have the firstfruits of the Spirit, even we ourselves groan within

ourselves, waiting for the adoption, to wit, the redemption of
our body. [24]For we are saved by hope: but hope that is seen is
not hope: for what a man seeth, why doth he yet hope for?
[25]But if we hope for that we see not, then ~~do we~~ with patience
{we do} wait for it. [26]Likewise the Spirit also helpeth our infirmities: for we know not what we should pray for as we ought:
but the Spirit itself maketh intercession for us with groanings
/sighings/ which cannot be uttered. [27]And he that searcheth the
hearts knoweth ~~what is~~ the mind of the Spirit, because he
maketh intercession for the saints according to the will of God.

Calling and foreordination

Rom. 8:28–30 [28]And we know that all things work together for good to
them that love God, to them who are the called according to
his purpose. [29]For {him} whom he did foreknow, he also did
predestinate /appointed beforehand, foreordained/ to be
conformed to /to have the same form as/ ~~the~~ {his own} image
~~of his Son~~, that he might be the firstborn among many
brethren. [30]Moreover {him} whom he did predestinate
/appointed beforehand, foreordained/, ~~them~~ {him} he also
called: and {him} whom he called, ~~them~~ {him} he also ~~justi-
fied~~ {sanctified}: and whom he ~~justified~~ {sanctified}, ~~them~~
{him} he also glorified.

The Transforming Power of Christ

Paul's desire that all know Christ through personal revelation

Eph. 1:15–23 [15]Wherefore I also, after I heard of your faith in the Lord
Jesus, and love unto all the saints, [16]Cease not to give thanks for
you, making mention of you in my prayers; [17]That the God of
our Lord Jesus Christ, the Father of glory, may give unto you
the spirit of wisdom and revelation in the knowledge of him:
[18]The eyes of your understanding being enlightened; that ye
may know what is the hope of his calling, and what the riches of
the glory of his inheritance in the saints, [19]And what is the
exceeding greatness of his power to usward who believe,
according to the working of his mighty power, [20]Which he
wrought in Christ, when he raised him from the dead, and set

him at his own right hand in the heavenly places, [21]Far above all
principality, and power, and might, and dominion, and every
name that is named, not only in this world, but also in that
which is to come: [22]And hath put all ~~things~~ under his feet, and
gave him to be the head over all ~~things~~ to the church, [23]Which is
his body, the fulness of him that filleth all in all.

The gift of salvation and new life in Christ

[1]And you ~~hath he quickened~~, who were dead in trespasses Eph.
and sins; [2]Wherein in time past ye walked according to the 2:1–10
course of this world, according to the prince of the power of the
air, the spirit that now worketh in the children of disobedience:
[3]Among whom also we all had our conversation in times past in
the lusts of our flesh, fulfilling the desires of the flesh and of the
mind; and were by nature the children of wrath, even as others.
[4]But God, who is rich in mercy, for his great love wherewith he
loved us, [5]Even when we were dead in sins, hath quickened us
together with Christ, (by grace ye are saved;) [6]And hath raised
us up together, and made us sit together in heavenly places in
Christ Jesus: [7]That in the ages to come he might shew the
exceeding riches of his grace in ~~his~~ kindness toward us through
Christ Jesus. [8]For by grace are ye saved through faith; and that
not of yourselves: {but} it is the gift of God: [9]Not of works, lest
any man should boast. [10]For we are his workmanship, created in
Christ Jesus unto good works, which God hath before ordained
that we should walk in them.

Paul's prayer that all know the love of Christ

[14]For this cause [recognizing the privilege of being in the Eph.
household of God] I bow my knees unto the Father \of our 3:14–21
Lord Jesus Christ\, [15]Of whom the whole family in heaven and
earth is named, [16]That he would grant you, according to the
riches of his glory, to be strengthened with might by his Spirit in
the inner man; [17]That Christ may dwell in your hearts by faith;
that ye, being rooted and grounded in love, [18]May be able to
comprehend with all saints ~~what is~~ the breadth, and length, and
depth, and height; [19]And to know the love of Christ, which

passeth knowledge, that ye might be filled with all the fulness of God. [20]Now unto him that is able to do exceeding abundantly above all that we ask or think, according to the power that worketh in us, [21]Unto him be glory in the church by Christ Jesus throughout all ages, world without end. Amen.

We are complete in Christ

Col. 2:9–15; 3:1–4

[9]For in him [Jesus Christ] dwelleth all the fulness of the Godhead bodily. [10]And ye are complete in him, which is the head of all principality and power: [11]In whom also ye are circumcised with the circumcision made without hands, in putting off the body of the sins of the flesh by the circumcision of Christ: [12]Buried with him in baptism, wherein also ye are risen with him through the faith of the operation of God, who hath raised him from the dead. [13]And you, being dead in your sins and the uncircumcision of your flesh, hath he quickened /caused to become alive/ together with him, having forgiven you all trespasses; [14]Blotting out the handwriting of ordinances that was against us, which was contrary to us, and took it out of the way, nailing it to his cross; [15]~~And~~ having spoiled principalities and powers, he made a shew of them openly, triumphing over them in it. [1]If ye then be risen with Christ, seek those things which are above, where Christ sitteth on the right hand of God. [2]Set your affection /mind/ on things above, not on things on the earth. [3]For ye are dead, and your life is hid with Christ in God. [4]When Christ, who is our life, shall appear, then shall ye also appear with him in glory.

The basis of the Christian moral life

Titus 2:11–15

[11a]For the grace of God that bringeth salvation {[11c]}to all men [11b]hath appeared. [12]Teaching us that, denying ungodliness and worldly lusts, we should live soberly, righteously, and godly, in this present world; [13]Looking for that blessed hope, and the glorious appearing of the great God and our Saviour Jesus Christ; [14]Who gave himself for us, that he might redeem us from all iniquity, and purify unto himself a peculiar people, zealous of good works. [15]These things speak, and exhort, and rebuke /disregard/ with all authority. Let no man despise thee.

Living and Walking with God

Be a living sacrifice to God

[1]I beseech you therefore, brethren, by the mercies of God, Rom.
that ye present your bodies a living sacrifice, holy, acceptable 12:1–2
unto God, which is your reasonable service. [2]And be not conformed to this world: but be ye transformed by the renewing of
your mind, that ye may prove /test, try, prove/ what ~~is~~ that
good, and acceptable, and perfect, will of God {is}.

Submit to God

[6]But he [God] giveth more grace. Wherefore he saith, James
"God resisteth the proud, but giveth grace unto the humble" 4:6–10
[Proverbs 3:34 LXX]. [7]Submit yourselves therefore to God.
Resist the devil, and he will flee from you. [8]Draw nigh to God,
and he will draw nigh to you. Cleanse your hands, ye sinners;
and purify your hearts, ye double minded. [9]Be afflicted /endure
hardship, suffer harassment/, and mourn, and weep: let your
laughter be turned to mourning, and your joy to heaviness.
[10]Humble yourselves in the sight of the Lord, and he shall lift
you up.

The new life in Christ

[17]This I say therefore, and testify in the Lord, that ye Eph.
henceforth walk not as other Gentiles walk, in the vanity of 4:17–24
their mind, [18]Having the understanding darkened, being alienated from the life of God through the ignorance that is in them,
because of the blindness /hardness/ of their heart: [19]Who being
past feeling have given themselves over unto lasciviousness, to
work all uncleanness with greediness. [20]But ye have not so
learned Christ; [21]If so be that ye have ~~heard~~ {learned} him, and
have been taught by him, as the truth is in Jesus: [22b]{And now I
speak unto you} concerning the former conversation, {by
exhortation, [22a]}That ye put off {[22c]}the old man, [22d]which is
corrupt according to the deceitful lusts; [23a]And be renewed in
{[23d]}~~your~~ {the} mind {[23c]}of [23b]the spirit; [24]And that ye put on
the new man, which after God is created in righteousness and
true holiness.

Walk as children of light

Eph. 5:6–21

[6]Let no man deceive you with vain words: for because of these things cometh the wrath of God upon the children of disobedience. [7]Be not ye therefore partakers with them. [8]For ye were sometimes darkness, but now ~~are ye~~ light in the Lord: walk as children of light: [9](For the fruit of the \Spirit, light\ is in all goodness and righteousness and truth;) [10]Proving what is acceptable unto the Lord. [11]And have no fellowship with the unfruitful works of darkness, but rather reprove ~~them~~. [12]For it is a shame even to speak of those things which are done of them in secret. [13]But all things that are reproved are made manifest by the light: for whatsoever doth make manifest is light. [14]Wherefore he saith, Awake thou that sleepest, and arise from the dead, and Christ shall give thee light. [15]See then that ye walk circumspectly, not as fools, but as wise, [16]Redeeming the time, because the days are evil. [17]Wherefore be ye not unwise, but understanding what the will of the Lord is. [18]And be not drunk with wine, wherein is excess; but be filled with the Spirit; [19]Speaking to yourselves in psalms and hymns and spiritual songs, singing and making melody in your heart to the Lord; [20]Giving thanks always for all things unto God and the Father in the name of our Lord Jesus Christ; [21]Submitting yourselves one to another in the fear of God.

Walk in God's light

1 Jn. 1:5–7

[5]This then is the message which we have heard of him, and declare unto you, that God is light, and in him is no darkness at all. [6]If we say that we have fellowship with him, and walk in darkness, we lie, and do not the truth: [7]But if we walk in the light, as he is in the light, we have fellowship one with another, and the blood of Jesus Christ his Son cleanseth us from all sin.

Walk in truth and love through the doctrine of Christ

2 Jn. 1:4–11

[4]I rejoiced greatly that I found of thy children walking in truth, as we have received a commandment from the Father. [5]And now I beseech thee, lady /the church, congregation/, not as though I wrote a new commandment unto thee, but that

which we had from the beginning, that we love one another.
[6]And this is love, that we walk after his commandments. This is
the commandment, That, as ye have heard from the beginning,
ye should walk in it. [7]For many deceivers are entered into the
world, who confess not that Jesus Christ is come in the flesh.
This is a deceiver and an antichrist. [8]Look to yourselves, that we
lose not those things which we have wrought /performed/, but
that we receive a full reward. [9]Whosoever transgresseth, and
abideth not in the doctrine \of Christ\, hath not God. He that
abideth in the doctrine of Christ, he hath both the Father and
the Son. [10]If there come any unto you, and bring not this doctrine, receive him not into your house, neither bid him God
speed: [11]For he that biddeth him God speed is partaker of his
evil deeds.

Walk together in the Lord

[15]Let us therefore, as many as be perfect, be thus minded: Philip.
and if in any thing ye be otherwise minded, God shall reveal 3:15–4:1
even this unto you. [16]Nevertheless, whereto we have already
attained, let us walk by the same rule, let us mind the same
thing. [17]Brethren, be followers together of me, and mark them
which walk so as ye have us for an ensample. [18](For many walk,
of whom I have told you often, and now tell you even weeping,
~~that they are~~ {as} the enemies of the cross of Christ: [19]Whose
end is destruction, whose God is their belly, and who~~se~~ glory ~~is~~
in their shame, who mind earthly things.) [20]For our conversation is in heaven; from whence also we look for the Saviour, the
Lord Jesus Christ: [21]Who shall change our vile /humble, of low
estate/ body, that it may be fashioned like unto his glorious
body, according to the working whereby he is able even to subdue all things unto himself. [1]Therefore, my brethren dearly
beloved and longed for, my joy and crown, so stand fast in the
Lord, ~~my~~ dearly beloved.

Live by the spirit, not the flesh

[1]There is therefore now no condemnation to them which Rom.
are in Christ Jesus, who walk not after the flesh, but after the 8:1–13
Spirit. [2]For the law of the Spirit of life in Christ Jesus hath made

\me, you, us\ free from the law of sin and death. [3]For what the law could not do, in that it was weak through the flesh, God sending his own Son in the likeness of sinful flesh, and for sin, condemned sin in the flesh: [4]That the righteousness of the law might be fulfilled in us, who walk not after the flesh, but after the Spirit. [5]For they that are after the flesh do mind /watch, guard/ the things of the flesh; but they that are after the Spirit the things of the Spirit. [6]For to be carnally minded is death; but to be spiritually minded is life and peace. [7]Because the carnal mind is enmity against God: for it is not subject to the law of God, neither indeed can be. [8]So then they that are ~~in~~ {after} the flesh cannot please God. [9]But ye are not ~~in~~ {after} the flesh, but ~~in~~ {after} the Spirit, if so be that the Spirit of God dwell in you. Now if any man have not the Spirit of Christ, he is none of his. [10]And if Christ be in you, {though} the body ~~is dead~~ {shall die} because of sin; ~~but~~ {yet} the Spirit is life because of righteousness. [11]~~But~~ {And} if the Spirit of him that raised up Jesus from the dead dwell in you, he that raised up Christ from the dead shall also quicken /make alive/ your mortal bodies by his Spirit that dwelleth in you. [12]Therefore, brethren, we are debtors, not to the flesh, to live after the flesh. [13]For if ye live after the flesh {unto sin}, ye shall die /are at the point of whithering, dying/: but if ye through the Spirit do mortify /put to death, subdue/ the deeds of the body, ye shall live {unto Christ}.

Being Righteous

Be truly wise

James 3:17–18 [17]But the wisdom that is from above is first pure, then peaceable, gentle, and easy /pliant, easily persuaded/ to be intreated, full of mercy and good fruits, without partiality, and without hypocrisy. [18]And the fruit of righteousness is sown in peace of them that make peace.

Be honest

James 5:12 [12]But above all things, my brethren, swear not, neither by heaven, neither by the earth, neither by any other oath /thing/: but let your yea be yea; and your nay, nay; lest ye fall into condemnation.

Be holy

[13]Wherefore gird up the loins of your mind, be sober, and 1 Pet.
hope to the end /perfectly, completely/ for the grace that is to 1:13–16
be brought unto you at the revelation /appearance/ of Jesus
Christ; [14]As obedient children, not fashioning yourselves
according to the former lusts in your ignorance: [15]But as he
which hath called you is holy, so be ye holy in all manner of
conversation [conduct]; [16]Because it is written, "Be ye holy; for
I am holy" [Leviticus 11:44; 19:2].

Doing Good Works

Do good in God and boast not of yourself

[13]Go to now, ye that say, To day or to morrow we will go James
into such a city, and continue there a year, and buy and sell, 4:13–17
and get gain: [14]Whereas ye know not what shall be on the morrow. For what is your life? It is even a vapour, that appeareth
for a little time, and then vanisheth away. [15]~~For that~~ ye ought to
say, If the Lord will, we shall live, and do this, or that. [16]But
now ye rejoice in your boastings: all such rejoicing is evil.
[17]Therefore to him that knoweth to do good, and doeth it not,
to him it is sin.

Work for salvation and shine as a light in the world

[12]Wherefore, my beloved, as ye have always obeyed, not as Philip.
in my presence only, but now much more in my absence, work 2:12–18
out your own salvation with fear and trembling. [13]For it is God
which worketh in you both to will and to do of ~~his~~ good pleasure. [14]Do all things without murmurings and disputings:
[15]That ye may be blameless and harmless, the sons of God, without rebuke, in the midst of a crooked and perverse nation /gen-
eration/, among whom ye shine as lights in the world; [16]Holding
forth the word of life; that I may rejoice in the day of Christ,
that I have not run in vain, neither laboured in vain. [17a]Yea, and
if I be offered {[17c]a} sacrifice {[17b]}upon the [17d]~~and~~ service of
your faith, I joy, and rejoice with you all. [18]For the same cause
also do ye joy, and rejoice with me.

Be rich in good works

1 Tim. [17]Charge them that are rich in this world, that they be not
6:17–21 highminded, nor trust in uncertain riches, but in the living
God, who giveth us richly all things to enjoy; [18]That they do
good, that they be rich in good works, ready to distribute, willing to communicate; [19]Laying up in store for themselves a good
foundation against /for the future/ the time to come, that they
may lay hold on eternal life. [20]O Timothy, keep that which is
committed to thy trust, avoiding profane and vain babblings,
and oppositions of science falsely so called /disputations of what
is falsely called knowledge/: [21]Which some professing have
erred concerning the faith. Grace be with thee. Amen.

Christians should do good

Titus [1]Put them in mind to be subject to principalities and pow-
3:1–7 ers, to obey magistrates, to be ready to every good work, [2]To
speak evil of no man, to be no brawlers /not quarrelsome/, but
gentle, shewing all meekness unto all men. [3]For we ourselves
also were sometimes /once, formerly/ foolish, disobedient,
deceived, serving divers lusts and pleasures, living in malice
and envy, hateful, ~~and~~ hating one another. [4]But after that the
kindness and love of God our Saviour toward man appeared,
[5]Not by works of righteousness which we have done, but
according to his mercy he saved us, by the washing of regener-
ation, and renewing of the Holy Ghost; [6]Which he shed on us
abundantly through Jesus Christ our Saviour; [7]That being justified by his grace, we should be made heirs according to the
hope of eternal life.

Growing and Progressing

Grow as a child

1 Pet. [1]Wherefore laying aside all malice, and all guile, and
2:1–3 hypocrisies, and envies, and all evil speakings, [2]As newborn
babes, desire the sincere /pure, genuine/ milk of the word, that
ye may grow thereby: [3]If so be ye have tasted /experienced/ that
the Lord is gracious.

Confidence before God comes from a clear conscience

19And hereby we know that we are of the truth, and shall 1 Jn.
assure our hearts before him. 20For if our heart condemn us, 3:19–24
God is greater than our heart, and knoweth all things. 21Beloved, if our heart condemn us not, then ~~have~~ we {have} confidence toward God. 22And whatsoever we ask, we receive of him, because we keep his commandments, and do those things that are pleasing in his sight. 23And this is his commandment, That we should believe on the name of his Son Jesus Christ, and love one another, as he gave us commandment. 24And he that keepeth his commandments dwelleth in him, and he in him. And hereby we know that he abideth in us, by the Spirit which he hath given us.

Maturing in the gospel

11Of whom [about Melchizedek] we have many things to Heb.
say, and hard to be uttered /difficult to be explained/, seeing ye 5:11–6:8
are dull of hearing. 12For when for the time ye ought to be teachers, ye have need that one teach you again which be the first principles of the oracles of God; and are become such as have need of milk, and not of strong meat. 13For every one that useth milk is unskilful in the word of righteousness: for he is a babe. 14But strong meat belongeth to them that are of full age, ~~even~~ those who by reason of use have their senses exercised to discern both good and evil. 1Therefore {not} leaving /having left behind the beginning of the doctrine/ the principles of the doctrine of Christ, let us go on unto perfection; not laying again the foundation of repentance from dead works, and of faith toward God, 2Of the doctrine of baptisms, ~~and~~ of laying on of hands, and of {the} resurrection of the dead, and of eternal judgment. 3And ~~this~~ {we} will ~~we do~~ \let us do\ {go on unto perfection}, if God permit. 4For {he hath made} it ~~is~~ impossible for those who were once enlightened, and have tasted of the heavenly gift, and were made partakers of the Holy Ghost, 5And have tasted the good word of God, and the powers of the world to come, 6If they shall fall away, to {be} renew{ed} ~~them~~ again unto repentance; seeing they crucify {un}to themselves the Son

of God afresh, and put him to an open shame. 7For {the day
cometh that} the earth which drinketh in the rain that cometh
oft upon it, and bringeth forth herbs meet /suitable, fit, proper/
for them {who dwelleth thereon} by whom it is dressed /culti-
vated, tilled/, {who now} receiveth blessing from God {shall be
cleansed with fire}: 8~~But~~ {For} that which beareth thorns and
briers is rejected, and is nigh unto cursing; ~~whose~~ {therefore
they who bring not forth good friuts, shall be cast into the fire;
for their} end is to be burned.

Enduring to the End

Stand fast in the faith

Philip. 27~~Only~~ {Therefore} let your conversation be as it
1:27–30 becometh the gospel of Christ: that whether I come and see
you, or else be absent, I may hear of your affairs, that ye stand
fast in one spirit, with one mind striving together for the faith of
the gospel; 28And in nothing terrified by your adversaries:
~~which is to them an evident token of perdition, but to you of~~
{who reject the gospel, which bringeth on them destruction;
but you who receive the gospel,} salvation, and that of God.
29For unto you it is given in the behalf of Christ, not only to
believe on him, but also to suffer for his sake; 30Having the same
conflict /struggle/ which ye saw in me, and now ~~hear~~ {know} to
be in me.

The good fight of faith

1 Tim. 11But thou, O man of God, flee these things; and follow
6:11–16 after righteousness, godliness, faith, love, patience, meekness.
12Fight the good fight of faith, lay hold on eternal life, whereunto thou art also called, and hast professed a good profession
before many witnesses. 13I give thee charge in the sight of God,
who quickeneth /brings to life/ all things, and ~~before~~ Christ
Jesus, who before Pontius Pilate witnessed /testified/ a good
confession; 14That thou keep this commandment without spot,
unrebukeable, until the appearing of our Lord Jesus Christ:
15aWhich in his times he shall shew, who is the blessed and only

Potentate, the King of kings, and Lord of lords [16e]{[15b]}to whom be honor and power everlasting; {[16c]}Whom no man hath seen, nor can see, {[16b]}in the light which {unto whom} no man can approach ~~unto~~, {only he who hath the light and [16a]}~~Who only hath~~ {the hope of} immortality dwelling {in him.}. Amen.

Words of hope and encouragement

[9]But, beloved, we are persuaded {of} better things of you, Heb.
and things that accompany salvation, though we thus speak. 6:9–20
[10]For God is not unrighteous ~~to~~ {therefore he will not} forget your work and labour of love, which ye have shewed toward his name, in that ye have ministered to the saints, and do minister.
[11]And we desire that every one of you do shew the same diligence to the full assurance of hope unto the end: [12]That ye be not slothful, but followers of them who through faith and patience inherit the promises. [13]For when God made promise to Abraham, because he could swear /promise, confirm by an oath/ by no greater, he sware by himself, [14]Saying, Surely blessing I will bless thee, and multiplying I will multiply thee. [15]And so, after he had patiently endured, he obtained the promise. [16]For men verily swear by the greater: and an oath for confirmation ~~is~~ to them an end of all strife. [17]Wherein God, willing more abundantly to shew unto the heirs of promise the immutability of his counsel /design, purpose/, confirmed ~~it~~ by an oath: [18]That by two immutable things, in which it was impossible for God to lie, we might have a strong consolation, who have fled for refuge to lay hold upon the hope set before us: [19]Which hope we have as an anchor of the soul, both sure and stedfast, and which entereth into that within the veil; [20]Whither the forerunner is for us entered, even Jesus, made an high priest for ever after the order of Melchisedec.

The Christian opportunity

[19]Having therefore, brethren, boldness /license, authority/ Heb.
to enter into the holiest by the blood of Jesus, [20]By a new and 10:19–25
living way, which he hath consecrated for us, through the veil, that is to say, his flesh; [21]And having {such} an high priest over

the house of God; [22]Let us draw near with a true heart in full assurance of faith, having our hearts sprinkled /purified/ from an evil conscience, and our bodies washed with pure water. [23]Let us hold fast the profession of ~~our~~ faith /hope/ without wavering; (for he is faithful that promised;) [24]And let us consider /understand/ one another to provoke unto love and to good works: [25]Not forsaking the assembling of ourselves together, as the manner of some is; but exhorting ~~one another~~: and so much the more, as ye see the day approaching.

Motives for perseverance

Heb. 10:32–39 [32]But call to remembrance the former days, in which, after
ye were illuminated, ye endured a great fight of afflictions;
[33]Partly, whilst ye were made a gazingstock both by reproaches
and afflictions; and partly, whilst ye became companions of
them that were so used. [34]For ye had compassion of me in my
bonds, and took joyfully the spoiling of your goods, knowing in
yourselves that ye have in heaven a better and an enduring sub-
stance. [35]Cast not away therefore your confidence, which hath
great recompence of reward. [36]For ye have need of patience,
that, after ye have done the will of God, ye might receive the
promise. [37]For "yet a little while, and he that shall come will
come, and will not tarry. [38]Now the just shall live by faith: but if
any man draw back, my soul shall have no pleasure in him"
[Habakkuk 2:3–4]. [39]But we are not of them who draw back
/take in the sail, shrink back/ unto perdition /ruin, destruction/;
but of them that believe to the saving of the soul.

Encouragement to endure

2 Thes. 2:13–15 [13]But we are bound to give thanks alway to God for you,
brethren beloved of the Lord, because God hath from the
beginning chosen you to salvation through sanctification of the
Spirit and belief of the truth: [14]Whereunto he called you by our
gospel, to the obtaining of the glory of our Lord Jesus Christ.
[15]Therefore, brethren, stand fast, and hold the traditions which
ye have been taught, whether by word, or our epistle.

The Church and the mystery of the spiritual life

[14]These things write I unto thee, hoping to come unto 1 Tim.
thee shortly: [15a]But if I tarry long, that thou mayest know how 3:14–16
thou oughtest to behave thyself in the house of God, which is
the church of the living God: [15b]{[16]}the pillar and ground /foun-
dation/ of the truth {is} [16](And without controversy, great is the
mystery of godliness): God was manifest in the flesh, justified in
the /approved by the/ Spirit, seen of angels, preached unto the
Gentiles, believed on in the world, received up into glory.

The Christian's Loving Relationships with Others

Christian liberty in faith and charity

[1]Stand fast therefore in the liberty wherewith Christ hath Gal.
made us free, and be not entangled again with the yoke of 5:1–15
bondage. [2]Behold, I Paul say unto you, that if ye be circumcised, Christ shall profit you nothing. [3]For I testify again to
every man that is circumcised, that he is a debtor to do the
whole law. [4]Christ is become of no effect unto you, whosoever
of you are justified by the law; ye are fallen from grace. [5]For we
through the Spirit wait for the hope of righteousness by faith.
[6]For in Jesus Christ neither circumcision availeth /has any
power, validity, service/ anything, nor uncircumcision; but faith
which worketh by love. [7]Ye did run well; who did hinder you
that ye should not obey the truth? [8]This persuasion cometh not
of him that calleth you. [9]A little leaven leaveneth the whole
lump. [10]I have confidence in you through the Lord, that ye will
be none otherwise minded /will take no other view, will not
have a different opinion/: but he that troubleth you shall bear
his judgment, whosoever he be. [11]And I, brethren, if I yet
preach circumcision, why do I yet suffer persecution? then is
the offence /stumblingblock, cause of misery/ of the cross
ceased. [12]I would they were even cut off which trouble you.
[13]For, brethren, ye have been called unto liberty; only use not
liberty for an occasion to the flesh, but by love serve one
another. [14]For all the law is fulfilled in one word, even in this;
"Thou shalt love thy neighbour as thyself" [Leviticus 19:18].

15But if ye bite and devour one another, take heed that ye be not consumed one of another.

Aspects of Christian living

Eph. 4:25–5:5 25"Wherefore putting away lying, speak every man truth with his neighbour: for we are members one of another" [Zechariah 8:16]. 26"{Can ye} Be ~~ye~~ angry, and ~~sin~~ not {sin?}" [Psalm 4:4 LXX]: let not the sun go down upon your wrath: 27Neither give place to the devil. 28Let him that stole steal no more: but rather let him labour, working with his hands {for} the thing{s} which ~~is~~ {are} good, that he may have to give to him that needeth. 29Let no corrupt communication proceed out of your mouth, but that which is good to the use of edifying, that it may minister grace unto the hearers. 30And grieve not the holy Spirit of God, whereby ye are sealed unto the day of redemption. 31Let all bitterness, and wrath, and anger, and clamour, and evil speaking, be put away from you, with all malice: 32And be ye kind one to another, tenderhearted, forgiving one another, even as God for Christ's sake hath forgiven you. 1Be ye therefore followers /imitators/ of God, as dear children; 2And walk in love, as Christ also hath loved us, and hath given himself for us an offering and a sacrifice to God for a sweet-smelling savour. 3But fornication, and all uncleanness, or covetousness, let it not be once named among you, as becometh saints; 4Neither filthiness, nor foolish talking, nor jesting, which are not convenient: but rather giving of thanks. 5For this ye know, that no whoremonger, nor unclean person, nor covetous man, who is an idolater, hath any inheritance in the kingdom of Christ and of God.

General rules of Christian behavior

Col. 3:5–17 5Mortify /put to death/ therefore your members /the parts of you/ which are upon the earth; fornication, uncleanness, inordinate affection, evil concupiscence, and covetousness, which is idolatry: 6For which things' sake the wrath of God cometh on the children of disobedience: 7In the which ye also walked some time /formerly/, when ye lived in them. 8But now

ye also put off all these; anger, wrath, malice, blasphemy, filthy
communication out of your mouth. [9]Lie not one to another, seeing that ye have put off the old man with his deeds; [10]And have
put on the new ~~man~~, which is renewed in knowledge after the
image of him that created him: [11]Where there is neither Greek
nor Jew, circumcision nor uncircumcision, Barbarian, Scythian,
bond, ~~nor~~ free: but Christ is all, and in all. [12]Put on therefore, as
the elect of God, holy and beloved, bowels of mercies, kindness,
humbleness of mind, meekness, longsuffering; [13]Forbearing
one another, and forgiving one another, if any man have a quar-
rel against any: even as Christ forgave you, so also ~~do~~ ye. [14]And
above all these things ~~put on~~ charity, which is the bond of per-
fectness. [15]And let the peace of God rule in your hearts, to the
which also ye are called in one body; and be ye thankful. [16]Let
the word of Christ dwell in you richly in all wisdom; teaching
and admonishing one another in psalms and hymns and spiritual songs, singing with grace in your hearts to the Lord. [17]And
whatsoever ye do in word or deed, do all in the name of the
Lord Jesus, giving thanks to God and the Father by him.

Show charity to everyone, including enemies

[14]Bless them which persecute you: bless, and curse not. Rom.
[15]Rejoice with them that do rejoice, and weep with them that 12:14–21
weep. [16]Be of the same mind one toward another. Mind not
high things, but condescend /conforming willingly with the
humble/ to men of low estate. Be not wise in your own conceits.
[17]Recompense to no man evil for evil. "Provide things honest in
the sight of all men" [Proverbs 3:4 LXX]. [18]If it be possible, as
much as lieth in you, live peaceably with all men. [19]Dearly
beloved, avenge not yourselves, but ~~rather~~ give place unto
wrath [leave room for God's retribution]: for it is written,
"Vengeance is mine; I will repay" [Deuteronomy 32:35], saith
the Lord. [20]Therefore "if thine enemy hunger, feed him; if he
thirst, give him drink: for in so doing thou shalt heap coals of
fire on his head" [Proverbs 25:21–22]. [21]Be not overcome of
evil, but overcome evil with good.

Judge not

James 4:11–12 [11]Speak not evil one of another, brethren. He that speaketh evil of his brother, and judgeth his brother, speaketh evil of the law, and judgeth the law: but if thou judge the law, thou art not a doer of the law, but a judge. [12]There is one law-giver, who is able to save and to destroy: who art thou that judgest another?

Rom. 14:1–12 [1]Him that is weak in the faith receive ye, ~~but~~ not to doubtful disputations [2]For one believeth that he may eat all things: another, who is weak, eateth herbs /vegetables/. [3]Let not him that eateth despise him that eateth not; and let not him which eateth not judge him that eateth: for God hath received him. [4]Who art thou that judgest another man's servant? to his own master he standeth or falleth. Yea, he shall be holden up: for God is able to make him stand. [5]One man esteemeth one day above another: another esteemeth every day ~~alike~~. Let every man be fully persuaded in his own mind. [6]He that regardeth the day, regardeth it unto the Lord; and he that regardeth not the day, to the Lord he doth not regard it. He that eateth, eateth to the Lord, for he giveth God thanks; and he that eateth not, to the Lord he eateth not, and giveth God thanks. [7]For none of us liveth to himself, and no man dieth to himself. [8]For whether we live, we live unto the Lord; and whether we die, we die unto the Lord: whether we live therefore, or die, we are the Lord's. [9]For to this end Christ both died, and rose, and revived, that he might be Lord both of the dead and living. [10]But why dost thou judge thy brother? or why dost thou set at nought thy brother? for we shall all stand before the judgment seat of \Christ, God\. [11a]For {[11c]}I live, saith the Lord, {[11b]as} it is written, ~~as~~ [11d]"{and} every knee shall bow to me, and every tongue shall ~~confess~~ {swear} /praise, profess openly/ to God" [Isaiah 49:18; 45:23]. [12]So then every one of us shall give account of himself to God.

Avoid hypocrisy

Rom. 2:17–24 [17]Behold, thou art called a Jew, and restest in the law, and makest thy boast of God, [18]And knowest his will, and approvest the things that are more excellent, being instructed out of the law; [19]And art confident that thou thyself art a guide of the blind, a light of them which are in darkness, [20]An instructor of the foolish, a teacher of babes, which hast the form /system, appearance/ of knowledge and of the truth in the law. [21]Thou therefore which teachest another, teachest thou not thyself? thou that preachest a man should not steal, dost thou steal? [22]Thou that sayest a man should not commit adultery, dost thou commit adultery? thou that abhorrest idols, dost thou commit sacrilege /rob shrines, temples/? [23]Thou that makest thy boast of the law, through breaking the law dishonourest thou God? [24]"For the name of God is blasphemed among the Gentiles through you" [Isaiah 52:5], as it is written.

Talk is cheap and dangerous

[1]My brethren, ~~be not many masters~~ {strive not for the James 3:1–12
mastery}, knowing that {in so doing} we shall receive the greater condemnation. [2]For in many things we offend /stumble, err/ all. If any man offend not in word, the same is a perfect man, and able also to bridle the whole body. [3]Behold, we put bits in the horses' mouths, that they may obey us; and we turn about their whole body. [4]Behold also the ships, which though they be so great, and are driven of fierce winds, yet are they turned about with a very small helm, whithersoever the governor /helmsman, pilot/ listeth. [5]Even so the tongue is a little member, and boasteth great things. Behold, how great a matter /forest/ a little fire kindleth! [6]And the tongue ~~is a~~ {a}fire, a world of iniquity: so is the tongue among our members, that it defileth the whole body, and setteth on fire the course of nature /all of existance/; and it is set on fire of hell. [7]For every kind of beasts, and of birds, and of serpents, and of things in the sea, is tamed, and hath been tamed of mankind: [8]But the tongue can no man tame; it is an unruly /untameable, uncontrollable/ evil, full of deadly poison. [9]Therewith bless we God, even the Father; and therewith curse we men, which are made after the similitude of God. [10]Out of the same mouth proceedeth blessing and cursing. My brethren, these things ought not so to be. [11]Doth a fountain /spring, well/ send forth at the same place sweet

water and bitter? [12]Can the fig tree, my brethren, bear olive
berries? either a vine, figs? so ~~can~~ no fountain both yield salt
water and fresh.

Please your neighbors, not yourself

Rom. [1]We then that are strong ought to bear /remove, endure,
15:1–6 bear with/ the infirmities of the weak, and not to please ourselves. [2]Let every one of us please his neighbour for his good to
edification. [3]For even Christ pleased not himself; but, as it is
written, "The reproaches /revilings, insults/ of them that
reproached thee fell on me" [Psalm 69:9]. [4]For whatsoever
things were written aforetime were written for our learning,
that we through patience and comfort of the scriptures might
have hope. [5]Now the God of patience and consolation /comfort/
grant you to be likeminded one toward another according ~~to~~
{as was} Christ Jesus: [6]That ye may with one mind and one
mouth glorify God, even the Father of our Lord Jesus Christ.

On kindness, humility, and perseverance, bearing one another's burdens

Gal. [1]Brethren, if a man be overtaken in a fault /transgression,
6:1–10 trespass/, ye which are spiritual, restore such an one in the spirit
of meekness; considering /watching/ thyself, lest thou also be
tempted. [2]Bear ye one another's burdens, and so fulfil the law
of Christ. [3]For if a man think himself to be something, when he
is nothing, he deceiveth himself. [4]But let every man prove his
own work, and then shall he have rejoicing in himself alone,
and not in another. [5]For every man shall bear his own burden.
[6]Let him that is taught in the word communicate unto him that
teacheth in all good things. [7]Be not deceived; God is not
mocked: for whatsoever a man soweth, that shall he also reap.
[8]For he that soweth to his flesh shall of the flesh reap corruption; but he that soweth to the Spirit shall of the Spirit reap life
everlasting. [9]And let us not be weary in well doing: for in due
season we shall reap, if we faint not. [10]As we have therefore
opportunity, let us do good unto all ~~men~~, especially unto them
who are of the household of faith.

Forgive and comfort the offender

[5]But if any have caused grief, he hath not grieved me, but 2 Cor.
in part: that I may not overcharge you all. [6]Sufficient to such a 2:5–11
man is this punishment, which was inflicted of many. [7]So that
contrariwise ye ought rather to forgive him, and comfort him,
lest perhaps such a one should be swallowed up with overmuch
sorrow. [8]Wherefore I beseech you that ye would confirm your
love toward him. [9]For to this end also did I write, that I might
know the proof of you, whether ye be obedient in all things.
[10]To whom ye forgive any thing, I forgive also: for if I forgave
any thing, to whom I forgave it, for your sakes forgave I it in the
person /presence/ of Christ; [11]Lest Satan should get an advantage of us: for we are not ignorant of his devices.

Some demands made by life in community

[12]And we beseech you, brethren, to know them which 1 Thes.
labour among you, and are over you in the Lord, and admon- 5:12–22
ish you; [13]And to esteem them very highly in love for their
work's sake. ~~And~~ be at peace among yourselves. [14]Now we
exhort you, brethren, warn them that are unruly, comfort
/encourage, console/ the feebleminded /fainthearted, despon-
dent/, support /care for/ the weak /infirm, doubting, timid/, be
patient toward all ~~men~~. [15]See that none render evil for evil unto
any ~~man~~; but ever follow that which is good, both among yourselves, and to all ~~men~~. [16]Rejoice evermore. [17]Pray without ceasing. [18]In every thing give thanks: for this is the will of God in
Christ Jesus concerning you. [19]Quench /extinguish, hinder,
supress/ not the Spirit. [20]Despise not prophesyings. [21]Prove
/examine, put to the test/ all things; hold fast that which is good.
[22]Abstain from all appearance /kinds/ of evil.

Deal honestly with all people and rulers

[11]Dearly beloved, I beseech you as strangers and pilgrims 1 Pet.
/resident aliens, sojourners/, abstain from fleshly lusts, which 2:11–17
war against the soul; [12]Having your ~~conversation~~ {conduct}
honest among the Gentiles: that, whereas they speak against
you as evildoers, they may by your good works, which they shall

behold, glorify God in the day of visitation. [13]Submit yourselves to every ordinance /public law/ of man for the Lord's sake: whether it be to the king, as supreme /superior/; [14]Or unto governors, as unto them that are sent by him for the punishment of evildoers, and for the praise of them that do well. [15]For so is the will of God, that with well doing ye may put to silence the ignorance of foolish men: [16]As free, and not using your liberty for a cloke of maliciousness, but as the servants of God. [17]Honour all ~~men~~. Love the brotherhood. Fear God. Honour the king.

Be subject to civil authority

Rom. 13:1–7 [1]Let every soul be subject /be submissive, render obedience/ unto the higher powers /authorities/ {in the church}~~. For there is no power~~ but of God: the powers that be are ordained of God. [2]Whosoever therefore resisteth the power, resisteth the ordinance of God: and they that resist shall receive to themselves ~~damnation~~ {punishment}. [3]For rulers are not a terror to good works, but to the evil. Wilt thou then not be afraid of the power /authority/? do that which is good, and thou shalt have praise of the same: [4]For he is the minister /a servant/ of God to thee for good. But if thou do that which is evil, be afraid; for he beareth not the ~~sword~~ {rod} in vain: for he is the minister of God, a revenger to execute wrath upon him that doeth evil. [5]Wherefore ye must needs be subject \to distress or compulsion\, not only for wrath, but also for conscience sake. [6]For for this cause pay ye ~~tribute~~ {your consecrations} also {unto them}: for they are God's ministers, attending continually upon this very thing. [7]{But first,} Render ~~therefore~~ to all their dues {according to custom,}: tribute to whom tribute ~~is due~~; custom to whom custom {that your consecrations may be done in} fear {of him} to whom fear {belongs}; {and in} honour {of him} to whom honour {belongs}.

How to treat other Saints

1 Tim. 5:1–2 [1]Rebuke not an elder, but intreat ~~him~~ as a father; ~~and~~ the younger men as brethren; [2]The elder women as mothers; the younger as sisters, with all purity.

Chastity and charity

[1]Furthermore then we beseech you, brethren, and exhort 1 Thes.
you by the Lord Jesus, that as ye have received of us how ye 4:1–12
ought to walk and to please God, ~~so~~ ye would abound more and
more. [2]For ye know what commandments we gave you by the
Lord Jesus. [3]For this is the will of God, ~~even~~ your sanctification,
that ye should abstain from fornication /immorality/: [4]That
every one of you should know how to possess his vessel in sanctification and honour; [5]Not in the lust of concupiscence /passion
of lust/, even as the Gentiles which know not God: [6]That no
man go beyond /take advantage of, wrong/ and defraud his
brother in any /the/ matter: because that the Lord is the
avenger of all such, as we also have forewarned you and testified. [7]For God hath not called us unto uncleanness, but unto
holiness. [8]He therefore that despiseth /rejects, sets aside, vio-
lates/, despiseth not man, but God, who hath also given unto us
his holy Spirit. [9]But as touching brotherly love ye need not that
I write unto you: for ye yourselves are taught of God to love one
another. [10]And indeed ye do it toward all the brethren which
are in all Macedonia: but we beseech you, brethren, that ye
increase more and more; [11]And that ye study /strive, endeavor
earnestly/ to be quiet, and to do your own business, and to work
with your own hands, as we commanded you; [12]That ye may
walk honestly toward them that are without, and that ye may
have lack of nothing.

Show mercy

[12]So speak ye, and so do, as they that shall be judged by the James
law of liberty. [13]For he shall have judgment without mercy, that 2:12–13
hath shewed no mercy; and mercy rejoiceth against judgment.

Love one another

[22]Seeing ye have purified your souls in obeying the truth 1 Pet.
\through the Spirit\ unto unfeigned /unhypocritical/ love of the 1:22–23
brethren, ~~see that ye~~ love one another with a pure heart fervently: [23]Being born again, not of corruptible seed, but of incorruptible, by the word of God, which liveth and abideth for ever.

God loved us, so we should love

1 Jn. [7]Beloved, let us love one another: for love is of God; and
4:7–21 every one that loveth is born of God, and knoweth God. [8]He
that loveth not knoweth not God; for God is love. [9]In this was
manifested the love of God toward us, because that God sent his
only begotten Son into the world, that we might live through
him. [10]Herein is love, not that we loved God, but that he loved
us, and sent his Son to be the propitiation for our sins.
[11]Beloved, if God so loved us, we ought also to love one another.
[12]No man hath seen God at any time {except them who
believe.} If we love one another, God dwelleth in us, and his
love is perfected in us. [13]Hereby know we that we dwell in him,
and he in us, because he hath given us of his Spirit. [14]And we
have seen and do testify that the Father sent the Son to be the
Saviour of the world. [15]Whosoever shall confess that Jesus is the
Son of God, God dwelleth in him, and he in God. [16]And we have
known and believed the love that God hath to us. God is love;
and he that dwelleth in love dwelleth in God, and God in him.
[17]Herein is our love made perfect, that we may have boldness in
the day of judgment: because as he is, so are we in this world.
[18]There is no fear in love; but perfect love casteth out fear:
because fear hath torment /correction, punishment/. He that
feareth is not made perfect in love. [19]We love him, because he
first loved us. [20]If a man say, I love God, and hateth his brother,
he is a liar: for he that loveth not his brother whom he hath
seen, how can he love God whom he hath not seen? [21]And this
commandment have we from him, That he who loveth God
love his brother also.

Love one another in deed

1 Jn. [11]For this is the message /precept, doctrine/ that ye heard
3:11–18 from the beginning, that we should love one another. [12]Not as
Cain, who was of that wicked one, and slew his brother. And
wherefore slew he him? Because his own works were evil, and
his brother's righteous. [13]Marvel not, my brethren, if the world
hate you. [14]We know that we have passed from death unto life,
because we love the brethren. He that loveth not his brother

abideth in death. [15]Whosoever hateth his brother is a murderer:
and ye know that no murderer hath eternal life abiding in him.
[16]Hereby perceive we the love of ~~God~~ {Christ}, because he laid
down his life for us: and we ought to lay down our lives for the
brethren. [17]But whoso hath this world's good, and seeth his
brother have need, and shutteth up his bowels ~~of compassion~~
from him /is hardhearted, void of compassion/, how dwelleth
the love of God in him? [18]My little children, let us not love in
word, neither in tongue {only}; but in deed and in truth.

Service is well pleasing to God

[1]Let brotherly love continue. [2]Be not forgetful to entertain Heb.
strangers: for thereby some have entertained angels unawares. 13:1–16
[3]Remember them that are in bonds, as bound with them; and
them which suffer adversity, as being yourselves also ~~in~~ {of} the
body. [4]Marriage is honourable in all, and the bed undefiled: but
whoremongers and adulterers God will judge. [5]Let your con-
versation{s} be without covetousness; and be content with {giv-
ing} such things as ye have: for he hath said, I will never leave
thee, nor forsake thee. [6]So that we may boldly say, "The Lord is
my helper, and I will not fear what man shall do unto me"
[Psalm 118:6]. [7]Remember them which have the rule over you,
who have spoken unto you the word of God: whose faith follow,
considering the end of their conversation. [8]Jesus Christ the
same yesterday, and to day, and for ever. [9]Be not carried about
with divers and strange doctrines. For it is a good thing that the
heart be established with grace; not with meats, which have not
profited them that have been occupied therein. [10]We have an
altar, whereof they have no right to eat which serve the tabernacle. [11]For the bodies of those beasts, whose blood is brought
into the sanctuary by the high priest for sin, are burned without
the camp. [12]Wherefore Jesus also, that he might sanctify the
people with his own blood, suffered without /outside of/ the
gate. [13]Let us go forth therefore unto him without /outside of/
the camp /the tent city of wandering Israel/, bearing his
reproach /the insult and humiliation he bore/. [14]For here have we
no continuing city, but we seek one to come. [15]By him therefore

let us offer the sacrifice of praise to God continually, that is, the fruit of our lips giving thanks to his name. [16]But to do good and to communicate forget not: for with such sacrifices God is well pleased.

Love fulfills the law

Rom. [8]{Therefore} Owe no man any thing, but to love one
13:8–10 another: for he that loveth another hath fulfilled the law. [9]For
this, "Thou shalt not commit adultery, Thou shalt not kill,
Thou shalt not steal, Thou shalt not bear false witness, Thou
shalt not covet" [Exodus 20:13–15, 17]; and if ~~there be~~ any
other commandment, it is briefly comprehended in this saying,
namely, "Thou shalt love thy neighbour as thyself" [Leviticus
19:18]. [10]Love worketh no ill to his neighbour: therefore love is
the fulfilling of the law.

Love one another

1 Pet. [8]Finally, be ye all of one mind, having compassion one of
3:8–12 another, love as brethren, ~~be~~ pitiful /tenderhearted, compas-
sionate/, ~~be~~ courteous: [9]Not rendering evil for evil, or railing
for railing: but contrariwise blessing; knowing that ye are
thereunto called, that ye should inherit a blessing. [10]"For he
that will love life, and see good days, let him refrain his tongue
from evil, and his lips that they speak no guile: [11]Let him
eschew /turn away from, avoid/ evil, and do good; let him seek
peace, and ensue /pursue, follow eagerly/ it. [12]For the eyes of
the Lord are over the righteous, and his ears are open unto
their prayers: but the face of the Lord is against them that do
evil" [Psalm 34:12–16].

Unity in the Church

Avoid contention

James [13]Who is a wise man and endued [endowed] with knowl-
3:13–16 edge among you? let him shew out of a good conversation [con-
duct] /way of life/ his works with meekness of wisdom. [14]But if ye
have bitter envying and strife in your hearts, glory not /do not
assume superiority over/ and lie not against the truth. [15]This

wisdom descendeth not from above, but is earthly, sensual, devilish. [16]For where envying and strife is, there is confusion and every evil work.

A call to unity in body of Christ

[1]I therefore, the prisoner of the Lord, beseech you that ye walk worthy of the vocation /calling/ wherewith ye are called, [2]With all lowliness and meekness, with longsuffering, forbearing one another in love; [3]Endeavouring to keep the unity of the Spirit in the bond of peace. [4]~~There is~~ {In} one body, and one Spirit, even as ye are called in one hope of your calling; [5]One Lord, one faith, one baptism, [6]One God and Father of all, who is above all, and through all, and in you all. [7]But unto every one of us is given grace according to the measure of the gift of Christ. [8]Wherefore he saith, "When he ascended up on high, he led captivity captive, and gave gifts unto men" [Psalm 68:18]. [9](Now that he ascended, what is it but that he also descended \first\ into the lower parts of the earth? [10]He ~~that~~ {who} descended is the same also ~~that~~ {who} ascended up ~~far above all~~ {into heaven, to glorify him who reigneth over all} heavens, that he might fill all things.) [11]And he gave some, apostles; and some, prophets; and some, evangelists; and some, pastors and teachers; [12]For the perfecting of the saints, for the work of the ministry, for the edifying of the body of Christ: [13a]Till we {[13c]}in the unity of the faith, {[13b]}all come {[13d]}~~and of~~ {to} the knowledge of the Son of God, ~~[13e]unto a perfect man, unto the measure of the stature of the fulness of Christ:~~ [14]That we ~~henceforth~~ be no more children, tossed to and fro, and carried about with every wind of doctrine, by the sleight of men, and cunning craftiness, whereby they lie in wait to deceive; [15]But speaking the truth in love, may grow up into him in all things, which is the head, even Christ: [16]From whom the whole body fitly joined together and compacted by that which every joint supplieth, according to the effectual working in the measure of every part, maketh increase of the body unto the edifying of itself in love.

Eph. 4:1–16

Attain unity by following Christ's example of humility

Philip. 2:1–11

1If there be therefore any consolation in Christ, if any comfort of love, if any fellowship of the Spirit, if any bowels /tender affections of the heart, compassion/ and mercies, 2Fulfil ye my joy, that ye be likeminded, having the same love, ~~being~~ of one accord, of one mind. 3~~Let~~ nothing ~~be done~~ through strife or vainglory; but in lowliness of mind let each esteem other better than themselves. 4Look not every man on his own things, but every man also on the things of others. 5Let this mind be in you, which was also in Christ Jesus: 6Who, being in the form of God, thought it not robbery to be equal with God: 7But made himself of no reputation, and took upon him the form of a servant, and was made in the likeness of men: 8And being found in fashion /outward appearance/ as a man, he humbled himself, and became obedient unto death, even the death of the cross. 9Wherefore God also hath highly exalted him, and given him a name which is above every name: 10That at the name of Jesus "every knee should bow, ~~of things~~ in heaven, and ~~things~~ in earth, and ~~things~~ under the earth; 11And ~~that~~ every tongue should confess" [Isaiah 45:23] ~~that~~ Jesus Christ is Lord, to the glory of God the Father.

Reconciliation of all people with each other and with God

Eph. 2:11–22

11Wherefore remember, that ye {were} ~~being~~ in time past Gentiles in the flesh, who are called Uncircumcision by that which is called the Circumcision in the flesh made by hands; 12That at that time ye were without Christ, being aliens from the commonwealth of Israel, and strangers from the covenants of promise, having no hope, and without God in the world: 13But now in Christ Jesus ye who sometimes were far off are made nigh by the blood of Christ. 14For he is our peace, who hath made both one, and hath broken down the middle wall of partition ~~between us~~; 15Having abolished in his flesh the enmity, even the law of commandments ~~contained~~ in ordinances; for to make in himself of twain one new man, so making peace; 16And that he might reconcile both unto God in one body by the cross, having slain the enmity thereby: 17And came and preached peace to you which were afar off, and to them that were nigh. 18For through him we both have access by one Spirit unto the Father. 19Now therefore ye are no more strangers and foreigners, but fellowcitizens with the saints, and of the household of God; 20And are built upon the foundation of the apostles and prophets, Jesus Christ ~~himself~~ being the chief corner ~~stone~~; 21In whom all the building fitly framed together groweth unto an holy temple in the Lord: 22In whom ye also are builded together for an habitation of God through the Spirit.

Love the poor

1My brethren, {ye cannot have} the faith of our Lord James
Jesus Christ, the Lord of glory, ~~with~~ {and yet have} respect 2:1–9
/partiality/ to persons. 2~~For~~ {Now} if there come unto your assembly a man with a gold ring, in goodly apparel, and there come in also a poor /dirty/ man in vile raiment; 3And ye have respect to him that weareth the gay /splendid/ clothing, and say unto him, Sit thou here in a good place; and say to the poor, Stand thou there, or sit here under my footstool: 4aAre ye not then {4c}in yourselves {4b}partial {4e}judges {4dand} ~~are~~ {become} 4f~~of~~ evil {in your} thoughts? 5Hearken, my beloved brethren, Hath not God chosen the poor of this world rich in faith, and heirs of the kingdom which he hath promised to them that love him? 6But ye have despised the poor. Do not rich men oppress you, and draw you before the judgment seats? 7Do not they blaspheme that worthy name by the which ye are called? 8If ye fulfil the royal law according to the scripture, "Thou shalt love thy neighbour as thyself, ye do well" [Leviticus 19:18]: 9But if ye have respect /favoritism/ to persons, ye commit sin, and are convinced /convicted/ of the law as transgressors.

Warning to the corrupt rich

1Go to now, ~~ye~~ rich men, weep and howl for your miseries James
that shall come upon you. 2Your riches are corrupted, and your 5:1–6
garments are motheaten. 3Your gold and silver is cankered /rusted, tarnished/; and the rust /venom, poison/ of them shall be a witness against you, and shall eat your flesh as it were fire.

Ye have heaped treasure together for the last days. 4Behold, the
hire of the labourers who have reaped down your fields, which
is of you kept back by fraud, crieth: and the cries of them which
have reaped are entered into the ears of the Lord of sabaoth.
5Ye have lived in pleasure /luxuriously/ on the earth, and been
wanton /indulgent/; ye have nourished your hearts, as in a day
of slaughter. 6Ye have condemned and killed the just; ~~and~~ he
doth not resist you.

Against factions in the Church

1 Cor. 10Now I beseech you, brethren, by the name of our Lord
1:10–16 Jesus Christ, that ye all speak the same thing, and ~~that~~ there be
no divisions /factions, schisms/ among you; but ~~that~~ ye be perfectly joined together in the same mind and in the same judgment. 11For it hath been declared unto me of /about,
concerning/ you, my brethren, by them ~~which are of the house~~
~~of~~ {in} Chloe, that there are contentions among you. 12Now this
I say, that ~~every one~~ {many} of you saith, I am of Paul; and I of
Apollos; and I of Cephas; and I of Christ. 13Is Christ divided?
was Paul crucified for you? or were ye baptized in the name of
Paul? 14I thank God that I baptized none of you, but /except/
Crispus and Gaius; 15Lest any should say that I had baptized in
mine own name. 16And I baptized also the household of
Stephanas: besides, I know not whether I baptized any other.

1 Cor. 1And I, brethren, could not speak unto you as unto spiri-
3:1–23 tual, but as unto carnal, ~~even~~ as unto babes in Christ. 2I have
fed you with milk, and not with meat: for hitherto ye were not
able to ~~bear~~ {receive} it, neither yet now are ye able. 3For ye are
yet carnal: for whereas there ~~is~~ among you envying, and strife,
\and divisions\, are ye not carnal, and walk as men? 4For while
one saith, I am of Paul; and another, I am of Apollos; are ye not
carnal? 5Who then is Paul, and who ~~is~~ Apollos, but ministers
/servants/ by whom ye believed, even as the Lord gave to every
man? 6I have planted, Apollos watered; but God gave the
increase /caused gave growth/. 7So then neither is he that
planteth any thing, neither he that watereth; but God that
giveth the increase. 8Now he that planteth and he that watereth

are one: and every man shall receive his own reward according to his own labour. 9For we are labourers together with God: ye are God's husbandry /cultivated field, farm/, ~~ye are~~ God's building. 10According to the grace of God which is given unto me, as a wise masterbuilder, I have laid the foundation, and another buildeth thereon. But let every man take heed how he buildeth thereupon. 11For other foundation can no man lay than that is laid, which is Jesus Christ. 12Now if any man build upon this foundation gold, silver, precious stones, wood, hay, stubble; 13Every man's work shall be made manifest: for the day shall declare it, because it shall be revealed by fire; and the fire shall try /test, put to proof/ every man's work of what sort it is. 14If any man's work abide which he hath built thereupon, he shall receive a reward. 15If any man's work shall be burned, he shall suffer loss: but he himself ~~shall~~ {may} be saved; yet so as by fire. 16Know ye not that ye are the temple of God, and ~~that~~ the Spirit of God dwelleth in /within, among/ you? 17If any man defile /spoil, corrupt, deprave/ the temple of God, him shall God destroy; for the temple of God is holy, which {T}emple ye are. 18Let no man deceive himself. If any man among you seemeth to be wise in this world, let him become a fool, that he may be wise. 19For the wisdom of this world is foolishness with God. For it is written, "He taketh the wise in their own craftiness /cunning, villainy; cleverness (LXX)/" [Job 5:13]. 20And again, "The Lord knoweth the thoughts" of the wise, "that they are vain /deceptive, fruitless/" [Psalm 94:11]. 21Therefore let no man glory in men. For all things are yours; 22Whether Paul, or Apollos, or Cephas, or the world, or life, or death, or things present, or things to come; all are yours; 23And ye are Christ's; and Christ is God's.

One in Christ

27For as many of you as have been baptized into Christ have put on Christ. 28There is neither Jew nor Greek, there is neither bond nor free, there is neither male nor female: for ye are all one in Christ Jesus. 29And if ye ~~be~~ {are} Christ's, then are ye Abraham's seed, and heirs according to the promise. Gal. 3:27–29

An appeal for unity between Jews and Gentiles

Rom. 7Wherefore receive ye one another, as Christ also received
15:7–13 us to the glory of God. 8Now I say that Jesus Christ was a minister of the circumcision for the truth of God, to confirm /estab-
lish, make constant/ the promises made unto the fathers: 9And
that the Gentiles might glorify God for his mercy; as it is written, "For this cause I will confess /profess openly, praise/ to thee
among the Gentiles, and sing unto thy name" [Psalm 18:49].
10And again he saith, "Rejoice, ye Gentiles [nations], with his
people" [Deuteronomy 32:43]. 11And again, "Praise the Lord,
all ye Gentiles [nations]; and laud him, all ye people" [Psalm
117:1]. 12And again, Esaias saith, "There shall be a root of Jesse,
and he that shall rise to reign over the Gentiles; in him shall the
Gentiles trust" [Isaiah 11:10]. 13Now the God of hope fill you
with all joy and peace in believing, that ye may abound in hope,
through the power of the Holy Ghost.

Paul preaches the mystery to the Gentiles

Eph. 1aFor this cause I Paul, {am} the prisoner of Jesus Christ
3:1–13 ~~for~~ {among} you Gentiles, 2{1b}~~If ye have heard of~~ {for} the dispensation of the grace of God which is given me to you-ward:
3~~How~~ {As ye have heard} that by revelation he made known
unto me the mystery {of Christ}; (as I wrote ~~afore~~ {before} in
few words, 4Whereby, when ye read, ye may understand my
knowledge in the mystery of Christ) 5Which in other ages was
not made known unto the sons of men, as it is now revealed
unto his holy apostles and prophets by the Spirit; 6That the
Gentiles should be fellowheirs, and of the same body, and partakers of his promise in Christ by the gospel: 7Whereof I was
made a minister, according to the gift of the grace of God given
unto me by the effectual working of his power. 8Unto me, who
am less than the least of all saints, is this grace given, that I
should preach among the Gentiles the unsearchable riches of
Christ; 9And to make all ~~men~~ see what is the fellowship of the
mystery, which from the beginning of the world hath been hid
in God, who created all things by Jesus Christ: 10To the intent
that now unto the principalities and powers in heavenly places

might be known by the church the manifold wisdom of God, [11]According to the eternal purpose which he purposed in Christ Jesus our Lord: [12]In whom we have boldness and access with confidence by the faith of him. [13]Wherefore I desire that ye faint not at my tribulations for you, which is your glory.

Forbidding recourse to the pagan law courts

[1]Dare any of you, having a matter against another, go to 1 Cor.
law before the unjust, and not before the saints? [2]Do ye not 6:1–8
know that the saints shall judge the world? and if the world shall be judged by you, are ye unworthy to judge the smallest matters? [3]Know ye not that we shall judge angels? how much more things that pertain to this life? [4]If then ye have judgments of things pertaining to this life, set them to judge who are least esteemed in the church. [5]I speak to your shame. Is it so, that there is not a wise man among you? no, not one that shall be able to judge between his brethren? [6]But brother goeth to law with brother, and that before the unbelievers. [7]Now therefore there is utterly a fault among you, because ye go to law one with another. Why do ye not rather take wrong? why do ye not rather suffer yourselves to be defrauded? [8]Nay, ye do wrong, and defraud, and that ~~your~~ [you do to] brethren.

Spiritual Gifts

God loved us so we should love

[1]Beloved, believe not every spirit, but try /test, prove by 1 Jn.
trial, discern/ the spirits whether they are of God: because many 4:1–6
false prophets are gone out into the world. [2]Hereby know ye the Spirit of God: Every spirit that confesseth that Jesus Christ is come in the flesh is of God: [3]And every spirit that \confesseth not, sets aside\ that Jesus Christ \is come in the flesh\ is not of God: and this is that spirit of antichrist, whereof ye have heard that it should come; and even now ~~already~~ it is {already} in the world. [4]Ye are of God, little children, and have overcome them: because greater is he that is in you, than he that is in the world. [5]They are of the world: therefore speak they of the world, and the world heareth them. [6]We are of God: he that knoweth God

heareth us; he that is not of God heareth not us. Hereby know we the spirit of truth, and the spirit of error /deception, sin/.

The variety and the unity of gifts

1 Cor. 12:1–11 [1]Now concerning spiritual ~~gifts~~ {things}, brethren, I would not have you ignorant. [2]Ye know that ye were Gentiles, carried away /led astray/ unto these dumb idols, even as ye were led. [3]Wherefore I give you to understand, that no man speaking by the Spirit of God calleth Jesus accursed: and ~~that~~ no man can say that Jesus is the Lord, but by the Holy Ghost. [4]Now there are diversities of gifts, but the same Spirit. [5]And there are differences of administrations, but the same Lord. [6]And there are diversities of operations, but it is the same God which worketh all in all. [7]But the manifestation of the Spirit is given to every man to profit withal. [8]For to one is given by the Spirit the word of wisdom; to another the word of knowledge by the same Spirit; [9]To another faith by the same Spirit; to another the gifts of healing by the same Spirit; [10]To another the working of miracles; to another prophecy; to another discerning of spirits; to another ~~divers~~ kinds of tongues; to another the interpretation of tongues: [11]But all these worketh that one and the selfsame Spirit, dividing to every man severally as he will.

The body and its members as an analogy of the church

1 Cor. 12:12–30 [12]For as the body is one, and hath many members, and all the members of that one body, being many, are one body: so also ~~is~~ Christ. [13]For by one Spirit are we all baptized into one body, whether ~~we be~~ Jews or Gentiles /Greeks/, whether ~~we be~~ bond /slaves/ or free; and have been all made to drink into one Spirit. [14]For the body is not one member, but many. [15]If the foot shall say, Because I am not the hand, I am not of the body; is it therefore not of the body? [16]And if the ear shall say, Because I am not the eye, I am not of the body; is it therefore not of the body? [17]If the whole body ~~were~~ an eye, where ~~were~~ the hearing? If the whole ~~were~~ hearing, where ~~were~~ the smelling? [18]But now hath God set the members every one of them in the body, as it hath pleased him. [19]And if they were all one member, where ~~were~~ the body? [20]But now ~~are they~~ many members, yet

but one body. [21]And the eye cannot say unto the hand, I have no need of thee: nor again the head to the feet, I have no need of you. [22]Nay, much more those members of the body, which seem to be more feeble /weaker/, are necessary: [23]And those members of the body, which we think to be less honourable, upon these we bestow more abundant honour; and our uncomely parts have more abundant comeliness. [24]For our comely parts have no need: but God hath tempered the body together, having given more abundant honour to that part which lacked: [25]That there should be no schism in the body; but ~~that~~ the members should have the same care one for another. [26]And whether one member suffer, all the members suffer with it; or one member be honoured, all the members rejoice with it. [27]Now ye are the body of Christ, and members in particular. [28]And God hath set some in the church, first apostles, secondarily prophets, thirdly teachers, after that miracles, then gifts of healings, helps, governments, diversities of tongues. [29]Are all apostles? ~~are~~ all prophets? ~~are~~ all teachers? ~~are~~ all workers of miracles? [30]Have all the gifts of healing? do all speak with tongues? do all interpret?

Love, the most important spiritual gift

[31a]~~But~~ {I say unto you, nay, [31c]for} ~~and yet shew~~ I {have shewn} unto you a more excellent way [31b]{therefore} covet /seek earnestly, be zealous for/ earnestly the best gifts. [1]Though I speak with the tongues of men and of angels, and have not charity /love/, I am become ~~as~~ sounding brass, or a tinkling cymbal. [2]And though I have ~~the gift of~~ prophecy, and understand all mysteries, and all knowledge; and though I have all faith, so that I could remove mountains, and have not charity, I am nothing. [3]And though I bestow all my goods to feed the poor, and though I give my body to be burned, and have not charity, it profiteth me nothing. [4]Charity suffereth long, ~~and~~ is kind; charity envieth not; charity vaunteth not itself, is not puffed up, [5]Doth not behave itself unseemly /indecently, unbecomingly/, seeketh not her own, is not easily provoked, thinketh no evil; [6]Rejoiceth not in iniquity /injustice, unrighteousness/,

1 Cor. 12:31–13:13

but rejoiceth in the truth; [7]Beareth all things, believeth all things, hopeth all things, endureth all things. [8]Charity never faileth /falls down, collapses/: but whether ~~there be~~ prophecies, they shall fail; whether ~~there be~~ tongues, they shall cease; whether ~~there be~~ knowledge, it shall vanish away. [9]For we know in part, and we prophesy in part. [10]But when that which is perfect is come, then that which is in part shall be done away. [11]When I was a child, I spake as a child, I understood as a child, I thought as a child: but when I became a man, I put away childish things. [12]For now we see through a glass, darkly /obscurely, enigmatically/; but then face to face: now I know in part; but then shall I know even as also I am known. [13]And now abideth faith, hope, charity, these three; but the greatest of these is charity.

Prophecy greater than speaking in tongues

1 Cor. 14:1–25

[1]Follow after /pursue, follow eagerly, earnestly/ charity, and desire spiritual gifts, but rather that ye may prophesy. [2]For he that speaketh in an ~~unknown~~ {another} tongue speaketh not unto men, but unto God: for no man understandeth him; howbeit in the spirit he speaketh mysteries. [3]But he that prophesieth speaketh unto men to edification, and exhortation, and comfort. [4]He that speaketh in an ~~unknown~~ {another} tongue edifieth himself; but he that prophesieth edifieth the church. [5]I would /wish/ that ye all spake with tongues, but rather that ye prophesied: for greater is he that prophesieth than he that speaketh with tongues, except he interpret, that the church may receive edifying.

[6]Now, brethren, if I come unto you speaking with tongues, what shall I profit you, except /unless/ I shall speak to you either by revelation, or by knowledge, or by prophesying, or by doctrine? [7]And even things without life giving sound, whether pipe or harp, except they give a distinction in the sounds, how shall it be known what is piped or harped? [8]For if the trumpet give an uncertain sound, who shall prepare himself to the battle? [9]So likewise ye, except ye utter by the tongue words easy to be understood, how shall it be known what is spoken? for ye shall

speak into the air. [10]There are, it may be, so many kinds of
voices in the world, and none of them is without signification.
[11]Therefore if I know not the meaning of the voice, I shall be
unto him that speaketh a barbarian, and he that speaketh ~~shall
be~~ a barbarian unto me. [12]Even so ye, forasmuch as /since/ ye
are zealous of spiritual gifts, seek that ye may excel to the edifying of the church. [13]Wherefore let him that speaketh in an
~~unknown~~ {another} tongue pray that he may interpret. [14]For if
I pray in an ~~unknown~~ {another} tongue, my spirit prayeth, but
my understanding /mind/ is unfruitful. [15]What is it then? I will
pray with the spirit, and I will pray with the understanding
also: I will sing with the spirit, and I will sing with the understanding also. [16]Else when thou shalt bless with the spirit, how
shall he that occupieth the room of the unlearned say Amen at
thy giving of thanks, seeing he understandeth not what thou
sayest? [17]For thou verily givest thanks well, but the other is not
edified. [18]I thank my God, I speak with tongues more than ye
all: [19]Yet in the church I had rather speak five words with my
understanding, that ~~by my voice~~ I might teach others also, than
ten thousand words in an ~~unknown~~ {another} tongue.

[20]Brethren, be not children in understanding: howbeit in
malice /wickedness, depravity/ be ye children, but in understanding be men. [21]In the law it is written, "With ~~men of~~ other
tongues and other lips will I speak unto this people; and yet for
all that will they not hear /listen to, heed/ me" [Isaiah 28:11–12],
saith the Lord. [22]Wherefore tongues are for a sign, not to them
that believe, but to them that believe not: but prophesying
~~serveth~~ not for them that believe not, but for them which
believe. [23]If therefore the whole church be come together into
one place, and all speak with tongues, and there come in ~~those
that are~~ unlearned, or unbelievers, will they not say that ye are
mad? [24]But if all prophesy, and there come in one that believeth
not, or ~~one~~ unlearned, he is convinced of all, he is judged of all:
[25]And thus are the secrets of his heart made manifest; and so
falling down on his face he will worship God, and report that
God is in you of a truth.

Regulating spiritual gifts and showing restraint

1 Cor. 14:26–40

26How is it then, brethren? when ye come together, every-
one of you hath a psalm, hath a doctrine, hath a tongue, hath a
revelation, hath an interpretation. Let all things be done unto
edifying. 27If any man speak in an ~~unknown~~ {another} tongue,
~~let it be~~ by two, or at the most ~~by~~ three, and ~~that~~ by course; and
let one interpret. 28But if there be no interpreter, let him keep
silence in the church; and let him speak to himself, and to God.
29Let the prophets speak two or three, and let the other judge.
30If any thing be revealed to another that sitteth by, let the first
hold his peace. 31For ye may all prophesy one by one, that all
may learn, and all may be comforted. 32And the spirits of the
prophets are subject to the prophets. 33For God is not the
author of confusion, but of peace, as in all churches of the
saints, 34Let your women keep silence in the churches /assem-
blies/: for it is not permitted unto them to ~~speak~~ {rule}; but
~~they are commanded~~ to be under obedience /to be submissive/,
as also saith the law. 35And if they will learn any thing /some-
thing/, let them ask their husbands at home: for it is a shame for
women to ~~speak~~ {rule} in the church. 36What? came the word of
God out from you? or came it unto you only? 37If any man think
himself to be a prophet, or spiritual, let him acknowledge that
the things that I write unto you are the commandments of the
Lord. 38But if any man be ignorant, let him be ignorant.
39Wherefore, brethren, covet to prophesy, and forbid not to
speak with tongues. 40Let all things be done decently /appropri-
ately/ and in order.

Charity and humility in exercising gifts

Rom. 12:3–13

3For I say, through the grace given unto me, to every man
that is among you, not to think ~~of himself~~ more highly than he
ought to think; but to think soberly, according as God hath
dealt to every man the measure of faith. 4For as we have many
members in one body, and all members have not the same
office /function, operation/: 5So we, being many, are one body
in Christ, and every one members one of another. 6Having
then gifts differing according to the grace that is given to us,

whether prophecy, ~~let us prophesy~~ according to the proportion of faith; 7Or ministry, ~~let us wait~~ on ~~our~~ ministering: or he that teacheth, on teaching; 8Or he that exhorteth, on exhortation: he that giveth, ~~let him do it~~ with simplicity; he that ruleth, with diligence; he that sheweth mercy, with cheerfulness. 9Let love be without dissimulation /sincere, unfeigned, real/. Abhor that which is evil {and} cleave to that which is good. 10Be kindly affectioned one to another with brotherly love; in honour preferring one another; 11Not slothful in business /haste, diligence/; fervent in spirit; serving the Lord; 12Rejoicing in hope; patient in tribulation; continuing instant in /constantly persisting in/ prayer; 13Distributing to the necessity of saints; given to hospitality.

The Struggle to Overcome Sin

Tests build faith through patience

2My brethren, count it all joy when ye fall into ~~divers temptations~~ {many afflictions}; 3Knowing ~~this,~~ that the trying /approval by trial/ of your faith worketh patience. 4But let patience have ~~her~~ {its} perfect work, that ye may be perfect and entire, wanting nothing. James 1:2–4

Trials refine faith

6bThough now for a season, if need be, ye are in heaviness through manifold /various/ temptations /trials, afflictions/: 7That the trial of your faith, being much more precious than of gold that perisheth, though it be tried with fire, might be found unto praise and honour and glory at the appearing /revelation/ of Jesus Christ: 8Whom having not seen, ye love; in whom, though now ye see ~~him~~ not, yet believing, ye rejoice with joy unspeakable and full of glory: 9Receiving the ~~end~~ {object} /goal, purpose, consummation/ of your faith, even the salvation of your souls. 1 Pet. 1:6b–9

Be patient

7Be patient therefore, brethren, unto the coming of the Lord. Behold, the husbandman waiteth for the precious fruit of James 5:7–11 the earth, and hath long patience for it, until he receive the early and latter rain. [8]Be ye also patient; stablish /strengthen, fix firmly/ your hearts: for the coming of the Lord draweth nigh. [9]Grudge not one against another, brethren, lest ye be condemned: behold, the judge standeth before the door. [10]Take, my brethren, the prophets, who have spoken in the name of the Lord, for an example of suffering affliction, and of patience. [11]Behold, we count them happy which endure. Ye have heard of the patience of Job, and have seen the end of the Lord; that "the Lord is very pitiful, and of tender mercy" [Exodus 34:6].

Baptism, dead to sin, alive in Christ

Rom. 6:1–11

[1]What shall we say then? Shall we continue in sin, that grace may abound? [2]God forbid /May it not be!/. How shall we, that are dead to sin, live any longer therein? [3]Know ye not, that so many of us as were baptized into Jesus Christ were baptized into his death? [4]Therefore we are buried with him by baptism into death: that like as Christ was raised up from the dead by the glory of the Father, even so we also should walk in newness of life. [5]For if we have been planted together in the likeness of his death, we shall be also ~~in the likeness~~ of his resurrection: [6]Knowing this, that our old man is crucified with him, that the body of sin might be destroyed /brought to an end, freed/, that henceforth we should not serve sin. [7]For he that is dead {to sin} is freed /acquitted, cleared/ from sin. [8]Now if we be dead with Christ, we believe that we shall also live with him: [9]Knowing that Christ being raised from the dead dieth no more; death hath no more dominion over him. [10]For in that he died, he died unto sin once: but in that he liveth, he liveth unto God. [11]Likewise reckon ye also yourselves to be dead indeed unto sin, but alive unto God through Jesus Christ our Lord.

Let holiness, not sin, have dominion over you

Rom. 6:12–14

[12]Let not sin therefore reign in your mortal body, that ye should obey it in the lusts thereof. [13]Neither yield ye your members as instruments /weapons/ of unrighteousness unto sin: but yield yourselves unto God, as those that are alive from the dead, and your members as instruments of righteousness unto God.

[14]For {in so doing} sin shall not have dominion over you: for ye
are not under the law, but under grace.

The Christian becomes servant of righteousness

[15]What then? shall we sin, because we are not under the Rom.
law, but under grace? God forbid /May it not be!/. [16]Know ye 6:15–19
not, that to whom ye yield yourselves servants to obey, his servants ye are to whom ye obey; whether of sin \unto death\, or of
obedience unto righteousness? [17]But God be thanked, that ye
~~were~~ {are not} the servants of sin, ~~but~~ {for} ye have obeyed
from the heart that form of doctrine which was delivered you.
[18]Being then made free from sin, ye became the servants of
righteousness. [19]I speak after the manner of men because of the
infirmity of your flesh: for as ye have {in times past} yielded
your members servants to uncleanness and to iniquity unto
iniquity; even so now yield your members servants to righteousness unto holiness.

The fruit of sin and of holiness

[20]For when ye were the servants of sin, ye were free from Rom.
/unrestricted by/ righteousness. [21]What fruit /benefit, reward/ 6:20–23
had ye then in those things whereof ye are now ashamed? for
the end of those things is death. [22]But now being made free
from sin, and become servants to God, ye have your fruit unto
holiness, and the end everlasting life. [23]For the wages of sin is
death; but the gift /benefit, reward/ of God is eternal life
through Jesus Christ our Lord.

The inward struggle

[14]For we know that the ~~law~~ {commandment} is spiritual: Rom.
but {when I was under the law,} I ~~am~~ {was yet} carnal, sold 7:14–25
under /devoted to, a slave to/ sin. [15a]{But now I am spiritual,}
For that /what I produce, achieve/ which I do {am commanded
to do, I do, and that which I am commanded not to allow,} I
allow /know, understand/ not: [15b]{[16]}for what I {know is not
right I} would /choose, intend, design/ {not do;} ~~that do I not;~~
~~but~~ {for} ~~what I hate~~ {that which is sin}, ~~that do~~ I {hate}.

[16]{[17]}If then I do {not} that which I would not {allow} /choose, intend, design/, I consent unto the law that it is good {and I am not condemned}. [17]{[18]}Now then it is no more I that do ~~it~~ {sin}, but {I seek to subdue that} sin that dwelleth in me. [18]{[19]}For I know that in me (that is, in my flesh,) dwelleth no good thing: for to will is present with me; but ~~how~~ to perform that which is good I \find not, know not\, {only in Christ}. [19a]{[20]}For the good that I would /intend, choose/ {have done when under the law, I find not to be good; therefore,} I do {it} not: [19b]{[21]}but the evil which I would not {do under the law, I find to be good}, that I do. [20]{[22]}Now if I do that /what I do not intend, choose/ {through the assistance of Christ,} I would not {do under the law, I am not under the law; and}, it is no more that I ~~do~~ {seek} /produce, work/ {to do} ~~it~~ {wrong}, but {to subdue} sin that dwelleth in me. [21]{[23a]}I find then {that under} ~~a~~ {the} law, that, when I would do good, evil ~~is~~ {was} present with me. [22]{[23b]}For I delight in the law of God after the inward man: [23a]{[24]}~~But~~ {And now} I see another law {even the commandment of Christ, and it is inprinted} in {my mind.} [23b]{[25]But} my members, {are} warring against the law of my mind, and bringing me into captivity ~~to~~ the law of sin which is in my members. [24]{[26]And if I subdue not the sin which is in me, but with the flesh serve the law of sin;} O wretched man that I am! who shall deliver me from the body of this death? [25]{[27]}I thank God through Jesus Christ our Lord {then, that} So ~~then~~ with the mind I myself serve the law of God~~; but with the flesh the law of sin~~.

The example of Jesus Christ

Heb. 12:1–4

[1]Wherefore seeing we also are compassed about with so great a cloud of witnesses, let us lay aside every weight, and the sin which doth so easily beset ~~us~~, and let us run with patience the race that is set before us, [2]Looking unto Jesus the author and finisher of /one who completes, perfects/ ~~our~~ faith; who for the joy that was set before him endured the cross, despising the shame, and is set down at the right hand of the throne of God. [3]For consider him that endured such contradiction /rebellion,

opposition/ of sinners against himself, lest ye be wearied and faint in your minds. [4]Ye have not yet resisted unto blood, striving against sin.

A warning, and the lessons of Israel's history

[1]Moreover, brethren, I would not that ye should be igno- 1 Cor.
rant, how that all our fathers were under the cloud, and all 10:1–13
passed through the sea; [2]And were all baptized unto Moses in
the cloud and in the sea; [3]And did all eat the same spiritual
meat; [4]And did all drink the same spiritual drink: for they
drank of that spiritual Rock that followed them: and that Rock
was Christ. [5]But with many of them God was not well pleased:
for they were overthrown /strewn, buried/ in the wilderness.
[6]Now these things were our examples /types/, to the intent we
should not lust after /desire, long for/ evil things, as they also
lusted. [7]Neither be ye idolaters, as were some of them; as it is
written, "The people sat down to eat and drink, and rose up to
play" [Exodus 32:6]. [8]Neither let us commit fornication, as
some of them committed, and fell in one day three and twenty
thousand. [9]Neither let us tempt Christ, as some of them also
tempted, and were destroyed of serpents. [10]Neither murmur
ye, as some of them also murmured, and were destroyed of the
destroyer. [11]Now all these things happened unto them for
ensamples /types/: and they are written for our admonition
{also, and for an admonition for those} upon whom the end~~s~~ of
the world ~~are~~ {shall} come. [12]Wherefore let him that thinketh
he standeth take heed lest he fall. [13]There hath no temptation
taken /seized upon/ you but such as is common to man: but God
is faithful, who will not suffer you to be tempted above that ye
are able; but will with the temptation also make a way to escape,
that ye may be able to bear ~~it~~.

Fruit of spirit and works of flesh

[16]~~This~~ I say then, Walk in the Spirit, and ye shall not fulfil Gal.
the lust of the flesh. [17]For the flesh lusteth against the Spirit, 5:16–26
and the Spirit against the flesh: and these are contrary the one
to the other: so that ye cannot do the things that ye would. [18]But
if ye be led of the Spirit, ye are not under the law. [19]Now the

works of the flesh are manifest, which are ~~these~~; Adultery, fornication, uncleanness, lasciviousness, [20]Idolatry, witchcraft,
hatred, variance, emulations, wrath, strife, seditions, heresies,
[21]Envyings, murders, drunkenness, revellings, and such like: of
the which I tell you before, as I have also told you in time past,
that they which do such things shall not inherit the kingdom of
God. [22]But the fruit of the Spirit is love, joy, peace, longsuffering, gentleness, goodness, faith, [23]Meekness, temperance /self-
control/: against such there is no law. [24]And they that are
Christ's have crucified the flesh with the affections /sufferings,
afflictions, passions/ and lusts. [25]If we live in the Spirit, let us
also walk in the Spirit. [26]Let us not be desirous of vain glory,
provoking one another, envying one another.

Separate yourself from uncleanliness

2 Cor. [11]O ~~ye~~ Corinthians, our mouth is open unto you, our heart
6:11–7:4 is enlarged. [12]Ye are not straitened in us, but ye are straitened in
your own bowels. [13]Now for a recompence in the same, (I speak
as unto ~~my~~ children,) be ye also enlarged. [14]Be ye not unequally
yoked together with unbelievers: for what fellowship hath
righteousness with unrighteousness? and what communion
hath light with darkness? [15]And what concord hath Christ with
Belial [wickedness]? or what part hath he that believeth with an
infidel? [16]And what agreement hath the temple of God with
idols? for ye are \the temple, a temple, temples\ of the living
God; as God hath said, "I will dwell in them, and walk in them;
and I will be their God, and they shall be my people" [Leviticus
26:12]. [17]"Wherefore come out from among them, and be ye
separate," saith the Lord, "and touch not the unclean ~~thing~~;
and I will receive you" [Isaiah 52:11], [18]And will be a Father
unto you, and ye shall be my sons and daughters, saith the
Lord Almighty. [1]Having therefore these promises, dearly
beloved, let us cleanse ourselves from all filthiness /pollution,
stain, defilement/ of the flesh and spirit, perfecting holiness in
the fear of God. [2]Receive us; we have wronged no man, we have
corrupted no man, we have defrauded no man. [3]I speak not
~~this~~ to condemn you: for I have said before, that ye are in our
hearts to die and live with you. [4]Great ~~is~~ my boldness of speech

toward you, great ~~is~~ my glorying of you: I am filled with comfort, I am exceeding joyful in all our tribulation.

The spiritual war against evil

[10]Finally, my brethren, be strong in the Lord, and in the Eph.
power of his might. [11]Put on the whole armour of God, that ye 6:10–20
may be able to stand against the wiles of the devil. [12]For we
wrestle not against flesh and blood, but against principalities,
against powers, against the rulers of the darkness of this
world, against spiritual wickedness in high places. [13]Where-
fore take unto you the whole armour of God, that ye may be
able to withstand in the evil day, and having done all, to stand.
[14]Stand therefore, having your loins girt about with truth, and
having on the breastplate of righteousness; [15]"And your feet
shod with the preparation of the gospel of peace" [Isaiah
52:7]; [16]Above all, taking the shield of faith, wherewith ye shall
be able to quench all the fiery darts of the wicked. [17]And take
the helmet of salvation, and the sword of the Spirit, which is
the word of God: [18]Praying always with all prayer and supplication in the Spirit, and watching thereunto with all perseverance and supplication for all saints; [19]And for me, that
utterance may be given unto me, that I may open my mouth
boldly, to make known the mystery \of the gospel\, [20]For which
I am an ambassador in bonds: that therein I may speak boldly,
as I ought to speak.

Godly sorrow brings repentance

[8]For though I made you sorry with a letter, I do not 2 Cor.
repent, though I did repent: for I perceive that the same epistle 7:8–16
hath made you sorry, though ~~it were~~ but for a season. [9]Now I
rejoice, not that ye were made sorry, but that ye sorrowed to
repentance: for ye were made sorry after a godly manner, that
ye might receive damage by us in nothing. [10]For godly sorrow
worketh repentance to salvation not to be repented of: but the
sorrow of the world worketh death. [11]For behold this selfsame
thing, that ye sorrowed after a godly sort, what carefulness it
wrought in you, yea, ~~what~~ clearing of yourselves, yea, ~~what~~
indignation, yea, ~~what~~ fear, yea, ~~what~~ vehement desire, yea,

~~what~~ zeal, yea, ~~what~~ revenge! In all ~~things~~ ye have approved
yourselves to be clear in this matter. [12]Wherefore, though I
wrote unto you, ~~I did it~~ not for his cause that had done the
wrong, nor for his cause that suffered wrong, but that our care
for you in the sight of God might appear unto you. [13]Therefore
we were comforted in your comfort: yea, and exceedingly the
more joyed we for the joy of Titus, because his spirit was
refreshed by you all. [14]For if I have boasted any thing to him of
you, I am not ashamed; but as we spake all things to you in
truth, even so our boasting, which I made before Titus, is found
a truth. [15]And his inward affection /heart, tender affections,
compassion/ is more abundant toward you, whilst he remem-
bereth the obedience of you all, how with fear and trembling ye
received him. [16]I rejoice therefore that I have confidence in you
in all things.

Resisting sin brings the crown of life

James [12]Blessed is the man that ~~endureth~~ {resisteth} temptation:
1:12–18 for when he is tried, he shall receive the crown of life, which \the
Lord, God\ hath promised to them that love him. [13]Let no man
say when he is tempted, I am tempted of God: for God cannot be
tempted with evil, neither tempteth he any man: [14]But every man
is tempted, when he is drawn away of his own lust, and enticed.
[15]Then when lust hath conceived, it bringeth forth sin: and sin,
when it is finished /has run its course/, bringeth forth death. [16]Do
not err, my beloved brethren. [17]Every good gift and every perfect
gift is from above, and cometh down from the Father of lights,
with whom is no variableness, neither shadow of turning /caused
by rotation/. [18]Of his own will begat he us with the word of truth,
that we should be a kind of firstfruits of his creatures.

Let us labor to enter into God's rest

Heb. [7]Wherefore (as the Holy Ghost saith, "To day if ye will
3:7–4:11 hear his voice, [8]Harden not your hearts, as in the provocation,
in the day of temptation in the wilderness: [9]When your fathers
tempted me, proved me, and saw my works forty years.
[10]Wherefore I was grieved with that generation, and said, They
do alway err in ~~their~~ heart; and they have not known my ways.

11So I sware in my wrath, They shall not enter into my rest" [Psalm 95:7–11].) 12Take heed, brethren, lest there be in any of you an evil heart of unbelief, in departing /apostatizing, withdrawing/ from the living God. 13But exhort one another daily, while it is called To day; lest any of you be hardened through the deceitfulness of sin. 14For we are made partakers of Christ, if we hold the beginning of our confidence stedfast unto the end; 15While it is said, "To day if ye will hear his voice, harden not your hearts, as in the provocation" [Psalm 95:7–8]. 16For some, when they had heard, did provoke: howbeit not all that came out of Egypt by Moses. 17But with whom was he grieved forty years? ~~was it~~ not with them that had sinned, whose carcases fell in the wilderness? 18And to whom sware he that they should not enter into his rest, but to them that believed not? 19So we see that they could not enter in because of unbelief. 1Let us therefore fear, lest, a promise being left ~~us~~ of entering into his rest, any of you should seem to come short of it. 2For unto us was the ~~gospel~~ {rest} preached, as well as unto them: but the word preached did not profit them, not being mixed with faith in them that heard it. 3For we ~~which~~ {who} have believed do enter into rest, as he said, "As I have sworn in my wrath, if they shall {harden their hearts they shall not} enter into my rest" [Psalm 95:11]: {also, I have sworn, If they will not harden their hearts, they shall enter into my rest;} although the works {of God} were {prepared, or} finished from the foundation of the world. 4For he spake in a certain place of the seventh day on this wise, And God did rest the seventh day from all his works. 5And in this place again, If they {harden not their hearts they} shall enter into my rest. 6Seeing therefore it remaineth that some must enter therein, and they /those who formerly were taught the gospel/ to whom it was first preached entered not in because of unbelief /disobedience, obstinancy/: 7Again, he limiteth /appoints, decrees, constitutes/ a certain day, saying in David, "To day, after so long a time"; as it is said, "To day if ye will hear his voice, harden not your hearts" [Psalm 95:7–8]. 8For if Jesus had given them rest, then would he not afterward have spoken of another day. 9There remaineth therefore a rest to the people of God. 10For he that is entered into his rest, he

also hath ceased from his own works, as God did from his. [11]Let
us labour /hasten, be eager/ therefore to enter into that rest,
lest any man fall after the same example of unbelief /obsti-
nancy, disobedience/.

Overcome the world by faith and obedience

1 Jn. [1]Whosoever believeth that Jesus is the Christ is born of
5:1–5 God: and every one that loveth him that begat loveth him also
that is begotten of him. [2]By this we know that we love the children of God, when we love God, and \keep, do\ his commandments. [3]For this is the love of God, that we keep his
commandments: and his commandments are not grievous /bur-
densome, oppressive/. [4]For whatsoever is born of God overcometh the world: and this is the victory that overcometh the
world, ~~even~~ our faith. [5]Who is he that overcometh the world,
but he that believeth that Jesus is the Son of God?

Be born unto eternal life

1 Jn. [13]These things have I written unto you that believe on the
5:13–21 name of the Son of God; that ye may know that ye have eternal
life, and that ye may {continue to} believe on the name of the
Son of God. [14]And this is the confidence that we have in him,
that, if we ask any thing according to his will, he heareth us:
[15]And if we know that he hear us, whatsoever we ask, we know
that we have the petitions that we desired of him. [16]If any man
see his brother sin a sin ~~which~~ is not unto death, he shall ask,
and he shall give him life for them that sin not unto death.
There is a sin unto death: I do not say that he shall pray for it.
[17]All unrighteousness is sin: and there is a sin not unto death.
[18]We know that whosoever is born of God ~~sinneth~~ {continueth}
not {in sin}; but he that is begotten of God {and} keepeth
/guards, shields/ himself, that wicked one ~~toucheth~~ {over-
cometh} him not. [19]And we know that we are of God, and the
whole world lieth in wickedness. [20]And we know that the Son of
God is come, and hath given us an understanding, that we may
know him that is true, and we are in him that is true, ~~even~~ in his
Son Jesus Christ. This is \the true God, the true one\, and eternal life. [21]Little children, keep yourselves from idols. \Amen.\

10

Closing Personal Remarks

Greetings and Good Wishes

[1]I commend unto you Phebe our sister, which is a servant Rom.
of the church which is at Cenchrea: [2]That ye receive her in the 16:1–16
Lord, as becometh saints, and that ye assist her in whatsoever
business she hath need of you: for she hath been a succourer of
many, and of myself also. [3]Greet Priscilla and Aquila my
helpers in Christ Jesus: [4]Who have for my life laid down their
own necks: unto whom not only I give thanks, but also all the
churches of the Gentiles. [5]Likewise ~~greet~~ the church that is in
their house. Salute my wellbeloved Epaenetus, who is the firstfruits of Achaia unto Christ. [6]Greet Mary, who bestowed much
labour on us. [7]Salute Andronicus and Junia, my kinsmen, and
my fellowprisoners, who are of note among the apostles, who
also were in Christ before me. [8]Greet Amplias my beloved in
the Lord. [9]Salute Urbane, our helper in Christ, and Stachys my
beloved. [10]Salute Apelles approved in Christ. Salute them
which are of Aristobulus' ~~household~~ {church}. [11]Salute Hero-
dion my kinsman. Greet them that be of the ~~household~~
{church} of Narcissus, which are in the Lord. [12]Salute
Tryphena and Tryphosa, who labour in the Lord. Salute the
beloved Persis, which laboured much in the Lord. [13]Salute
Rufus chosen in the Lord, and his mother and mine. [14]Salute
Asyncritus, Phlegon, Hermas, Patrobas, Hermes, and the
brethren which are with them. [15]Salute Philologus, and Julia,
Nereus, and his sister, and Olympas, and all the saints which
are with them. [16]Salute one another with an holy ~~kiss~~ {saluta-
tion}. The churches of Christ salute you.

A warning and first postscript

Rom. 16:17–20

17Now I beseech you, brethren, mark /watch, beware of/
them which cause divisions and offences /stumbling blocks,
scandals/ contrary to the doctrine which ye have learned; and
avoid them. 18For they that are such serve not our Lord Jesus
Christ, but their own belly; and by good words and fair
speeches deceive the hearts of the simple /innocent, guileless/.
19For your obedience is come abroad unto all men. I am glad
therefore on your behalf: but yet I would have you wise unto
that which is good, and simple /blameless, innocent/ concerning
evil. 20And the God of peace shall bruise /break the power of,
crush/ Satan under your feet shortly. The grace of our Lord
Jesus Christ be with you. Amen.

Last greetings and second postscript

Rom. 16:21–24

21Timotheus my workfellow, and Lucius, and Jason, and
Sosipater, my kinsmen, salute you. 22I Tertius, who wrote this
epistle, salute you in the Lord. 23Gaius mine host, and ~~of~~ the
whole church, saluteth you. Erastus the chamberlain of the city
saluteth you, and Quartus a brother. 24The grace of our Lord
Jesus Christ be with you all. Amen.

Glorifying God

Rom. 16:25–27

25Now to him that is of power to stablish you according to
~~my~~ {the} gospel, and the preaching of Jesus Christ, according
to the revelation of the mystery, which was kept secret since the
world began, 26But now is made manifest, and by the scriptures
of the prophets, according to the commandment of the everlasting God, made known to all nations for the obedience of
faith: 27To God only wise, be glory through Jesus Christ for
ever. Amen.

News, good wishes, and greetings

Heb. 13:20–25

20Now the God of peace, that brought again from the dead
our Lord Jesus, that great shepherd of the sheep, through the
blood of the everlasting covenant, 21Make you perfect in every
good \work and word\ to do his will, working in you that which

is wellpleasing in his sight, through Jesus Christ; to whom be
glory for ever and ever. Amen. 22And I beseech you, brethren,
suffer the word of exhortation: for I have written a letter unto
you in few words. 23Know ye that our brother Timothy is set at
liberty; with whom, if he come shortly, I will see you. 24Salute all
them that have the rule over you, and all the saints. They of
Italy salute you. 25Grace be with you all. Amen.

Final request and greetings

13Watch ye, stand fast in the faith, quit /behave/ you like 1 Cor.
men, be strong. 14Let all your things be done with charity. 15I 16:13–24
beseech you, brethren, (ye know the house of Stephanas, that it
is the firstfruits of Achaia, and ~~that~~ they have addicted /devoted,
appointed/ themselves to the ministry of the saints,) 16That ye
submit yourselves unto such, and to every one that helpeth with
us, and laboureth. 17I am glad of the coming of Stephanas and
Fortunatus and Achaicus: for that which was lacking on your
part they have supplied. 18For they have refreshed my spirit
and yours: therefore acknowledge ye them that are such. 19The
churches of Asia salute you. Aquila and Priscilla salute you
much in the Lord, with the church that is in their house. 20All
the brethren greet you. Greet ye one another with an holy ~~kiss~~
{salutation}. 21The salutation of ~~me~~ Paul with mine own hand.
22If any man love not the Lord Jesus Christ, let him be Anath-
ema Maranatha /Aramaic: 'The Lord will come,' or 'Come, O
Lord!'/. 23The grace of our Lord Jesus Christ be with you. 24My
love be with you all in Christ Jesus. Amen.

Paul's concern for the Corinthian Church

11I am become a fool in glorying; ye have compelled me: 2 Cor.
for I ought to have been commended of you: for in nothing am 12:11–21
I behind the very chiefest apostles, though I be nothing. 12Truly
the signs of an apostle were wrought among you in all patience,
in signs, and wonders, and mighty deeds. 13For what is it
wherein ye were inferior to other churches, except it be that I
myself was not burdensome to you? forgive me this wrong.
14Behold, the third time I am ready to come to you; and I will
not be burdensome to you: for I seek not yours, but you: for the

children ought not to lay up for the parents, but the parents for the children. 15And I will very gladly spend and be spent for you; though the more abundantly I love you, the less I be loved. 16But be it so, I did not burden you: nevertheless, being crafty, I caught you with guile. 17Did I make a gain of you by any of them whom I sent unto you? 18I desired Titus, and with him I sent a brother. Did Titus make a gain of you? walked we not in the same spirit? walked we not in the same steps? 19Again, think ye that we excuse ourselves unto you? we speak before God in Christ: but we do all things, dearly beloved, for your edifying. 20For I fear, lest, when I come, I shall not find you such as I would, and that I shall be found unto you such as ye would not: lest there be debates, envyings, wraths, strifes, backbitings, whisperings, swellings, tumults: 21And lest, when I come again, my God will humble me among you, and that I shall bewail many which have sinned already, and have not repented of the uncleanness and fornication and lasciviousness which they have committed.

Paul's fears and anxieties

2 Cor. 13:1–10

1This is the third time I am coming to you. "In the mouth of two or three witnesses shall every word be established" [Deuteronomy 19:15]. 2I told you before, and foretell you, as if I were present, the second time; and being absent now I write to them which heretofore have sinned, and to all other, that, if I come again, I will not spare: 3Since ye seek a proof of Christ speaking in me, which to you-ward is not weak, but is mighty in you. 4For though he was crucified through weakness, yet he liveth by the power of God. For we also are weak in him, but we shall live with him by the power of God toward you. 5Examine yourselves, whether ye be in the faith; prove your own selves. Know ye not your own selves, how that Jesus Christ is in you, except ye be reprobates? 6But I trust that ye shall know that we are not reprobates. 7Now I pray to God that ye do no evil; not that we should appear approved, but that ye should do that which is honest, though we be as reprobates. 8For we can do nothing against the truth, but for the truth. 9For we are glad, when we are weak, and ye are strong: and this also we wish,

even your perfection. [10]Therefore I write these things being
absent, lest being present I should use sharpness, according to
the power which the Lord hath given me to edification, and not
to destruction.

Recommendations, greetings, final good wishes

[11]Finally, brethren, farewell. Be perfect, be of good com- 2 Cor.
fort, be of one mind, live in peace; and the God of love and 13:11–14
peace shall be with you. [12]Greet one another with an holy ~~kiss~~
{salutation}. [13]All the saints salute you. [14]The grace of the Lord
Jesus Christ, and the love of God, and the communion of the
Holy Ghost, be with you all. Amen.

Warning and blessing

[11]Ye see how large a letter I have written unto you with Gal.
mine own hand. [12]As many as desire to make a fair shew in the 6:11–18
flesh, they constrain you to be circumcised; only lest they
should suffer persecution for the cross of Christ. [13]For neither
they themselves who are circumcised keep the law; but desire to
have you circumcised, that they may glory in your flesh. [14]But
God forbid that I should glory, save in the cross of our Lord
Jesus Christ, by whom the world is crucified unto me, and I
unto the world. [15]For in Christ Jesus neither circumcision
availeth anything, nor uncircumcision, but a new creature.
[16]And as many as walk according to this rule, peace be on them,
and mercy, and upon the Israel of God. [17]From henceforth let
no man trouble me: for I bear in my body the marks of the
Lord Jesus. [18]Brethren, the grace of our Lord Jesus Christ be
with your spirit. Amen.

Personal news and final salutation

[21]But that ye also may know my affairs, and how I do, Eph.
Tychicus, a beloved brother and faithful minister in the Lord, 6:21–24
shall make known to you all things: [22]Whom I have sent unto
you for the same purpose, that ye might know our affairs, and
that he might comfort your hearts. [23]Peace ~~be~~ to the brethren,
and love with faith, from God the Father and the Lord Jesus

Christ. [24]Grace be with all them that love our Lord Jesus Christ
in sincerity. Amen.

Last advice

Philip. 4:2–9

[2]I beseech Euodias, and beseech Syntyche, that they be of
the same mind in the Lord. [3]And I intreat thee also, true yoke-
fellow /associate/, help those women which laboured with me in
the gospel, with Clement also, and with other my fellowlabourers, whose names are in the book of life. [4]Rejoice in the Lord
alway: and again I say, Rejoice. [5]Let your moderation /gentle-
ness/ be known unto all men. The Lord is at hand. [6]Be ~~careful~~
{afflicted} for nothing /Do not be unduly concerned about any-
thing/; but in every thing by prayer and supplication with
thanksgiving let your requests be made known unto God. [7]And
the peace of God, which passeth all understanding, shall keep
/guard/ your hearts and minds through Christ Jesus. [8]Finally,
brethren, whatsoever things are true, whatsoever ~~things are~~
honest, whatsoever ~~things are~~ just, whatsoever ~~things are~~ pure,
whatsoever things ~~are~~ lovely, whatsoever things ~~are~~ of good
report; ~~if there be~~ any virtue, and if ~~there be~~ any praise, think
on these things. [9]Those things, which ye have both learned, and
received, and heard, and seen in me, do: and the God of peace
shall be with you.

Praise and blessing for help received

Philip. 4:10–20

[10]But I rejoiced in the Lord greatly, that now at the last
your care of me hath flourished again; wherein ye were also
careful, but ye lacked opportunity. [11]Not that I speak in respect
of want: for I have learned, in whatsoever state I am, ~~therewith~~
to be content. [12]I know both how to be abased /humble/, and I
know how to abound: every where and in all things I am
instructed both to be full and to be hungry, both to abound and
to suffer need. [13]I can do all things through Christ which
strengtheneth me. [14]Notwithstanding ye have well done, that ye
did communicate /participate/ with my affliction. [15]Now ye
Philippians know also, that in the beginning of the gospel,
when I departed from Macedonia, no church communicated

with me as concerning giving and receiving, but ye only. 16For
even in Thessalonica ye sent once and again unto my necessity.
17Not because I desire a gift: but I desire fruit that may abound
to your account. 18But I have all, and abound: I am full, having
received of Epaphroditus the things ~~which were~~ sent from you,
an odour of a sweet smell, a sacrifice acceptable, wellpleasing to
God. 19But my God shall supply all your need according to his
riches in glory by Christ Jesus. 20Now unto God and our Father
be glory for ever and ever. Amen.

Salutations and final wish

21Salute every saint in Christ Jesus. The brethren which Philip.
are with me greet you. 22All the saints salute you, chiefly they 4:21–23
that are of Caesar's household. 23The grace of our Lord Jesus
Christ be with you all. Amen.

Greetings and final wishes

10Aristarchus my fellowprisoner saluteth you, and Marcus, Col.
sister's /cousin, kinsman/ son to Barnabas, (touching whom ye 4:10–18
received commandments: if he come unto you, receive him;)
11And Jesus, which is called Justus, who are of the circumcision.
These only are my fellowworkers ~~unto~~ {in} the kingdom of
God, which have been a comfort unto me. 12Epaphras, who is
~~one~~ of you, a servant of Christ, saluteth you, always labouring
fervently for you in prayers, that ye may stand perfect and complete in all the will of God. 13For I bear him record, that he hath
a great zeal for you, and them ~~that are~~ in Laodicea, and them in
Hierapolis. 14Luke, the beloved physician, and Demas, greet
you. 15Salute the brethren which are in Laodicea, and
Nymphas, and the church which is in his house. 16And when
this epistle is read among you, cause that it be read also in the
church of the Laodiceans; and that ye likewise read the epistle
from Laodicea. 17And say to Archippus, Take heed to the ministry which thou hast received in the Lord, that thou fulfil it.
18The salutation by the hand of me Paul. Remember my bonds.
Grace be with you. Amen.

Closing prayer and farewell

1 Thes. 5:23–28 23And the very God of peace sanctify you wholly; and ~~I pray God~~ your whole spirit and soul and body be preserved blameless unto the coming of our Lord Jesus Christ. 24Faithful is he that calleth you, who also will do it. 25Brethren, pray for us. 26Greet all the brethren with an holy ~~kiss~~ {salutation}. 27I charge you by the Lord that this epistle be read unto all the holy brethren. 28The grace of our Lord Jesus Christ be with you. Amen.

Pray for us

2 Thes. 2:16–3:5 16Now our Lord Jesus Christ himself, and God, even our Father, which hath loved us, and hath given ~~us~~ everlasting consolation and good hope through grace, 17Comfort your hearts, and stablish you in every good word and work. 1Finally, brethren, pray for us, that the word of the Lord may have ~~free~~ course /may progress freely, rapidly/, and be glorified, even as ~~it is~~ with you: 2And that we may be delivered from unreasonable /unsuitable, absurd, improper/ and wicked men: for all ~~men~~ have not faith. 3But the Lord is faithful, who shall stablish you, and keep you from evil /the evil one, the devil/. 4And we have confidence in the Lord touching you, that ye both do and will do the things which we command you. 5And the Lord direct your hearts into the love of God, and into the patient waiting for Christ.

Prayer and farewell wishes

2 Thes. 3:16–18 16Now the Lord of peace himself give you peace always by all means. The Lord be with you all. 17The salutation of Paul with mine own hand, which is the token in every epistle: so I write. 18The grace of our Lord Jesus Christ be with you all. Amen.

Final greetings

2 Tim. 4:19–22 19Salute Prisca and Aquila, and the household of Onesiphorus. 20Erastus abode at Corinth: but Trophimus have I left at Miletum sick. 21Do thy diligence to come before winter. Eubu-

lus greeteth thee, and Pudens, and Linus, and Claudia, and all
the brethren. [22]The Lord Jesus Christ be with {you, and} ~~thy
spirit.~~ Grace be with you {all}. Amen.

Practical recommendations, farewells and good wishes

[12]When I shall send Artemas unto thee, or Tychicus, be Titus
diligent to come unto me to Nicopolis: for I have determined 3:12–15
there to winter. [13]Bring Zenas the lawyer and Apollos on their
journey diligently, that nothing be wanting unto them. [14]And let
ours /our people/ also learn to maintain good works for necessary uses, that they be not unfruitful. [15]All that are with me
salute thee. Greet them that love us in the faith. Grace be with
you all. Amen.

Final greetings

[11]To him be glory \power\ and dominion for ever and ever. 1 Pet.
Amen. [12]By Silvanus, a faithful brother unto you, as I suppose, I 5:11–14
have written briefly, exhorting, and testifying that this is the
true grace of God wherein ye stand. [13]~~The church that is~~
{They} at Babylon, elected together with you, saluteth you; and
so doth Marcus my son. [14]Greet ye one another with a kiss of
charity. Peace be with you all that are in Christ Jesus. \Amen\.

Remember, remember

[12]Wherefore I will not be negligent to put you always in 2 Pet.
remembrance of these things, though ye know them, and be 1:12–15
established in the present truth. [13]Yea, I think it meet /right, just,
righteous/, as long as I am in this tabernacle, to stir you up by
putting you in remembrance; [14]Knowing that shortly I must put
off this my tabernacle, even as our Lord Jesus Christ hath shewed
me. [15]Moreover I will endeavour that ye may be able after my
decease /death/ to have these things always in remembrance.

Final greetings

[12]Having many things to write unto you, I would not write 2 Jn.
with paper and ink: but I trust /hope/ to come unto you, and 1:12–13
speak face to face, that our joy may be full. [13]The children of thy
elect sister greet thee. Amen.

3 Jn. [13]I had many things to write, but I will not with ink and
1:13–14 pen write unto thee: [14]But I trust I shall shortly see thee, and we
shall speak face to face. Peace be to thee. Our friends salute
thee. Greet the friends by name.

Do God's will

Jude [20]But ye, beloved, building up yourselves on your most
1:20–23 holy faith, praying in the Holy Ghost, [21]Keep yourselves in the
love of God, looking for the mercy of our Lord Jesus Christ
unto eternal life. [22]And of some \have compassion, convince or
reprove\, making a difference: [23]And others save \with fear\,
pulling them out of the fire; hating /abhorring, loathing/ even
the garment spotted by the flesh.

Benediction and praising God

Jude [24]Now unto him that is able to keep you from falling, and
1:24–25 to present you faultless before the presence of his glory with
exceeding joy, [25]To the only wise God our Saviour, be glory and
majesty, dominion and power, both now and ever. Amen.

Scripture Index

New Testament

Pearl of Great Price

Subject Index

— D —

— E —

— R —